STUDENT EDITION

Copyright © 2012 Jerome Dumetz

All rights reserved.

ISBN: 1479159689

ISBN 13: 9781479159680

CROSS-CULTURAL MANAGEMENT TEXTBOOK

Edited and co-authored by Jerome Dumetz

Co-authored by:

MEREDITH BELBIN
STEPHEN M.R. COVEY
DEAN FOSTER
CHARLES HAMPDEN-TURNER
OLGA SAGINOVA
EDGAR SCHEIN
JOERG SCHMITZ
CRAIG STORTI
JULIETTE TOURNAND
FONS TROMPENAARS
PETER WOOLLIAMS

To Bernard and Marie-Louise
My cultural roots,

Anna
My cross-cultural better half,

Alexandra and Valéria
My multicultural wonders.

PART 1
PREAMBLE

Preface

Why this textbook?

Cross-cultural management is a fascinating topic. It is increasingly taught in the curriculum of students and also used to explain the roots of communication and management misunderstandings in a globalized corporate world.

Academic and business worlds rarely mingle well. Usually the corporate world is applying academic theories to their practice. In the field of cross-cultural management the opposite has taken place: universities and other learning organizations, are adapting professional management books to their classroom. A practical, easy-to-use, structured, yet illustrated textbook was missing among the numerous specialized publications.

What began as an improbable endeavor has turned into a great adventure, thanks to the support of my fellow contributors, respected authors coming from both worlds: the academics and the practitioners.

Book objectives

Synthesizing today's best concepts, A *Cross-Cultural Management Textbook* is primarily intended for students and instructors, in particular, instructors looking for an outline for their management courses. Professionals, consultants, managers, and trainers, whose daily work involves international and cross-cultural challenges, will benefit from this text as well.

This textbook is designed to prepare readers from diverse backgrounds to comprehend the influence of culture in management and communication. It will also help them develop the behaviors and skills necessary to adapt rapidly to a world where cultures mix as never before.

This extensive, authoritative textbook is the missing link between various writings of renowned academics and specialists and the pragmatic approach of real-world practitioners who are confronted daily with intercultural situations.

What this textbook is not

This book is about cross-cultural communication and management in general. By culture, we mean, of course, ethno-related ones such as national cultures, but also corporate culture (Chap. 8) and cultures within organizations (departments). Depending on the context, cultures can also be generational or social. The aim of this textbook is to present how to better communicate and manage across cultures, any cultures.

Thus, this book is not about comparative management where cultures are measured and compared one with another. Some graphics with lists of countries are displayed here and there but they should be understood solely as illustrations. They are not the core of the textbook.

In our opinion, cross-cultural management is more about our attitude towards the "other" than an, often stereotyped, comparison between cultures. Focusing on elements comprising a culture is, we think, more fruitful to understand how to better communicate and manage across cultures.

Academic and practitioners support

Several European universities closely monitored the creation of this textbook. The FH Wurzburg-Schweinfurt university of applied science in Germany and the Plekhanov Russian Economic University are the primary supporters. We also received significant input from the FH Steyr university of applied science in Austria as well as Unicorn College in the Czech Republic.

All the theory presented in this publication has been thoroughly verified and applied in an academic environment. Not all the contributors pursue a full academic career, however, all of them are giving lectures in their respected fields in universities around the world.

In parallel, to make sure that what we present is useful in the real world, we have selected the latest theories accepted by practitioners. This is why all the contributors are confronting their input also in the business world, as consultants.

Our contributors are therefore a group of seasoned specialists, some more inclined to the academic world, others more in touch with that of business, but all knowing both worlds.

A detailed biography of each author can be found at the end of the textbook. You'll find useful information about their experience, and also about their current work.

Structure of the text

Most textbooks are written by a single author who regroups the work of past and current theorists. Luckily, cross-cultural management is a relatively recent field. Most of the great ideas linked to it come from authors that are still around.

This is why so many contributors participated. Not only to give different angles to a common topic, but also to share their authoritative knowledge on a precise topic. This work presents a view as to what cross-cultural management is today. Naturally, with each author contributing his or her own chapter, the writing styles do vary, reflecting one's personality.

Cases & Workshop

We wanted this textbook to be as practical as possible, with a plurality of views. Each chapter features several real-life examples, quoted directly by the authors or extracted from publications.

At the end of each chapter, there are longer cases, either in the form of articles or group workshops:

- The case studies are meant to be getaways for presentations, discussions and self-reflection. Discussion questions are intended to trigger interest but are by no mean exclusive.

- The workshops are exercises to be completed individually or in group. Just like the case studies, those workshops are designed to ideally be debriefed and analyzed in groups, in order to be related back to the content of the reviewed chapter.

All the case studies are available for reprint on our associated website www.crossculturaltextbook.org . (Registration code: crossculture)

Online extension

Because we did not want the textbook to become a thick compilation of everything related to cross-cultural management, we will be presenting extra resources on an associated website.

This web site has several objectives:

- All the case studies and workshops presented in the book can be easily accessed and legally downloaded to be used in class or in training.

- The numerous publications of our contributors can be accessed through their online biography to make it easier to find out more about a particular topic.

- Many extra texts and chapters, authored by contributors of this textbook on related fields that couldn't be published in this edition but might be of some interest for the readers, are also available on the site.

- Research work, based on online questionnaires (such as the "work goals" workshop in Chapter 1), can also be accessed. Researchers wishing to present their work in the field of cross-cultural management are also welcome to publish their article in the academic section.

- There are opportunities to share your own results and examples to enrich the field of cross-cultural management. You can upload and share your own case studies and cultural dialogues.

A special Q&A section allows you to contact the contributors of this textbook and to ask them questions.

Log on to **www.crossculturaltextbook.org**, enter the code: **crossculture** and register to access the extra information and documents linked to this textbook.

Cross-cultural Dialogues

Throughout the textbook short dialogues are showcased between individuals from different cultures.

Craig Storti published those dialogues to illustrate cultural misunderstandings in real life[1]. In the course of each of these conversations, the speakers make comments that reveal significant differences in their values and attitudes or in how they view or understand the world around them. The speakers are not *trying* to express these differences—they are in fact quite unaware of them—but the differences manifest themselves all the same as each speaker responds in a completely natural manner to the particular situation. After reading a few dialogues, one begins to wonder if what is "completely natural" to a person from one culture is indeed all that natural to someone from a different culture.

Which is, in fact, the central lesson of these dialogues: that when we are merely "being ourselves," acting according to our deepest instincts, human beings reveal fundamental differences in what we all tend to think of as normal behavior. In other words, we learn that, much of what we assumed was universal in human behavior, is, in fact, peculiar to a particular group or culture. With the inevitable consequence, of course, that whenever we leave that group—to live, work, or do business abroad, for example—or come into contact with people from another group, much of our behavior necessarily becomes suspect.

And that is just what happens over and over again in these dialogues: individuals come face to face with the fact that many of their most cherished instincts don't travel very well; that what is expected and understood in one culture may be shocking and incomprehensible in another. These cultural differences inevitably lead to all manner of misunderstandings, and these misunderstandings, in turn, often result in a wide variety of unpleasant emotional and practical consequences - everything from hurt feelings and missed opportunities, to failed negotiations and lost profits, to anger and hostility and even to organized warfare.

---

1 C. Storti, 1994, Cross-cultural Dialogues, Intercultural Press, Nicholas Brealey Publ.

By the same token, if we could avoid these misunderstandings, then we would stand a very good chance of sidestepping all the unpleasant consequences they lead to. And that, in a nutshell, is the purpose of those examples: to alert readers to the misunderstandings lurking in the most common interactions we have with people from other cultures—and to jar us, as a consequence, into being a little less sure of our instincts.

If we look at a sample dialogue, all of this will start to become clear.

DEAN SMITH:	I asked Professor Desai yesterday to discuss his new course.
MISS SINGH:	How was the meeting?
DEAN SMITH:	He was very charming. But he avoided the subject of the new course whenever I tried to bring it up.
MISS SINGH:	He may be upset that you didn't consult him in advance.
DEAN SMITH:	I don't think so. He didn't say anything.

The facts here are simple: Dean Smith, evidently the chair of a department in a college or some other educational institution, decided to have one of his faculty, Professor Desai, teach a new course, apparently without consulting him ahead of time. But when the Dean met with Professor Desai to raise the subject, Desai avoided it. Miss Singh, a compatriot of Professor Desai, thinks he must be upset at not being consulted, but the Dean feels sure he isn't because the Professor "didn't say anything."

But, in fact, he did say something quite clearly, only Dean Smith didn't hear it. In refusing to discuss the new course, Desai—by the standards of his culture—is signaling his extreme displeasure in a most direct manner. Smith misses the signal because by his standards it is too indirect and also because Professor Desai has been his usual charming self. In other words, Smith assumes that someone who is upset is going to say so and that someone who is angry is not going to be charming.

But these are norms—that people will be direct and that angry people won't be charming—and norms, which is where we get our idea of *norm*al behavior, vary from culture to culture. Indeed, in Professor Desai's culture it is very important not to embarrass another person through any kind of overt confrontation. For him to declare outright that he was upset about the new course would make Dean Smith feel very uncomfortable, something that is simply not done (not the norm). Instead, Desai communicates his displeasure indirectly, in this case by not talking about the new course, thus avoiding any kind of unpleasant incident. And all the while he maintains the most correct exterior so as not to betray the slightest sign of his wounded feelings, which would only make the Dean feel uneasy if he detected them. It's quite likely, by the way, that Professor. Desai has made his feelings very clear to Miss Singh, who is in all likelihood speaking for him (not for herself) when she says to the Dean, "He may be upset when you didn't consult him in advance."

Dean Smith and Professor Desai have had a classic cultural misunderstanding, caused by the usual culprit: the fact that each of them assumes the other looks at the world exactly as he does. While such misunderstandings can, of course, occur between two people from the same culture, they are much more common between two people from different cultures. And these misunderstandings, as we have noted, lead to all manner of unfortunate consequences which quickly sour—and even poison—relations between people from different cultures.

But if we could stop assuming that other people are like us—if we could begin to believe that we don't necessarily understand how foreigners are thinking and that they don't always understand how we are thinking—then we would be well on our way to avoiding cultural misunderstandings and all the problems they give rise to.

However, it isn't altogether true that all people think and behave the way we do. And, for the sake of successful intercultural interaction, the sooner we stop expecting them to the better. All of which is much easier said than done, for this habit of being right about how people are going to behave—a cornerstone of our being able to function in the world—isn't easy to displace. In fact, it takes a very strong dose of being *wrong* about people to bring about the necessary changes in attitude.

The dialogues are inserted within the chapters to illustrate a particular topic and to trigger some questions from the readers. All the dialogues are constructed in such a way that the key to the conversation—the clue to what's not quite right—is contained in the exchange itself. In other words, the reader does not have to know about Arab culture or Chinese culture in order to see what the problem is.

They can be the basis of group discussions where such issues can be analyzed:

- Whom do I feel the closer in the dialogue?
- Where is the misunderstanding? (If cultural mistakes like these were obvious, most of us wouldn't make them!)
- Can I relate this dialogue with a real-life, personal experience?
- What cultural element could help explain the misunderstanding?
- What alternative answers would I consider not to make the same mistake?

If you wish to read Craig Storti's own analysis of those dialogues, log on to www.crossculturaltextbook.org (Regsitration code: crossculture) and go to the Craig Storti's section.

Acknowledgements

This textbook would not exist without the active support of many colleagues, friends and fellow cross-culturalists. Out them, my 11 co-authors deserve a special tribute for their trust and enthusiasm into this endeavor. Edgar, Craig, Juliette, Fons, Joerg, Stephen, Peter, Meredith, Charles, Olga and Dean I can only say:

Thank you, Merci, Danke, Bedankt and Спасибо !

This textbook is also a mosaic of many pieces contributed by people from around the world. Many thanks to everyone:

Claudine ANDRE – Belgium/RD Congo • Tatyana ANDREEVA – Russia • Gilles ASSELIN – France/USA • Fatiha BADOUH – France/Morocco • Marek BERANEK – Czech Republic • Agnes BODA – Czech Republic • Jan CADIL – Czech Republic • Zanna CLAY – U.K. • Vladislav DAVYDOV – Russia • Marie-Pierre DILLENSEGER – France/USA • Huyen DO THU – Vietnam/Czech Republic • Terje ENGLUND – Norway/Czech Republic • Bill ETHERIDGE – U.K./Czech Republic • Paul EVANS – U.K. • Helen FARROW – U.K./France • Martina GAISCH – Austria • Patricia GLASEL – France • Pearl HARRIS – South Africa • Hannes HOFSTADLER – Austria • Jo KEELER – U.K. • Manfred KET-DE-VRIES – The Netherlands • Manfred KIESEL – Germany • Guillaume KERBOUL – Bretagne/France • Rochelle KOPP – USA • Rob LAAS – The Netherlands • LALZARZOVA – India • Fanny LINCOLN – France • Annemieke LOF-DE KOK – The Netherlands • Marielle van der MEER – The Netherlands • Anna MOOSER – Austria • Roald van de MUNT – The Netherlands/Czech Republic • Benjamin PELLETIER – France • Roland PFEIFHOFER – Austria • Jeta PRAKASH – India • Anelia RIMINCHAN – Bulgaria/Russia • Roisin SAUNIER – Ireland/France • Laurence SICOT – France/Brazil • Stéphanie SINGLETON – China/USA • Anja SPITZER – Austria • Phyllis STEWART – Singapore/U.K. • Nicholas STRANGE – UK/Germany • Ladislav STRATIL – Czech Republic • John VOELCKER – USA • Frans de WAAL – The Netherlands • Sophie WIESINGER – Austria • Rainer WEHNER – Germany

A special thank for their crucial support to:

Davina FAIRWEATHER – U.K. & David MARLATT – USA

Brief Contents

PART 1: PREAMBLE

Part 1: Preamble vii
Preface ix
Online extension xiii
Cross-cultural Dialogues xv
Acknowledgements xix
Brief Contents xxi
Contents: Chapters' overview xxiii
Workshops and Case studies xxvii

PART 2: THE CHAPTERS

Introduction 3
Prologue: The intelligence of cooperation 5
Chapter 1: Comparing cultures 19
Chapter 2: Cross-culture research as of today 53
Chapter 3: Culture and communication 81
Chapter 4: Cultural dimensions relating to people 117
Chapter 5: Cultural dimensions relating to time 147
Chapter 6: Cultural dimensions relating to the world 169
Chapter 7: Trust as a cultural dimension 199
Chapter 8: Organizational Culture 227
Chapter 9: Teams and culture 255
Chapter 10: Reconciliation of Cultural Dichotomies 273
Chapter 11: Culture and Marketing 303
Chapter 12: The challenge of culture in expatriation 331
A final word 355

PART 3: APPENDICES

About the Contributors 359
Bibliography 381
Index 385

Contents

Chapters' overview

We have thought of this textbook as a true guide. It can be used step-by-step, chapter after chapter, or randomly, following your needs and wishes.

Prologue – The intelligence of cooperation

Most literature about cross-culture begins with the unsaid postulate that readers want to communicate and cooperate better across cultures. Yet rarely is it explained that cooperation is a winning strategy in itself. So, before willingness to improve co-operation across cultures, it is worth understanding why cooperation is needed in the first place. **Juliette Tournand,** an executive coach, explains in this opening chapter, how the conjunction of theories and research from three larger than life experts, Sun Tsu, Axelrod and Rapoport leads us to the evidence that working together is always the right thing to do.

Chapter 1 – Comparing cultures

The introductory chapter presents culture as a concept that has multiple shapes. Culture is represented in different ways and all are equally valid even if one paradigm remains: culture has layers. From superficial elements to its core, culture is analyzed exclusively through its artifacts. With the help of ethology, **Jerome Dumetz** explains how we came to compare one culture with another, introducing the concept of cultural dimensions as an essential step to comprehend the rest of the textbook.

Chapter 2 – Cross-cultural research as of today

If this textbook is a true multicultural collective work, this chapter is its ultimate representation. Coordinated by the **Cross-Cultural Management and Emerging Markets Center of the University of Applied Science of Steyr**, in Austria, it is has been sourced by nearly all the co-authors of the book. In this chapter we review all the early and contemporary authors who made cross-cultural research what it is today. From ethnology, sociology or semiotics, all the roots of cross-culture are explored. Several key models of cross-cultural management are also presented to give the reader a plurality of options with neutral pros and cons analysis.

Chapter 3 – Culture and communication

Communication is usually associated with management where culture is concerned. It is true that a great deal of management has to do with communication. How we communicate our ideas will influence how our management is understood. This is why **Jerome Dumetz** focuses on communication in a cultural context. As well as verbal and non-verbal communication, the chapter also provides many examples of paralinguistic communication.

Chapter 4 - Cultural dimensions relating to people

Fons Trompenaars, renowned cross-cultural guru, shares his understanding of the key cultural dimensions impacting our interaction with others. Do we value more common rules or our particular relationship with people? Should our decisions serve the community or should the individual be placed before the group? How much do we allow others to be engaged in our private life and how do we accord status to important people? All of these issues are approached from a cross-cultural perspective.

Chapter 5 – Cultural dimensions relating to time

Time is also a key cultural element. Cultures around the world have a very different comprehension of this physical dimension. We are all confronted by various types of time, and we review many of them. Also in this chapter, **Fons Trompenaars** presents the cultural dimensions that are linked with time. He addresses a number of questions: Do we prefer to "see" time as a linear process or a circular one? What is our appreciation of the past, the present and future? And finally, what is our time perspective: long or short term?

Chapter 6 - Cultural dimensions relating to the world

Joerg Schmitz, consultant and author of one of the mostly used cross-cultural models, introduces the various cultural dimensions related to the world. In detail, this chapter questions our values regarding the relative control (or lack) of our own life. Locus of control, uncertainty avoidance and how we relate to space around us are described in detail and with practical examples.

Chapter 7 – Trust as a cultural dimension

One more dimension is presented in this textbook: Trust. Not always recognized as an academic cultural dimension, yet most practitioners made reference to it when describing behaviors. Acclaimed specialist **Stephen M. R Covey** shares his insights into this essential dimension.

Chapter 8 - Organizational culture

Each of us belongs to several cultures. In a managerial environment the organizational culture often takes front stage. **Peter Woolliams**, both an academic and a consultant, explores how this concept emerged and how much it is fundamental to our understanding of norms and values in the corporate world. He also goes on to combine Trompenaars' dimensions to create four main types of organizational culture to help us interpret the dynamics of our own institutions.

Chapter 9 – Teams and culture

What makes a successful team?, How can each member play a particular and necessary role especially when the team is multi-cultural? **Meredith Belbin** is the world authority on team roles and is the creator of this management concept. In this chapter he details the nine roles comprising the perfect team and provides tools to help us compare the various roles as we compare cultures in the rest of the book.

Chapter 10 – Reconciliation of cultural dichotomies

Author of many publications in the field of management, **Charles Hampden-Turner** is the creator of the Dilemma Theory presented in this chapter co-written with Raymond Abelin and Haihua Zhang. With the use of multiple examples and illustrations from previous chapters, they investigate the gap between the Western and the Asian perspective in cross-cultural research. Key cultural dimensions presented earlier in the textbook are reconciled in order to provide practical answers to theoretical questions.

Chapter 11 – Culture and marketing

In this very hands-on chapter, marketing professor **Olga Saginova** puts into practice the many concepts presented in the previous chapters. Following the classic Marketing mix 4Ps (product, price, place and promotion), she provides countless illustrations of cross-cultural management in marketing and links concepts with real-life cases.

Chapter 12 – The challenge of culture in expatriation

One of the most respected practitioners of cross-cultural training, **Dean Foster** contributes practical and useful tips that can be applied when confronting a new culture. Taken from his extensive experience, the chapter concludes the textbook with advice that can be put into practice immediately outside the classroom or in the workplace.

Workshops and Case studies

Case study: 0.1 Training in Yemen *15*
Workshop 1.1: Work Goals *47*
Workshop 1.2: Your own cultural Artifacts *49*
Workshop 2.1 : My Metaphor: *79*
Workshop 2.2 : Generations of Onions: *79*
Case Study 3.1: Why Do Japanese Fall Asleep In Meetings? *109*
Case Study 3.2: Kissing Across Cultures *112*
Case Study 4.1: Indians find it difficult to say no to their superiors *142*
Case study 4.2: Japan Company's 'Energy Saving' Staff Haircut *144*
Case study 5.1: Touareg time *163*
Case Study 5.2: A bag's time *165*
Case study 6.1: Locus of control in a Korean-US leadership team *194*
Case study 6.2: Re-coding the hidden language of space *196*
Case Study 7.1: Trust in the supermarket *221*
Case Study 7.2: International finance and trust *223*
Case study 8.1: French Railways change timetable *249*
Case study 8.2: Corporate culture changes at Steel-Roll *251*
Workshop 9.1: Create your dream team! *270*
Workshop 10.1: Reconciling your own dilemmas *299*
Case study 11.1: Oh, Audi, How Could You? *324*
Case Study 11.2: Puma's intercultural gaffe *326*
Workshop 12.1: Expats checklist *351*
Workshop 12.2: Ask around *354*

PART 2
THE CHAPTERS

Introduction

By Edgar H. Schein

In a world that is rapidly becoming multi-cultural it is very important to have a clear understanding of just what we mean when we throw the C word (culture) around glibly. It has come to mean practically anything that the speaker wants to convey that has to do with goals (we want a team culture) with values (we want a culture of ethical behavior) or with behavior (we want a culture of customer service). Implied in all of these uses is the notion that one can want a culture and create it. The problem is that, if we use the concept loosely in this way, we are in danger of missing what culture actually is and does and of ignoring crucial areas where culture makes a difference.

If we think of culture as what a given group has learned and has stabilized in its behavior, thought processes and values then it becomes immediately apparent that we can't just "create" a culture in the way that the loose definitions imply. If we accept culture as what one has learned then we must recognize that in today's world different people are learning different things yet are expected to work together. This matters especially in tomorrow's world because more and more work is being required of group members who are interdependent and yet come from different cultures.

What is involved when a multicultural team is sent by the United Nations to solve health problems in a culture different from that of any of their members? What is involved if we find that occupations also create strong cultures, which means that a surgical team may consist of an American surgeon, a Latino Nurse, an Indian anesthesiologist, and several technicians of unknown background? What if it is discovered that the tensions between nationalities are much less than the tension between the doctor and the nurse because of their occupational cultural training?

The point is that culture is a powerful force and has to be properly understood. If we do not manage culture, then culture manages us without our even knowing it. This used to matter only if we traveled. We did not want to offend people in other countries and we wanted to understand them better because becoming more sophisticated culturally was a good thing. But today, it is a matter far more serious. The work of the world is becoming more complex and more global. This has two major impacts culturally. Globalism means that work will increasingly be done by people from different nationalities, ethnicities and religions. If they are to work together they must develop common understanding of space, time, authority, human nature and the essence of human relationships. Complexity means that work will increasingly involve the meshing of expertise from different occupations. If they are to work together they must develop a common language, status system, rules of authority and decision making. None of this will happen without good, clear teaching materials that give culture its due.

What I have found of special value in this textbook is the combining of concepts that were developed for international comparisons with dimensions that have been primarily used to compare organizations and occupations. When I first wrote about organizational culture the focus was clearly on comparing organizations within a given culture. But the rapid growth of globalism has created the reality that organizations today are multicultural entities. To understand them requires all the tools of researchers who have international comparisons with the tools used to study organizations. This textbook is an excellent beginning in defining this new intercultural space.

One of the great dilemmas in analyzing cultures is to choose dimensions. There have been many typologies proposed and none has yet come to capture the whole field. What I have found valuable in this textbook is the effort to represent many of these typologies to give us many dimensions along which to think about culture. Some dimensions are universal across all cultures such as concepts of space and time. But others, such as the nature of authority, are specially relevant to the social and organizational worlds in which we all live. By looking at many different dimensions we learn not only how complex cultures are but also sharpen our own abilities to decipher new cultures we encounter. Teachers, students, travelers, managers, leaders and entrepreneurs will all find in this book a wealth of important information and concepts to aid their thinking and cross-cultural behavior.

EDGAR H. SCHEIN
Professor Emeritus
MIT Sloan School of Management
Spring 2012

Prologue

The intelligence of cooperation

By Juliette Tournand de Rouyn

Introduction

My knowledge of how to manage successfully across cultures began to form in my school years. By the time I was fourteen, I had attended more schools than there had been school years. And each school seemed to have its own values, references and beliefs that were considered good and bad.

Much later, in 2001, the CEO of a very successful fashion, fragrance and beauty company, requested a program to improve the cooperation among the company's executives coming from artistic, scientific, engineering, finance, management, HR, marketing, sales and communication cultures. What common guide could be accepted by all? What guidelines might help them rise above their differences and lead them to achieve excellence? Here was my chance to clarify this thrilling question.

It brought me on a cross-cultural journey through time and place that began in ancient China, crossed 20th century Russia and North America, and may offer a new understanding for you to build a cross-cultural 21st century. Along the way, I gathered evidence that the best universal way to succeed is to manage cooperation. And, thanks to three outstanding cross-cultural champions, I could discern four forces, consistent guidelines that mark out the safe ways of cooperation and the risks inherent to it.

Ancient China, source of the human science of success: Strategy

Some of the first rational thinking about success was elaborated around 500 B.C. in The Art of War[2] by Sun Tzu. His theories turned out to be a tremendous success, having managed the double intercultural achievement of crossing the cultures of continents and ages to become a reference for leaders all over the world.

Don't be frightened by the title, The Art of War. According to Chinese wisdom, extremes contain the beginning of their opposites[3]. Written at the time of warring states in China, this "art of war" represents an extreme of war culture, so chances are that it also shelters the germ of peaceful encounters, the condition for sustainable success in life and business.

Indeed, Sun Tzu wrote that "all warfare is based on deception" and that "the height of skill is to win without a fight." A common interpretation is that "to win without a fight" means driving the enemy to self-sabotage, but this neglects "warfare is based on deception." In fact, Sun Tzu advises to make alliances where the ways cross.

Crossroads contain as many dangers as opportunities, however, and the enigmatic master also advises: "He who knows when to fight, and when not to, will be victorious."

When should we fight? As seldom as possible, perhaps, since Sun Tzu advises to save a town, a brigade or a soldier rather than destroy them. Offering only tactical advice, such as, "Don't confront who occupies a high ground," "Don't attack the elites," and "In death ground, fight," Sun Tzu doesn't give a clear guidelines concerning when to fight and when not to.

Western twentieth century takes over with Game Theory

I recognized Sun Tzu's question, however, culturally worlds apart from ancient China, when I read the report[4] of a tournament organized at the University of Michigan in 1979.

---

2 Sun Tzu, The Art of War, translated from Chinese by Jean Joseph Amiot 1772, Samuel B. Griffith 1963, Valérie Niquet Cabestan 1990, Tsai Chi Chung 1991. From a Chinese text to occidental language, it is worth using different translations to reduce cultural bias.
3 More about reconciliation of dichotomies in chapter 10
4 R. Axelrod, The Evolution of Cooperation, Basic Books, 1984.

Participants included game theorists in economics, sociology, political science and mathematics. Each had contributed a computer program containing his decision rules, or strategy, that the tournament had then confronted one on one to all others, to itself and to a random program in a multiple moves competition. Echoing Sun Tzu's dilemma, the game consisted simply of choosing at each move, "I cooperate" or "I refuse to cooperate."

The game simulated life's crossroads: players had to decide their move before knowing what the others would do, and their score depended on their own move as well as the opposing player.

- When two players refused to cooperate they received only one point each.

- When two players cooperated they received three points each. As in life, mutual cooperation scored better than going alone.

- If one player refused to cooperate when the other cooperated, however, then the refusal brought five points to the refusing player and zero points to the cooperating one. The scoring took into account the risk of defeat when one player offers cooperation to a player who refuses it.

The winner would be the player who's strategy collects the highest amount of points.

The organizer, Professor[5] Robert Axelrod, intended to run three sets, and, after each set, to disclose all strategies and their scores in order to improve the strategies as the tournament progressed.

A surprise awaited the organizers at the end of the first set: the strategies that restrained from refusing cooperation until having received a refusal—Axelrod qualified them as "nice"– performed significantly better than those which searched the five/zero gain and initiated a refusal. The common belief that "the best defense is attack" was scientifically defeated. I saw in this result a scientific confirmation of one of Sun Tzu's most mysterious declarations, "The loser searches the victory in the fight," completed by his surprising, "the winner wins before seeking the fight." Moreover, the winner of the first set won without seeking a fight

---

5 Professor for the Study of Human Understanding at the University of Michigan in 1979.

(without ever initiating a refusal), and increased his lead the longer the game lasted, showing a way to win in Sun Tzu's manner.

As expected, the strategies and their respective performances were published before the second set. Meanwhile, the first set had produced such a buzz in the scientific communities that the second set gathered a cross-cultural melting pot of 64 competitors, including economists, biologists, sociologists, psychologists, computer scientists, and mathematicians, mostly from America, but also Canada, Europe and New-Zealand. All were aware of the winning program and eager to beat it, yet, the same strategy won again! There was no point in playing a third set.

Proposed by Russian-born bio-mathematician Anatol Rapoport, the winning strategy resisted multiple and long-lasting exchanges, a multitude of players and the being revealed. Moreover, it took advantage of these circumstances (simulating real life conditions) to win even more

Intriguingly, it never scored better than the opposing player in one on one play. It assured its victory by gathering the most long lasting cooperative games, those that offer a high score to both. Now, I understood why "the winner wins before seeking to fight." He seeks fruitful alliances before fighting. And manages to maximize the potential of overall cooperation.

Rapoport knows when to cooperate and when not to. This know-how generates enough alliances for him to win the tournament while many other players, of course, chose to fight. So when to cooperate? Here is his strategy, the simplest of the tournament:

- He starts the game with a cooperative move and cooperates as long as he receives cooperative moves. He cooperates as long as he receives cooperation in return.

- When a player sends him a refusal, he immediately sends a refusal; and comes back to cooperation as soon as he gets a cooperative move again.

PROLOGUE

How to implement this in life?

Robert Axelrod described Rapoport's mechanism as "cooperating on the first move and then doing whatever the other player did on the preceding move." Although correct, this view was of little practical use for people with leadership ambitions, so Axelrod came up with some tips:

- Don't be envious
- Never be the first to defect (Axelrod's formula for refusing to cooperate)
- Practice reciprocity in cooperation as well as in defection
- Don't be too clever
- Don't try to be tricky

But, one "Do" and four "Don'ts" don't provide enough accuracy to achieve Anatol Rapoport's performance in real life. Where is the scientific difference between inefficient envy and the inspiration one feels from watching others success? Where is the line between "clever" and "too clever?" Robert Axelrod was focused on finding how a mastery of the game could promote cooperation in a population, rather than at giving clear guidelines to individuals.

Yet, each of us is a participant in the game of life, and life is a multiplayer game where the choice to cooperate is a gain if the other cooperates and a loss if the other doesn't. At each move, the decision to cooperate or not is personal and a leap of faith, so it could be useful to find an operational model of Rapoport's winning strategy in real life.

Other authors wrote about this famous tournament and strategy, and some identified positive combinations in Rapoport's strategy, such as goodwill, retaliation and forgiveness. But they didn't enlighten us as to how, in real life, retaliation coexists with goodwill and forgiveness, nor what to do when forgiveness is too difficult to achieve to serve as a starting point.

Altogether, the evidence that there was a treasure in Rapoport's strategy, mixed with the blanks left by the literature about it, opened the way to further research.

Indeed, Anatol Rapoport was not only a champion of cross-cultural success in theory, but also in practice. Born in Russia in 1911, he arrived in the U.S. in 1922. He studied as a future piano virtuoso in Chicago, then at the State Academy of Music and Performing Arts of Vienna, Austria. Back in North America, he switched disciplines to biomathematics and lived in Canada.

In 1979, when he won Axelrod's tournament of strategy in research on cooperation theory, he was an emeritus professor of biomathematics and psychology at the University of Toronto, Canada, having combined three complex professional cultures and at least four national ones.

And, as a member of the team of peacemakers who helped the negotiations between the Soviet and Western blocks to avoid a nuclear conflict during the Cold War, he managed that a major conflict didn't happen. Just as he did in the scientific tournament, Anatol Rapoport proved himself in eminently complex situations to rank among the "best of the strategists" according to Sun Tzu. And reached the epitome of his art: conflicts don't happen.

Anatol Rapoport's life demonstrates, if necessary, that cooperation is the key of excellence in cross-cultural communication and management. And, managing the same result in life and in the tournament (to maximize the potential of any cooperation), he must have had the same recipe in both fields.

His strategy in the game is difficult to implement in life because it was specifically designed for a very simple game. But it certainly contains the recipe.

A set of forces for cross-cultural management excellence: benevolence, reciprocity, clarity, creativity

What forces govern Rapoport's strategy from the inside? Let us pose the problem as mathematicians do and search the necessary and sufficient set of forces or values that lead to Rapoport's mechanism.

- Opening the game with a cooperative move, shows a first force: benevolence for the other.

- Maintaining cooperation when receiving cooperative moves, adds reciprocity to benevolence.

- When playing a refusal after each refusal, reciprocity shows itself again. At first, we may believe that this reciprocity pairs with malevolence. But refusing is the only way offered in the game to avoid one's own destruction when confronted to a non-cooperative move. Rapoport here displays elementary benevolence for himself. This move is the perfect reciprocal of the first move, which was benevolence for the other. Benevolence and reciprocity are still at work.

- When going back to cooperation as soon as the other players cooperates again, benevolence and reciprocity are clearly there.

Benevolence and reciprocity are obviously constants of Rapoport's strategy, necessary keys. Are they sufficient to obtain his success? Not quite, because there was another benevolent and reciprocal strategy in the tournament. It worked, too, but Rapoport scored better. Unlike Rapoport, this strategy waited for two refusals before switching to refusal itself. What difference does it make? By reacting immediately, Rapoport's strategy was much easier for competitors to read. Thus, all players who were more clever than tricky could see that when Rapoport played cooperation they were assured the three-point score. And, since they could also see that after a refusal against him, they couldn't hope more than one point, a significant number of players stabilized their game by cooperating with Rapoport, letting him accumulate the greatest number of high one-to-one scores. The third force of his game is clarity.

My quest had lead me to those three simple forces: benevolence, reciprocity and clarity. And they cope very well with real life. They are combined in any sustainable success.

Of course, when you switch from the game to real life, you are confronted to situations where you don't see how benevolence, reciprocity and clarity could meet. There, don't give up. You need one more force to succeed, the force of life: creativity.

CROSS-CULTURAL MANAGEMENT TEXTBOOK

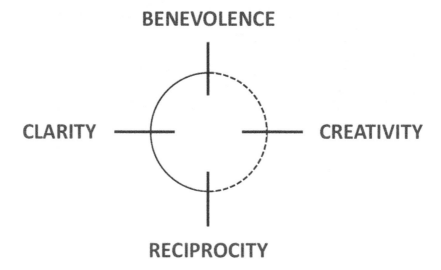

Fig. 0.1 Cross-cultural compass

Let us see that in a few examples:

Imagine you are a young American visiting France. You are invited for lunch at the home of your aunt, who you cherish. Upon entering, however, a smell turns your stomach. You are experiencing that, as far as food is concerned, generations and national habits have widened a cultural gap between you and aunt. After greeting you with a kiss on each cheek, she says with a smile, "I hope you like snails with garlic, darling" Snails with garlic! Her feast is a horror for you. Applying the rules of the game, what can you do?

1. Cooperate with an opponent that "doesn't cooperate" and eat the snails. "They are delicious," you might add, while guaranteeing a future of snails with garlic at auntie's house unless you sadly avoid future visits.

2. Attack and say, "How can you cook such special food without asking before if I like it? I hate snails with garlic!" And offend your aunt who will take it personally…

   In real life, you can say, "Aunty, I love you as much as I hate snails with garlic, so let's find a couple of eggs for me. I am so happy to see you!" After an initial surprise at your declaration (you had never told her you love her), she bursts into laughter and leads the way to the kitchen, thinking you are definitely her favorite niece or nephew.

This successful answer is benevolent for the aunt, benevolent for you, and perfectly clear. You can refuse to cooperate to what you experiment as a refusal of cooperation (here, to your taste), without attacking. Of course, it requires a small innovation: to say "I love you" to auntie.

Now let us increase the difficulty with another real world example, Chun-Hei at work.

Chun-Hei, a Korean lecturer, was confused when she started teaching an Erasmus class in Europe. In her native culture, students showed deference towards teachers, but this mix of European students seemed to ignore basic respect to her authority: silence when she speaks. The class's chattering surprised and disturbed her, but, "to be nice," she put up with some of it. Yet, the more chattering she accepted, the more there was, until she felt she had no choice but to protest to obtain silence. Her lectures alternated between growing murmurs (where she thought she was benevolent) and upset protestations (where she thought she was clear). Not realizing that she was never benevolent and clear at the same time, she believed she was both, and, receiving no satisfaction in return, complained that reciprocity didn't work with benevolence. Aware of the three forces that govern Rapoport's strategy, she decided to keep them together at the same time. Of course, it led her to be creative.

At her next lecture, when the first chatting occurred, Chun-Hei stood silent. At the beginning it felt odd. But since it was the first chatting, she was able to stand with a smile on her, watching the chattering people who eventually returned her smile with gentle apologies. She accepted the apologies in another silent smile (apologizing, they were cooperating again; so reciprocity worked when she was clear and benevolent) and went on. When more chatting started in another part of the room, she stopped again, smiling. This time, instead of apologizing, the chatterboxes asked her a question that was perfectly on the subject. All Chun-Hei had to do was to cooperate with the question by clarifying her point, which was a pleasure. So she continued, lecturing to her students who felt allowed to interrupt with questions that concerned the content.

By stopping her speech when the chatting began, Chun-Hei had not attacked, just refused to cooperate with the very first refusal to cooperate with her lecture. To her surprise, this led to better behavior than using what she thought was a nice attitude. Solving the complex problem of contagious chatting was as simple as that, and it created the conditions of true cooperation, arousing the perfect attentive and active audience that any speaker dreams of.

Consistent with the core of Rapoport's strategy, Chun-Hei, had joined the elite set of commanders, according to Sun Tzu. She used "the normal forces to engage"[6]—her normal forces being the knowledge she shared—and "the extraordinary forces to win."[11] "Extraordinary" is the Western translation for Qi, a Chinese word and key concept of this culture: life-force or energy flow. And, indeed, by putting herself at the crossroads of the three forces braided in the core of Rapoport's strategy, Chun-Hei created and nourished the conditions for the Qi to rise. As a result she acquired in her lectures one of the most desirable skills praised by Sun Tzu, "victory from the situation without demanding it of subordinates"[12].

Conclusion

Sun Tzu, Robert Axelrod, Anatol Rapoport, three worldwide authorities in strategy—the science of success—,and belonging to very different cultures, converge to put us on the fast track of success whatever the culture differences: the track of cooperation.

My research has led me to identify four forces: Reciprocity, Clarity and Benevolence, and Creativity at the rescue. Combined together, they lead the way to innovative and effective cooperation management.

They form a new understanding of cooperation between people and also between cultures[7], prerequisite to any successful cross-cultural relationship.

---

6 Sun Tzu, The Art of War.
7 Find more about Juliette Tournand's work on the associated website www.crossculturaltextbook.org and by reading "La Stratégie de la Bienveillance", Dunod Ed.

PROLOGUE

CASE STUDY 0.1: TRAINING IN YEMEN

During her internship at a European consulting company, Fanny was asked to assist a senior consultant sent to Yemen for a much needed two week "budget and cost control" training session at an important local company.

Fanny's first surprise was to discover that whatever the interest of the attendees, which they formally expressed, they always took valuable time out of the course for the multiple daily prayers required by their Muslim culture. The second surprise, more difficult to deal with, was that, in spite of the attention that the attendees showed during the course, when it came to practice it was almost as if the course had not taken place. This observation, combined with the frequent breaks, started to dampen Fanny's and the consultant's spirit. The time left for the task, which was reducing day by day, increased their stress and they began to lose their grip. Of course, the critical question which arose was: who is wrong? Is it us, the trainers, or the attendees?

Realizing that they were about to tend to reciprocal malevolence (like criticizing the attendees, then each other's teaching, then suffer the pain of guilt) they decided to do themselves some good and to relax during the next prayer meeting. Then, they had a stress-free conversation about the culture issues they were encountering. They observed the fact, probably related to Muslim culture, that the attendees were all men. They also noted that these were proud people and, despite having little money, considered prayer more important than budget and cost control. Their rank of values was completely different.

In a flash, Fanny understood. In this culture not only prayers but also pride were more important than budget management. Maybe was it simply impossible for these men to disclose what they didn't know or understand in the presence of a young European woman? Was *she* then the problem? Or could she choose to be the solution?

She suggested that the consultant continued the teaching alone. Fanny would assist him by actually assisting *the audience*. She would be the one to ask the questions. The only unknown was how the attendees would welcome such a change of role. They didn't even seem to notice it… apart from the fact that from then on everything taught was put into practice. The course became a success for both the attendees and the consulting company. And for Fanny it turned out to be a rewarding experience.

CASE STUDY 0.1: TRAINING IN YEMEN

Discussion questions:

- What are the cultural differences preventing the training taking place as expected?
- How does creativity enter in action?
- How do you explain that the participants didn't seem to notice Fanny's change of role?
- Can you think of a similar situation near you?

Chapter 1: Comparing cultures

CHAPTER CONTENTS

Highlights
Introduction

WHAT IS CULTURE?
    Definitions
    The grocery store theory
    Ethnocentrism
    Stereotypes
    Cultural Intelligence

CULTURE AS A MULTI-LAYER CONCEPT
    The superficial layer: the Artifacts
    The middle layers
    The inner layers
    Taboos
    Cultural archetypes
    Religion and culture

COMPARING CULTURES
    Observing and generalizing
    Culture as a normal distribution
    How apes can help humans in understanding themselves
    Behavioral dimensions
    Culture and nations

    Conclusion
    Recap
    Workshop 1.1: Work Goals
    Workshop 1.2: Your own cultural artifacts

CHAPTER 1

COMPARING CULTURES

By Jérôme Dumetz

Highlights:

After reading this chapter, you should be able to:

- Explain why there are several ways to define culture
- Make a better use of stereotypes
- Recognize the various layers of culture
- Comprehend the concept of cultural dimensions

Introduction

Humans are social animals. We live in families, in groups, in neighborhoods, in countries, in societies. We work in companies, we study in class and we play sports in teams. Interaction between people is constant, and we are used to it.

Every day we need skills to connect two apparently different situations: sometimes a problem and a solution; more often two conflicting ideas. Psychologists call this cognitive dissonance, and it is absolutely common. Everyone is concerned; it is part of our human nature.

Most of us are trained from birth to deal with those situations. Our personalities play a important role here. Some feel more comfortable than others to face such circumstances but overall we cope quite well.

Things get tricky when we are driven to face a new type of dissonance - when we are brought to a new environment. This might mean a move to a new town, to another region, or even to another country. It is also the case when we join a new school, a new company, or when we welcome someone from a different culture. Closer to our private life, it is also true when we join a new family (in-laws).

Suddenly, interrogations ("Why do they dress this way?"), misunderstandings ("They show so much disrespect to the professor!"), and outright shock ("I won't eat this!") seem to multiply. Something has supercharged the complexity of the interactions.

Selected definitions of culture:

1. "Culture is the collective programming of the mind which distinguishes the members of one group from another."

    Geert Hofstede

2. "Culture is an integrated system of learned behavior patterns that are characteristic of the members of any given society. Culture refers to the total way of life of a particular group of people. It includes everything that a group of people thinks, says, does, and makes–its customs, language, material artifacts, and shared system of attitudes and feelings. Culture is learned and transmitted from generation to generation."

    Robert Kohls

3. "Culture refers to whatever an identifiable group of people shares in order to meet its basic human needs and maintain its sense of identity."

    Jean-Claude Arteau

4. "Culture hides more than it reveals, and strangely enough, what it hides, it hides most effectively from its own participants."

    Edward T. Hall

What is yours?

This "thing" that makes the difference is culture.

COMPARING CULTURES

WHAT IS CULTURE?

Definitions

Ask around and you'll be surprised at how many definitions of culture you can find. In fact, there are easily more than one hundred definitions of culture.

Generally, these definitions relate to the way people understand the reality of the world around them. This is associated with our understanding of culture related to civilization. For example:

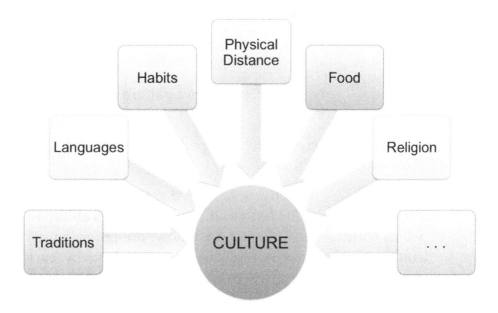

Fig. 1.1 – Culture synthesizes one's civilization

The Latin root of the word "culture" has something to do with the tilling of the soil; it is linked to cultivation. So, if we dig deeper, we can understand culture in a different way, related to something a lot more personal, halfway between our human natures characteristics and our personality preferences. Therefore, culture can also be associated with patterns of thinking, feeling, and acting toward others.

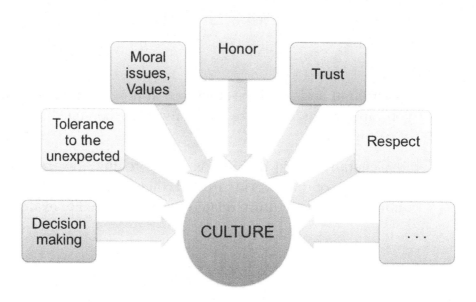

Fig. 1.2 – **Culture as a pattern of behaviors**

Renowned cross-cultural specialist Geert Hofstede calls culture "software of the mind."[8]

Despite its attractiveness, this definition can be rather narrow. It doesn't give enough credit to the human mind's ability to react. Indeed, while software is designed to follow pre-programmed automations, culture isn't a perfectly replicated process. Actually, each member of a given culture often carries a different version of it!

Earlier, cultural anthropologists Florence Kluckhohn and Fred Strodtbeck developed their Values Orientation Theory with three basic assumptions:[9]

1. There is a limited number of common human problems for which all peoples must at all times find some solution.

2. While there is variability in the solutions to all the problems, this variability is neither limitless nor random but is definitely variable within a range of possible solutions.

---

8   Hofstede, 1991, *Cultures and Organizations: Software of the Mind*
9   Hills, M.D. (2002). Kluckhohn and Strodtbeck's Values Orientation Theory. *Online Readings in Psychology and Culture*

3. All alternatives of all solutions are present in all societies at all times but are differentially preferred.

Here is an application in your daily life:

The grocery store theory

You are in your local grocery store. It's the end of the afternoon and several people are lining up in front of the cashier. You are fourth in line. In front of you stands a young mother with a young child. The boy is approximately five years old and all of a sudden he gets into hysterics. You understand from his cries that he wants a chocolate bar.

Immediately the atmosphere in the shop is changing. Each client exchanges amused looks and smiles. All but one: the mother!

Now, imagine it is you in this situation playing the part of the mother. What options are offered to you?

- To buy the chocolate bar?
- To ignore the child?
- To spank the boy?
- To leave the shop?
- Any others?

All those options are possible, yet our upbringing, our personalities, and also our cultures shape us to choose one solution.

This leads us to a commonly accepted definition of culture: "**Culture is the way we solve problems.**"[10]

But we can go one step further. Granted, our culture is influencing our decisions. However, we don't always act the way we think we should. Our "software of the mind" is indeed confronted by the unexpected: the context. The context (the child is sick and you have just come back from the doctor; it's the third time today such a crisis has happened and you have warned him to stop; you are running for local elections and you wish to show your family values, etc) will ultimately influence your decision, too. But your preference stands no matter what.

---

10 Edgar H. Schein, 1985, *Organizational Culture and Leadership*

Actually, all the options are possible. However, ask around, and most people will confirm the second assumption of Kluckhohn and Strodtbeck that, in fact, a limited number of options is available. This is an illustration of what psychologists call *availability heuristics*, here applied to culture: when confronted with a problem, we usually choose our solution from the most easily accessible ones.

Let's go back to the grocery store and ask ourselves another question. Not only "What would I do in such situation," but also "How would I rank my choices?" Once again, if you ask other clients in the shop, you'll find that most of them not only have the same options in mind but also a similar ranking. Statistically, fellow-clients of your local store are likely to approve the mother's decision, whatever it is.

It is when you go to another store located in a different region or another country that problems might arise. Not because people have different options in mind, but because they have a different ranking in mind! In other words, if a Dutch mother will shock fellow clients in an Italian grocery store by ignoring the cries, it is not because of her decision itself (they can easily imagine having to act that way), but because of her decision in this **context**.

When reaching out to other cultures, the challenge isn't only to understand their cultural elements but actually to understand their ranking. **Being able to adapt your ranking to the other's is what cross-culture is all about.**

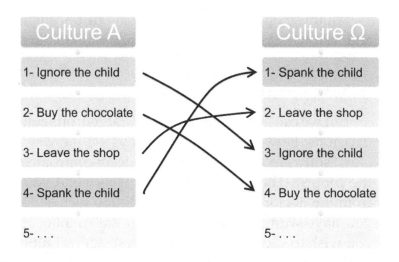

Fig. 1.3 – Connecting with the other's ranking

Failing to understand the other's mindset leads, in the best of cases, to guaranteed disillusions. Despite the numerous signs of globalization surrounding us, the increased knowledge of foreign languages, the soar in international traveling and the "flattening" of the world thanks to new technologies, despite it all, we remain different from one culture to another with cross-cultural blunders heard regularly in the news.

Ethnocentrism

When in contact with other cultures, and whenever we face difficulties in comprehending or accepting the manners or habits of others, we have a common tendency to see the world through the prism of our own culture. Understanding other cultures is not an easy process and as human beings we will often try to reduce the dissonance, by either denying the differences or by deciding their culture is simply better than the other, (and so removing the need for adaptation). This behavior is called ethnocentrism and it is the prime obstacle to cross-cultural management.

Stereotypes

Ethnocentrism is a global and widespread phenomenon because it is related to inherited culture. Expressions of ethnocentrism are stereotypes, mockeries or ridicule, toward the one who is different. If this occurrence is already hard to tolerate within a day-to-day relationship, it can become a major problem in the field of management.

Ethnocentrism is by essence intolerant toward others, and this is hardly compatible with the conduct of cross-cultural studies. People who claim to engage into cross-cultural relationships ought to respect and accept different views.

For all our positive intentions, this is not always an easy task. All of us use shortcuts to simplify our understanding of our environment. We set up a mental binary system: men/women, manager/subordinate, happy/sad, hardworking/lazy, etc. So that when we face a different culture for the first time, we naturally observe (and often judge) through the lenses of our mental binary system. And as far as culture is concerned, these shortcuts often lead to the establishments of stereotypes.

A stereotype is a cut-and-dried opinion. It is the result of a categorization that guides our behavior, particularly with regard to a given group or population of a given country. The stereotype never describes the behavior of an individual; it describes only the standard of behavior that one allots to all the members of a given group[11].

Stereotypes are often negative but may also be positive. Indeed, they can be helpful as a starting point to understanding new situations. The key issue is not whether stereotypes are useful or dangerous but actually not to question them. Candidly questioning the validity of stereotypes gently leads to engaging discussions in a cross-cultural encounter.

Sadly, a number of stereotypes related to the ethnic characteristics or the superiority of a culture over others should be considered so intolerant that they are not compatible with the open-mindedness required in cross-cultural communication and management. Being ignorant is not an excuse for insulting others.

Ultimately, stereotypes may inform more about the individual who comes up with the stereotype than the stereotyped person. Effectively, if one claims "all the rich people are lazy," the audience will react differently depending on whether this person making the claim is penniless or a known billionaire. When said by a poor man, one can always think, "Well, he is just jealous," but coming from a rich one, people may say, "Actually, he knows what he is talking about."

Once again, the context is intrinsically linked to our understanding of behaviors. Therefore, before discarding stereotypes, it is necessary to learn more about oneself and then to sort out the useful from the detrimental comments within stereotypes.

Cultural Intelligence

The study of cross-cultural management is a recent discipline and the processes to quantify the capacity to adapt to foreign cultures are seldom. An original concept is Cultural Intelligence (sometimes referred to as CQ, as in IQ). Calculating Cultural Intelligence is an attempt to measure how flexible and ready individuals are when confronted to a new culture.

---

11 Nancy Adler, 1991. *International Dimensions of Organizational Behavior.*

In 2003, Christopher Earley and Soon Ang[12] identified three features of a person's cultural intelligence:

- **Cognition**: "Do I know what is happening?" Understanding that cultural differences are happening in a given situation.

- **Motivation**: "Am I motivated to act?" Being prepared to relate and deal with people despite the difficulties imposed by cultural difference.

- **Behavior**: "Can I respond appropriately and effectively?" Learning how to relate and attend to people across cultures.

This approach is now the basis for most tools developed by researchers and practitioners to evaluate an individual's readiness to confront a new culture. The rationale being that the higher your cultural intelligence, the better you are prepared to experience a cross-cultural situation smoothly.

For instance, the Guidelines for Assessing Intercultural Communicative Competence (ICC) published by the Council of Europe[13] use three dimensions in their method:

- The intercultural "knowledge", aka "The know-what"
- The intercultural "know-how"
- The intercultural "know-being"

Completing this course and reading this textbook is designed to greatly enhance your QC but it will not be enough to "ride the waves of cultures[14]" easily. Some preliminary steps are necessary and before finding out how to reach out to another culture (by connecting the values as in Figure 1.3) we need to understand what culture is made of.

---

12   Early & Soon, 2003, *Cultural Intelligence: Individual Interactions Across Cultures*, Stanford business books

13   I. Lazar et al. , 2008, *Developing and Assessing Intercultural Communicative Competence: A Guide for Language Teachers and Teacher Educators*, Council of Europe edition

14   F. Trompenaars, 1993, *Riding The Waves of Culture: Understanding Diversity in Global Business*, The Economist Books

CULTURE AS A MULTI-LAYER CONCEPT

If everyone can make his or her own definition of culture, what definition of culture enjoys a consensus? Here is Edgar Schein's Level of Culture model.

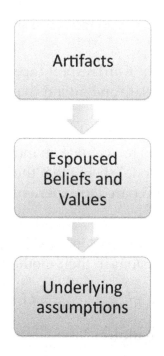

Fig. 1.4 – Ed. H. Schein model

Designed to describe organizational culture, this model is the root of many others. The paradigm, however, remains the same: culture can be analyzed through several different layers.

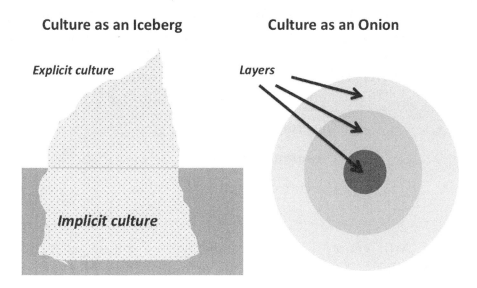

Fig. 1.5 – **Various models: culture as an iceberg and an onion**

Very common in North American courses, the "**cultural iceberg**" is very reminiscent of the 1960's "human motivation iceberg" of psychiatrist turned advertising guru Ernest Dichter[15]. The "**cultural onion**" (which looks more like a target actually) is a graphic re-design of Schein's model by cross-cultural pioneer Geert Hofstede.

Edgard Schein has his own metaphor of culture, that of a **lily pond**. And true enough, culture is anything but as frozen and static as an iceberg! As for the onion, dear to Dutchmen Hofstede and Trompenaars, well, maybe the bulb of the tulip had something to do with this image? In the lily pond, the elements are the flowers and leaves. These are connected through a root system to the bottom of the pond that is dynamic in providing the nutrients that create the flowers and leaves. Move one element and instantly ripples will transform the apparently static pond: **Culture is a dynamic system with hidden elements.**

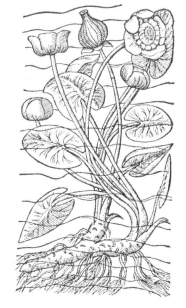

Fig. 1.6 – **A water lily**

---

15   E. Dichter, 2002, *The Strategy of Desire*, Transaction Publ.

When we are living and working in another culture we are usually very aware of obvious differences in dress, food, and basic behaviors. However, much more important for effective integration are the differences at a deeper, implicit level, which we are less likely to be aware of. Three distinct layers can be distinguished:

- The artifacts,
- The norms and values
- The core of the culture

The superficial layer: Artifacts

Artifacts represent the outer layer of culture, also called the explicit culture. As Schein states, it "includes all the phenomena that one sees, hears and feels when one encounters a new group with an unfamiliar culture."

In order to help us sort the artifacts they can be classified into three sub-categories: symbols, characters, and habits.

1. Symbols are words, gestures, pictures, or objects that carry a particular meaning that is only recognized by those who share the culture[16]. Among the endless examples, one can think of a country's flag, a regional drink, a traditional hairstyle, hand gestures, a typical house construction, and many others.

2. Characters are persons, dead or alive, real or fictional, who are closely associated with the surveyed culture. The term heroes, coined by Hofstede, is widely used but can be misleading, as heroes are usually associated with a positive image. Here, anyone, seen as good or bad, can qualify, from current politicians to sport legends, children's book heroes or local teams' mascots.

3. Habits (or rituals) are activities the members of the studied culture demonstrate in their natural environment. Ritualistic gatherings, such as religious ceremonies or sport events come to mind; also included are business etiquette or social practices.

---

16 Hofstede, 1991, *Cultures and Organizations: Software of the Mind*

> **Watch your shoes!**
>
> *An illustration of cultural habits*
>
> "If you are invited to a Czech home and your hosts urge you not to take off your sneakers, they are almost certainly expressing courtesy to their guest and expecting you to say something like 'Oh, that's alright,' and then leave your outdoor shoes by the doorstep. If you don't, and march into their flat with your own shoes on, you'll risk eternal damnation. Most Czech households have extra pairs of slippers, which guests are supposed to put on their feet during the visit."
>
> *Terje B. Englund, 2004, The Czech in a Nutshell*

The middle layers

If artifacts are often referred as explicit culture, the deeper layers are labeled implicit culture. It is because these elements of culture, unlike the artifacts, are more difficult to observe.

Schein, in his model, wrote about "espoused beliefs and values." Today, most practitioners describe this area of culture in terms of two layers: norms and values.

- A norm is a common orientation of a group toward what **one should do.** This is a very binary concept, in that most of us think an attitude can be either **right or wrong**. Groups, in essence, are individuals sharing common norms. Norms are often external; each society superimposes them on its members, reinforced by measure of social control. In many ways, norms are rules (written or not).

- A value is a common orientation toward what one **would like to do**. This is a lot more personal. Values are not binary concepts; here there is more room for ambiguity. Values tend to be more internal than norms and most societies do not have many means of controlling their enforcement. Besides, values are philosophical notions that are, in principle, nearly impossible to entirely fulfill. This is why values are usually analyzed along an axis with plus and minus on each end.

Our upbringing is actually mostly about learning and applying norms and values. Culture is a learned process and since the superficial aspects of cultures are easy to spot, they rarely represent sources of misunderstanding. Norms and values, on the other side, are most likely the cause of shocks and astonishment.

In the case of the grocery store, clients are not only shocked by the mother's action, but also by what such action means to them. While an Italian mother decides to spank her child in order to show him, and the other clients, that a line was crossed, an American citizen present in the store might find this action utterly violent and inappropriate. Alternatively, the Italian mother would most likely be disapproving of the American lady who favors buying the sweet, so coming to the conclusion the mother has given up and showed no moral firmness.

The inner layer

Whether we describe culture as an onion, an iceberg, or any other graphical representation (see chapter 2), most models take into account elements of culture that are intended to have influenced the shaping of the culture.

If we dig deeper we unearth basic assumptions that will ultimately influence norms and values, and through a chain reaction, the artifacts. These basic assumptions are the ultimate sources of value and norms and if taken for granted, they are very difficult to distinguish.

Often such basic assumptions are directly related to topics such as:

- Geography (island, mountains, desert, etc)
- Climate (continental, tropical, etc)
- History (former empires, kingdoms or colonies, wars)

> **From trees to gift rituals**
>
> Origami is a Japanese tradition of creating beautiful shapes by paper folding. The Japanese show great skill when it comes to wrapping gifts and offering them in an encoded celebration (to be handed with both hands, wrapped, never in numbers of four or nine). Many Westerners are baffled by this elaborate demonstration.
>
> Across the Sea of Japan, in Russia, offering a gift is not so codified. Actually, if Russians offer many presents to each other, the focus is more on the act of offering and on the meaning of the gift, more than the way the gift is presented. Typically, small gifts are simply tossed into a pretty paper bag (with flowers or kittens printed on it) and handed over. Wrapping is not compulsory, unlike in Japan.
>
> Now, let's look at some core differences between these two cultures. While the countries are of similar population sizes, Japan is a small island with practically no resources and small forests (bonsais are an old tradition!), Russia is the largest country in the world, with forest covering most of its territory.
>
> Paper has a long history in Japan and has always been seen as an expensive resource. Creating elaborate wrappings in beautiful paper enhances the value and meaning of a gift. In Russia, paper is… paper. There is nothing special about it and so Russians do not associate paper with anything valuable.
>
> In other words, we could sum up the situation as such:
>
> ➢ Japan: Small territory and shortage of trees results in gift wrapping being very codified, furoshiki and origami
>
> ➢ Russia: Large territory and plenty of trees results in gift wrapping being very casual. Gifts are meant to be spontaneous, no cultural artifact linked to the wrapping.

Three other concepts may be associated with the inner layer of culture: Taboos, cultural archetypes and religions.

Taboos

"Taboo" is a relatively new word in English (it comes from "tapu" or "tabu" in Polynesian languages) but its meaning is not.

Originally, taboo referred to something forbidden, often related to religion. A place could be taboo (forbidden to go for the non-initiated), an object could be taboo (forbidden to use), a word could be taboo (e.g. using the name of God), and of course some behavior could be taboo.

Taboos have steadily become an element of cultural artifact used to identify a given culture. But taboos can also be understood as the negative equivalents to cultural artifacts. As such, taboos can refer to:

- Symbols (such as the swastika in Germany, legally forbidden to show),
- Characters (He-Who-Must-Not-Be-Named in Harry Potter...),
- Words (any word considered vulgar becomes a taboo in any culture),
- Norms (nudity in Muslim countries),
- Values (male's infertility),
- Rituals (Animal sacrifice in Western countries), and,
- Behavior (walking naked in most developed countries).

Breaking taboos is understood as not following the rules of a given culture. A stranger can be tolerated for doing so, but the repetition of such breaches of tradition will not.

While taboos are usually extreme cases, any disobeying of established rules can create unpleasant feelings among the hosts and a visitor is always well advised to inquire about them.

Cultural archetypes

Coming from the field of psychiatry, French-American Clotaire Rapaille is a marketing adviser to many international companies. Dr. Rapaille's psychiatric work, based on Jung's approach and research led him to develop a new process for understanding how individuals are imprinted for the first time by what he calls the Logic of Emotion - the code of each cultural archetype in the collective unconscious of a given culture[17].

Some neuroscientists assert that humans primarily take their decisions with their "reptilian brain", the part of the brain that controls our instinctual behaviors. Dr Rapaille played with this concept in various fields related to marketing and claimed that people's "reptilian" brain answers to cultural stimuli that can be identified through reseach.

Arguably, Rapaille's cultural archetypes have some similarities with the core assumptions of a culture. For instance:

- The English code for England is CLASS
- The French code for France is IDEA
- The American code for the USA is DREAM
- The German code for Germany is ORDER

Religion and culture

Religions have a clear influence on both personality and cultural levels, in particular in decision making. Religions separate differently the spiritual from the temporal powers, hence influencing at various degrees the daily life of individuals.

Deciding where religion lies when describing culture is a subjective issue, yet two approaches can be observed:

- Religion is understood as one of our "cultures". We don't belong to a single culture but to several, such as our national culture, our corporate culture, our family culture and so on. Religion is adding an extra level with its own artifacts, values and norms. Specific clothing linked to religion rituals or obligations such as the Dumalla (turbans) and the Five Ks (Pañj Kakār) of the Sikhs are explicit elements of a "culture". Belonging to a religion, then, determines your behaviors.

- Another approach describes religion as a personal commitment having direct influence firstly on our behaviors. This more secular,

---

17 Rapaille (2006), *The Culture Code*

freewill based, approach to religion postulates that individuals ultimately choose their course of action consciously. Such an indeterminist view would categorize religion solely as a social factor, influencing one's personality. For instance, the history of the Jewish people based on persecution, exodus and repression could be the roots of the Israeli culture which statistically displays a strong tendency to want to control their environment (see chapter 6)

Whichever view one prefers to follow, it is necessary to treat religious characteristics with the same care as cultural cues. Cross-cultural communication must take into account religious benchmarks as they can most certainly be sources of misunderstanding or even frustrations.

COMPARING CULTURES

Observing and generalizing

One can't talk about entire cultures without generalizing. However, while generalizations may be accurate about groups, they're never going to be wholly true of individuals. In other words, not all of the individual Japanese or Germans you meet do act according to the cultural profile described in cross-cultural publications.

This doesn't mean that all these surveys and models are wrong, but only that in any culture you will always find a broad range of behaviors vis-à-vis a particular characteristic. Take indirectness, for example; you will find some Japanese who are exceedingly indirect, some who are rather indirect (by Western standards, that is), and some who are blunt. Or, take Americans and the notion of individualism or self-reliance: some Americans are extremely self-reliant, many are rather self-reliant, and some are very dependent. What we mean, then, when we say the Japanese are indirect or that Americans are self-reliant is that this trait seems to *predominate*, that is to be true of more of the people more of the time than either of the other two extremes.

While generalization refers to behavior displayed by the majority of a population, stereotypes are an extrapolation of an extreme behavior. For instance, we could safely generalize about the French people who enjoy drinking wine at dinner but it would be a stereotype to believe they eat frog legs each evening.

This being said, one should beware of generalizations even if they are not as ill-defined as stereotypes. Indeed, culture is only one of many influences on one's behavior. Depending on the circumstances, any one or a combination of these other influences—such as social class, gender, age, level and type of education—may be the primary determining factor for any particular behavior.

Culture as a normal distribution

Culture may also be presented as a normal distribution curve (bell curve).

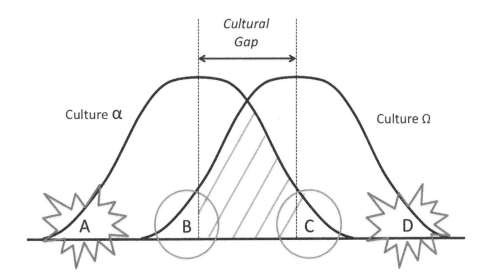

Fig. 1.7 – Culture as a normal distribution curve

In the graph above, each curve represents a culture. The difference in amplitude between the curves is the cultural gap. Thus, the further away two cultures are from each other, the greater the cultural gap.

However, when two cultures are separated by a small gap (USA and Canada, France and -French speaking region of Belgium- Wallonia, Germany and Austria, etc), it doesn't mean they are the same! Many managers make such assumptions when they go to a culture perceived as similar and pay a high price. While a big cultural gap is a guarantee of exoticism and cultural shocks, the differences are unmistakable. Two cultures with narrow gaps may lead to ignoring cultural differences altogether… until they come back in full force!

The central part of the graph, with stripes, is the cultural overlap, the common ground. In cross-cultural studies it is tempting to focus exclusively on cultural differences; however, most cultures share common norms and values. In most of your encounters with unfamiliar cultures the interactions will take place on this common ground. Here, misunderstandings are fewer.

This being said, if we represent culture with such a curve, it is because cultures also have extremities: extreme behaviors. For instance, in most European countries (culture α), it is expected to eat with forks and knives at the table. Eventually, in some extreme cases (when picnicking or at a fast-food restaurant), it is acceptable to eat with your hands. In other cultures, such as many Arabic cultures (culture Ω), a meal is shared as a group, and we expect guests and hosts to take food directly from the dish, by hand (and always the right hand).

When both cultures meet, each representative might tolerate the other "extreme" behavior: A European eating couscous with a fork, or a Yemenite eating a chicken wing by hand, at dinner.

Some extremes can be irreconcilable with other cultures. Religions can play a big role here: no matter how open-minded your Israeli guest is, s/he is unlikely to enjoy much of the Czech baked pork-knee served for dinner! Moreover, religion, superstitions and traditions are likely to be the main reasons for reacting to "extreme" behaviors.

> Behavior:
>
> 1. Manner of behaving or conducting oneself
>
> 2. On one's best behavior: behaving with good manners
>
> 3. *psychol* a. the aggregate of all the responses made by an organism in any situation b. a specific response of a certain organism to a specific stimulus or group of stimuli
>
> © *World English Dictionary, Collins*

It is useful to know your own extremes and limitations in order to engage with other cultures effortlessly. Meeting people in other cultures requires open-mindedness, but that doesn't mean you need to accept all the cultural elements of the others. Comparing cultures are the first steps to understanding each other.

How apes can help humans in understanding themselves

In the next chapter, we present the various fields of science that contributed to the creation of what cultural studies are today. Anthropology, sociology, communication, and modern business management are, of course, the main roots of this specialized field in management.

Cultural studies are, however undoubtedly, based on behavior analysis. This is not a precise science; it has little predictability, but the patterns created can reveal great practical use. The common point to all cross-cultural research is behavioral comparison.

Cross-cultural studies are actually not about analyzing cultures; this is impossible. "Culture," as Geert Hofstede often told his students, "does not exist."[18] Thus, cross-cultural studies exclusively use secondary data: behaviors are first observed and then analyzed. When we talk about cultural elements composing cultures such as values, we actually mean elements **stemming from the analysis of a specific behavior.**

Anthropology and ethnology have long involved the study of human behavior. Much can be learned about culture by studying these topics. However, in order to help us understand how culture can be compared, we can refer to the work of fellow scientists, the primatologists who study apes.

Primatology is the scientific study of primates, or apes. Apes are a family of primates, grouped into four genera: gorillas (Gorilla), chimpanzees (Pan), orangutans (Pongo), and humans (Homo). Primatologist Frans de Waal puts it succinctly: "We don't come from apes, we *are* apes."[19]

Scores of primatologists studied our closest kin, the chimpanzee. Chimpanzees share many features with humans. They live in social

---

18 Interculture magazine, Vol. 3, Num. 4
19 Frans de Waal, 2005, *Our Inner Ape*

groups, they have clear role definitions between males and females and an alpha male heads the group using aggression to maintain his position.

Sounds familiar? Many companies and governments today would fit this description! Many believe that our social organization and the relationships between one another are natural, almost genetic. If mankind is prone to conflict, it is because this is part of our core identity.

Things started to change in 1929 when a German anatomist, Ernst Schwarz, examined, a small skull in a museum that had been described as a juvenile chimpanzee because of its size. When Schwarz realized that it belonged to an adult he declared that he had stumbled on a new subspecies of chimpanzee. He named this new species the bonobo and the study of their behaviors was a revelation.

Bonobos, who can live up to sixty years, live in groups of about fifty individuals. They are not strongly territorial; so various groups often occupy similar range areas, allowing interactions between groups. A cluster of females, often older but not necessarily, heads each group. These females seem to have a strong character in common!

Males of the group, although physically stronger, usually submit to matriarchy, probably in fear of a cohesive group of females, but also because they get social and personal benefits from this situation. In fact, bonobo males stay closely bonded with their mothers and appear to gain benefits from the social position of the latter.

The bonobos are not only famous for this peaceful tendency. More troubling for early twentieth-century scientists, the bonobos appear to feature a highly sexualized social life. Bonobos have few serious conflicts as typically, conflicts are avoided by preemptive social negotiation. Such social negotiation includes cuddles, kisses, and frequent sexual contacts. Because juvenile females change groups, incestuous situations are prevented.

Sex, in other words, is used as a social tool to diffuse tensions and regulate social relationships.

Although males can sometimes dominate individual females, the formation of female alliances enables females to dominate the group. However, there are sometimes conflicts that take place and during female-female conflicts male bonobos sometimes play the role of peacekeepers. In this manner it appears that the desire for the maintenance of peaceful coexistence is shared among all members of the group. Most probably one of the great characteristics of bonobos is their ability to show empathy toward one other.

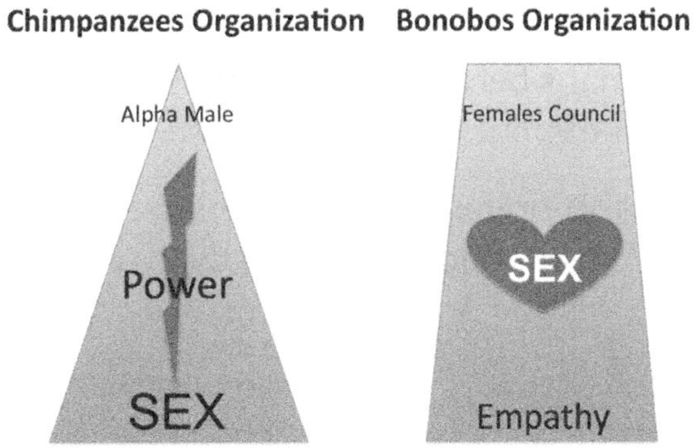

Chimpanzees Organization **Bonobos Organization**

Alpha Male / Power / SEX

Females Council / SEX / Empathy

Fig. 1.8 – Chimpanzees and Bonobos organizational structure

Chimpanzees and bonobos are members of the same genus, *Pan*, which means they can mate (although it has been rarely observed). Their differences in behavior, cannot therefore be solely linked to biology. Is it possible to say that chimpanzees and bonobos evolved with two different cultures?

> "Just imagine that we had never heard of chimpanzees or baboons and had known bonobos first. We would at present most likely believe that early hominids lived in female-centered societies, in which sex served important social functions and in which warfare was rare or absent. In the end, perhaps the most successful reconstruction of our past will be based not on chimpanzees or even on bonobos but on a three-way comparison of chimpanzees, bonobos, and humans."
> Frans de Waal, "Bonobo, Sex and Society[20]"

Behavioral dimensions

The differences in group behavior between bonobos and chimpanzees suddenly take a different meaning. A leading ethologist, Konrad Lorenz, theorized that aggression was a key element of human behavior. After

---

20 F. de Waal, 1995, *Bonobo, Sex and Society in Scientific American, Vol. 272, Issue 3*

observing chimpanzees who, like humans, can feature extreme violence leading to mutilating and murder, it sounds plausible. The analysis of the bonobo social organization reveals facts about our hominine ancestors that have often been forgotten: human beings are also very developed when it comes to showing empathy and caring for others. Possibly, most likely humans became the leading species on Earth not because of their fighting skills, but thanks to their cooperative ones.

From this opposition of behaviors, it is easy to create an axis labeled, "Conflict Resolution Style" with the two extremes of power and empathy.

Fig. 1.9 – A theoretical Power vs. Empathy cultural dimension

It is understood that each genus showcases both behaviors, and the individual preferences vary greatly. However, should we take a survey, one could position the chimps on the "power side" while the bonobos would be more on the "empathy side." If one goes to the jungle and has the opportunity to observe some chimpanzees and bonobos, it is possible that a bonobo alpha male will be dictating to the other with the help of his strength, while a chimpanzee is showing empathy to a youngster! However, there is a strong likelihood the opposite will happen.

The usefulness of such a diagram is not to forecast any specific behavior but merely to analyze observed behaviors.

This looks a lot like what cross-cultural specialists call a cultural dimension: an axis with two extreme types of behaviors.

Just as humans are neither completely chimpanzees nor bonobos, everyone hovers between two extremes when it comes to decision making. Remember, in the example of the mother in the shop the two extremes are to buy the chocolate bar or to spank the child, there is a wide variety of possibilities to choose from. You may favor one option, but it doesn't mean you'll act accordingly when the situation arises.

One of the risks inherent with cultural dimensions lies in the tendency to polarize cultures. It is worth remembering that cultures are not always opposite! Once again, the cultural gap between cultures is not always wide. When we split the behavioral analysis of two cultures into several dimensions, the cultural gap usually refers to only a few of those dimensions only. In other words, focusing too much on differences is not the best way to cooperate across cultures.

Many anthropologists, sociologists, and psychologists (see next chapter) have developed their own areas of study. Some studied our relationships toward social groups, others our understanding of time, and so on. Three main categories of dimensions can be isolated:

1. Focusing on people's interactions
2. Related to time
3. Related to our relationship with our environment

Geert Hofstede had the inspired idea of applying such anthropological tools to business management such that today, in most cross-cultural trainings, cultural dimensions are the main instruments to compare and analyze various cultures.

It is critical to understand that the extremes presented in cultural dimensions are not necessarily opposing forces. They are more like magnets attracting each other, each extreme representing a sub-category of the cohort surveyed. In any given culture, when one extreme tend to become the norm (culture is dynamic, the bell curve is moving along its axis), almost automatically a strong alternative emerges. Over time, the mainstream behavior swings from one side to another, like a pendulum.

Take vacations, for instance. On the one side of the spectrum we have camping, in essence an individualistic experience.. On the other hand we have organized, packaged group tourism. Any camper will agree that a true camper spirit exists worldwide and that campers will help each other if in trouble: the pattern of camping vacations is indeed very codified. Alternatively, while in a group, tourists in an organized trip rarely share much with many others; they stick to their companions or to one or two people in the group. When reviewing their trip, most tourists who traveled in groups will actually present a very personalized view of their trip. As you can see, deciding where to stand on the "camping-group experience continuum" is no easy task!

While dimensions are very useful tools to decipher cultures, the danger comes from transforming them into dogma. Once again, cross-cultural studies do not claim to be a hard science. Their purpose is only to note certain likelihoods of behaviors. Dimensions, the most widely used tool, should be handled with care, and only used as guidelines.

Culture and nations

While it is tempting to equate nationality with culture (i.e., national boundaries with cultural territory), it is potentially misleading, overly simplistic, and limiting. We have become used to framing cultural differences geographically and depicting them in terms of national boundaries. However, culture might be better understood as a dynamic process that often cuts across national borders or is not meaningfully described in geographic terms. We easily forget that the nation state is an invention with specific cultural roots and contexts in power dynamics among ethnic and religious groups. To understand, describe, and analyze culture, we may want to understand it as a dynamic process at numerous levels of human organization, including social identity groups, organizational, and business functions or professional groups.

No culture can be meaningfully described with pre-set models. Rather, cultures organize across the spectrum between both orientations in a unique way. We can, however, through careful observation and description, discern the intricate situational code in which both elements are arranged, managed, and balanced.

Conclusion

Anaïs Nin, not famous in the world of literature for her ethnological research, summarizes well our confrontation with other cultures in the following quotation: "We don't see things as they are, we see them as we are.[21]"

---

21 Nin, 1971, The Diary of Anais Nin, Vol. 3, Boston, MA. Harcourt.

Finding a perfect definition of culture is actually not bringing much added-value to the debate. However, trying to find ways to reduce our natural tendency for ethnocentrism is worth the effort to ensure that we better comprehend the other and so reduce the tensions that lead to misunderstanding.

Some of the keys to a successful cross-cultural experience are to enhance your knowledge about a culture, your communication skills (such as learning a foreign language) and keep an open attitude towards the unexpected.

Several approaches exist to better understand cultures; the next chapter will present how cultural studies have evolved over time.

RECAP

- There are **many definitions** of culture. All refer to elements in place during our interactions with others. These elements of cultures can be analyzed when we observe our **behaviors**.

- Culture has layers:

  - **The outer layer** contains those elements that people primarily associate with culture: the visual reality of behavior, clothes, food, language, architecture, and so on. This is the level of explicit culture.

  - **The middle layer** refers to the norms and values that a community holds: what is considered right and wrong (norms) or good and bad (values). In other words, values are the orientations of a group, defining what they like to do, while norms are the shared orientations of a group defining what they should do. However, they are not visible despite their influence on what happens at the observable surface in the outer layer of culture.

  - **The inner layer** is the deepest: the level of implicit culture. Understanding the core of a culture is the key to working successfully with other cultures. The core consists of basic assumptions, a series of rules and methods that a society has developed to deal with the regular problems that it faces. For an outsider, these basic assumptions can be very difficult to recognize.

- When we isolate a behavior, some extremes are easily recognizable. While each individual is influenced by personality, some **cultural patterns** can emerge when we compare preferred behavior in a particular situation. **Cultural dimensions** are analyzed this way.

WORKSHOP 1.1: WORK GOALS

In 1987, organizational behavior research was conducted to identify employee reward preferences by examining their work goals[22]. This slightly modified experience is a useful tool to analyze not only personalities but also cultural similarities.

Please rank each work goal according to your own preferences.

The first goal is ranked 1, the second 2 and so on till the last one, number 10.

		Your ranking
A	A lot of opportunities to learn new things	
B	Good interpersonal relations	
C	Good opportunities for upgrades or promotions	
D	Convenient work hours	
E	A lot of variety	
F	Good job security	
G	A good match between job requirements and your abilities and experience	
H	Good pay	
I	Good physical working conditions (such as light, temperature, cleanliness, low noise level)	
J	A lot of autonomy	

Fig. 1.10 – Work goals workshop

Discussion Questions:

- What is your own ranking? How does it differ from the person sitting next to you?
- Is there any pattern emerging when comparing results in a group? By age, gender, culture, etc.

---

22 MOW International Research Team. 1987. *The Meaning of Work.* London: Academic Press.

WORKSHOP 1.1: WORK GOALS

- Find real-life examples where knowing the other's ranking might influence your behavior

- Go to www.crossculturaltextbook.org and fill in the questionnaire to get access to the global results.

WORKSHOP 1.2: YOUR OWN CULTURAL ARTIFACTS

This workshop works best when participants come from two different cultures or if one culture is significantly more represented than others in the group.

Divide the group into two sub-groups, each representing one culture. In the case of a group with a dominant culture (Culture A), it is possible to set-up the workshop as Culture A vs. Rest of the world.

Using the model below, each group is given a few minutes to come up with a list of artifacts representing their own culture and those of the other culture (except if this is 'Rest of the World').

When all cells are completed each group exchanges their views of each other.

	Culture A seen by Culture A	Culture B seen by Culture A	Culture B seen by Culture B	Culture A seen by Culture B
Symbols				
Characters/ Heroes				
Rituals/ Traditions				

Fig. 1.11 - Your own artifacts

Discussion questions:
- Do we stereotype only others or also our own culture?
- What are the artifacts common to both grids?
- Why are those some artifacts known by all?
- What are the differences between the groups perspectives of each other?

Chapter 2: Cross-culture research as of today

CHAPTER CONTENTS

Highlights
Introduction

PRE-HISTORY OF CROSS-CULTURE
Gallic war
Montesquieu
Alexis de Tocqueville and Astolphe de Custine
Robert Michels
Thorstein Veblen

THE FIRST RESEARCHERS
Edward T. Hall
Claude Levi-Strauss
Franz Boas
Ruth Benedict
Margaret Mead
Konrad Lorenz
Edward Sapir
Charles Sanders Peirce
Ferdinand de Saussure
Max Weber
Emile Durkheim

EARLY MANAGEMENT WORKS
Frederick Taylor and Henri Fayol
Elton Mayo and Fritz Roethlisberger

THE MAIN MODELS

    About cross-cultural dimensions and standards
    Alexander Thomas
    Florence Kluckhohn and Fred Strodtbeck's Values Orientation Theory
    Edward T. Hall
    Edgar Schein
    Geert Hofstede
    Fons Trompenaars and Charles Hampden-Turner
    The GLOBE project
    The Etic/Emic perspectives
    The Steyr Intercultural Management Model (SIMM)
    The Cultural Orientations Indicator (COI)

Conclusion
Recap
Workshop 2.1: My metaphor
Workshop 2.2: Generations of onions

CHAPTER 2

CROSS-CULTURE RESEARCH AS OF TODAY

By the Cross-Cultural Management and Emerging Markets Center of the University of Applied Sciences Upper Austria (Sophie Wiesinger, Martina Gaisch, Anja Spitzer, Hannes Hofstadler) and Jerome Dumetz

Highlights:

After reading this chapter, you should be able to:

- Know the first steps taken by researchers in cross-cultural fields.
- Recount its pre-history and the early management works carried out by renowned scientists at the end of the nineteenth century.
- Comprehend the influence of anthropology theories in cross-culture, in particular the Value Orientations Theory
- Understand key cultural dimensions models
- Be familiar with the main concepts and theories of contemporary cross-cultural communication and management.

Introduction

As presented in the previous chapter many scientific works converged to create what is today called cross-cultural management. Cross-cultural management is a new field in the management domain and although it only appeared in the 1980s as a new management topic, its roots are much older.

Understanding the multiple influences of early researchers provides a wealth of information necessary to comprehend how the current models came to light.

These models stem from the same foundations and it is unfair to select one over the others: all models are worth using as they all have their advantages and disadvantages. This chapter is an overview of cross-culture research as of today.

PRE-HISTORY OF CROSS-CULTURE

Cross-cultural management is a new management field, and although it appeared only in the 1980s, its roots are much older.

Indeed, the logs of early travelers can be described as the first works on cultural comparison. We can find some fascinating reports from royal ambassadors to neighboring countries or eye-opening stories from missionaries and adventurers half-way across the world.

> "We have met the enemy, and he is us."
>
> *Pogo, by Walt Kelly*

Gallic War

One of the earliest accounts is probably *Commentarii de Bello Gallico* (*Commentaries on the Gallic War*) from Julius Caesar, written in 50 BC. It is today the main source of knowledge about the Gauls.

Later, some intellectuals used the exploratory style not only to describe the other but in reality to observe their own culture.

Montesquieu (1689-1755, French)

Persian Letters (*Lettres persanes*) is a book that comes to mind. Written in 1721 by the French thinker Montesquieu it recounts the experiences of two fictitious Persian noblemen, Usbek and Rica, traveling through France at that time. Their various letters comment on numerous aspects of Western and Christian society, particularly French politics. Ultimately, however, the reader understands that the analysis is actually one of French behaviors, not of Persian.

Closer to us, the controversial yet often misunderstood comedy movie *Borat*, with English actor Sacha Baron Cohen, is the modern version of

Montesquieu's style. Although of a different style, the movie follows the tribulation of a fictitious Kazahk reporter to the US. Behind the scandalous remarks of the character, it is criticism of the western world in general and the US in particular that is expressed in the movie.

Other older works could also be considered part of the genesis of cross-cultural studies.

Alexis de Tocqueville (1805-1859, French) and Astolphe de Custine (1790-1857, French)

Democracy in America, written in 1835 by the French thinker Alexis de Tocqueville, is widely considered an early work of sociology and political science. Its analysis of US sociological and political mechanisms has become a reference to US political science. Tocqueville being a French aristocrat, his work has indeed a place within the cross-cultural studies.

Another French aristocrat, the Marquis de Custine, went on a journey to Russia approximately at the same period than Tocqueville published his Democracy in America, with the firm intention to prove that autocracy remains the most appropriate type of governance. While his attitude towards autocracy evolves throughout his journey, *Empire of the Czar: A Journey Through Eternal Russia*. Published in 1839 is often considered as the parallel to Tocqueville.

Robert Michels (1876-1936, German-Italian)

A former student of Max Weber, the German sociologist Robert Michels became famous with his book *Political Parties*, in which he analyzed prewar socialism in Germany and coined the term "the iron law of oligarchy." His political theory suggests that specific precautions have to be taken in order to avoid oligarchical tendencies. His writings mainly dealt with fascism, nationalism, and elites, where he compared, among others, the working-class societies of Italy, France, and Germany.

Thorstein Veblen (1857-1929, Norwegian-American)

The son of Norwegian immigrants, Veblen taught political economy at the University of Chicago where he applied an innovative approach to the study of economics. In his first book, *The Theory of the Leisure Class*, Veblen argued that consumption plays a major role in gaining status; he applied Darwin's evolutionism to the study of modern economic life. As a social scientist, he coined phrases such as "conspicuous consumption" and "pecuniary emulation". Both expressions are still widely used among economists and social scientists.

THE FIRST RESEARCHERS

As presented earlier, many scientific works converged to create contemporary cross-cultural management. Several key authors are worth special attention.

Anthropology, the study of humankind, and ethnology, the study of the characteristics of various people, are the fundamental cornerstones of this field.

Edward T. Hall (1914-2009, American)

Edward Hall was a Professor of Anthropology at Northwestern University who lived and studied Native Americans in the 1930s. Working on reservations in the Southwest he witnessed the clash of four different cultures- Navajo, Hopi, Hispanic and Anglo. Hall drew a clear picture of the frugal and religiously faithful Hopi people with their isolated villages and the Navajos with their strict forms of respect. He later developed a cultural model focusing on non-verbal signals which pioneered the study of non-verbal communication and interactions between different ethnical groups. Based on his experiences in the Foreign Service he published two books, "The Silent Language" (1954) and "The Hidden Dimension" (1969) where he identified two key elements of cultural differences by describing low and high context cultures (also called rich and poor context). Furthermore, Hall defined the new field of "Proxemics," the study of man's experience of distance and his use of space as being a function of culture, status, and personality. Hall's cultural model and its concepts are described later in this chapter.

Claude Levi-Strauss (1908-2009, French)

Claude Levi-Strauss was a French anthropologist and philosopher who was a founder of modern structuralism. In his first work he demonstrated that the comparison of cultures was biased by old stereotypes. For instance, he explained that races had nothing to do with civilization but only with geographical location, hence discarding the notion of racism. Among his famous works, *Tristes Tropiques* and *Race and History* are certainly the most acclaimed.

Other famous anthropologists, such as Franz Boas, Ruth Benedict, and Margaret Mead, are famous for their studies that paved the way to a better understanding between people.

Franz Boas (1858-1942, German-American)

Another famous anthropologist is Franz Boas, a German-American researcher. He was such a pioneer in his field that people called him "the father of American anthropology" (Holloway 1997). His definition of culture made him, quite radically for his time, a cultural relativist, being against racism and cultural supremacy: "

He is well known for conducting one of the largest anthropological field studies of the nineteenth century, a five-year study called Jesup North Pacific Expedition, where he gained insights into Native Americans. Goldman (Goldman, MacDonald 1976) called his work one of the monumental achievements of the "grand era of American ethnography," and not only because his documentation of the Kwakiutl Indians comprises more than five thousand pages.

What made his approach special is that Boas believed that separate disciplines such as ethnography, archeology, and linguistics belong to "a unified discipline" (Goldman, MacDonald 1976). One of his most famous students was Margaret Mead (mentioned below).

Ruth Benedict (1887-1948, American)

Ruth Benedict, one of the pioneers of cultural anthropology, entered Columbia University in 1921 to begin her study of advanced societies under Franz Boas. Her works, dealing with the differences in temperament and national character of various groups, discuss the cultural implications of different nations. Her influential study, *The Chrysanthemum and the Sword: Patterns of Japanese Culture* (1946), is still considered compulsory reading for students of Japanese culture. Her strive for cross-cultural and racial equality can also be seen in other significant published works such as *Patterns of Culture* (1934), *Zuni Mythology* (1935), *Race: Science and Politics* (1940).

Margaret Mead (1901-1978, American)

Margaret Mead, an internationally renowned American anthropologist, started her career with the publication of her first book, *Coming of Age in Samoa*, in 1928. Influenced by both Franz Boas and Ruth Benedict, she observed the adolescent development of Samoan girls. Most of her works focused on sex roles, child development and education and their impact on culture and personality. Mead's particular interest in American education encouraged her to compare and contrast her own culture with that of other societies. Another influential book by Mead was *Sex and Temperament of Three Primitive Societies* (1935), where she undertook pioneer work in the field of gender consciousness. A deeper insight into her research work is given in *Male and Female* (1949), a book considered an early work of feminism.

"Courtesy, modesty, good manners, conformity to definite ethical standards are universal, but what constitutes courtesy, modesty, very good manners, and definite ethical standards is not universal." F. Boas in the foreword of *Coming of Age in Samoa* by M. Mead

A cousin of anthropology, **ethology,** the science of animal behavior, is also a component of what cross-cultural management is today. Understanding animal behavior can be useful in understanding human behavior.

Konrad Lorenz (1903-1989, Austrian) and *Nikolaas Tinbergen (1907-1988, Dutch)*

Most renowned are the works of Konrad Lorenz from Austria and his Dutch colleague Nikolaas "Niko" Tinbergen who were awarded with a Nobel prize in 1973. Pioneers in this field, they researched the differences between instinctive and learned behaviors and they theorized the concept of imprinting. These studies are of great help when studying human behavior, in particular cultural cues and rituals.

Edward Sapir (1884-1939, American)

Trained by Franz Boas, this American anthropologist and linguist showed that language is not only a study of culture and words but mainly a reflection of relations and influence. His contributions to both cultural studies and psychology were outstanding, however he is mostly known for his findings about North American Indian languages. Among his publications, *Language* (1921) was the most influential.

Also linked to anthropology, **semiotics** (the study of signs and symbols) interests any cross-cultural specialist. In order to understand the meaning of signs, semioticians usually compare signs from different cultures. If the aim of this science is to explain the meaning of signs, it is also useful as a means of illustrating cultural differences. For instance, color coding is highly related to culture. In general, in the West, white is associated with a positive connotation (birth, wedding, etc.), but in the Chinese, Japanese, and Indian traditions, white is the color of grief, death and ghosts.

Charles Sanders Peirce (1839-1914, American)

Charles Sanders Peirce was a multidisciplinary scientist, contributing not only significantly to mathematics, philosophy, statistics, but also to linguistics, the history of science, and semiotics. In his opinion, "logic in the broadest sense is to be equated with semeiotic (the general theory of signs), and […] logic in a much narrower sense (which he typically called "logical critic") is one of three major divisions or parts of semeiotic" (Burch 2010).

Ferdinand de Saussure (1857-1913, Swiss)

The most influential work of the Swiss linguistic Ferdinand de Saussure, *A Course in General Linguistics* (1916), was based on several of his courses held in Geneva. Saussure's innovative ideas were not only in accordance with those of his compatriot Claude Levi-Strauss but also with the Frenchman Emile Durkheim, considered the father of sociology. His research still exerts a considerable influence on various disciplines, in particular on linguistics, literary theory, philosophy, and the social sciences.

Sociology, the study of human society, is also an integral part of today's cross-cultural management research. In order to analyze and compare cultures, the work engaged in to understand societies becomes a valuable insight.

Max Weber (1864-1920, German)

Out of all the fathers of sociology, the German Max Weber comes to mind when focusing on cross-cultural management. In his famous book, *The Protestant Ethic and the Spirit of Capitalism*, he proposes that religion is one of the reasons Western cultures developed in distinct ways. In particular, he stresses the importance of ascetic Protestantism in the development of capitalism.

Emile Durkheim (1858-1917, French)

By many experts, the Frenchman Emile Durkheim is considered to be one of the most influential men in the evolution of sociology. Not only did he publish a number of important sociological studies, but he also established, together with Karl Marx and Max Weber, sociology as an academic discipline.

EARLY MANAGEMENT WORKS

Frederick Taylor (1856-1915, American) and *Henri Fayol (1841-1925, French)*

Much research has been conducted in the area of employee efficiency at the end of the nineteenth and beginning of the twentieth century. The beginning of the industrial revolution was marked by a need for increased productivity. A school of thought, best known as scientific management, emerged in which people like Frederick Taylor and Henri Fayol occupied themselves with questions about efficiency.

Taylor conducted many time and behavioral studies to determine how an employee could become more productive through a change in attitude and movement, while Fayol did good work on organizational issues, such as how many subordinates an employer should ideally have and how many individuals should form a fully operational team. Although these approaches fitted well into the considerations of the period, when productivity was seen as essential, they had their limitations.

First of all, an employee was considered a purely rational actor with specific (usually financial) motivations. The environment or context of the organization was set aside, which led to the conclusion that there was only one way of organizing.

Elton Mayo (1880-1949, Australian) and *Fritz Roethlisberger (1898-1974, American)*

During the 1920s and 1930s there was a change that, interestingly, came about by accident. Researchers of the scientific management school studied the effects of light intensity on productivity in an assembly line factory in Hawthorne in the US. The intensity of light seemed to have a positive correlation with productivity. However, productivity also rose after reducing the intensity of light. It became apparent that the attention that was given to the assembly line workers had more effect on their productivity than the intensity of the light. A new school of thought, the human relations school, was then formed under the influence of Elton Mayo and Fritz Roethlisberger. All kinds of motivational theories, like the ones of Maslow, McGregor, and Herzberg, were subsequently developed. Since then, much attention has been given to the social aspects that play a role in an organization.

As the result of a study, better known as the contingency theory, the end of the "one way of organizing" approach was in sight. Statistical correlations between organizational structure and environmental circumstances were found. The work of Lawrence and Lorsch[23] made it very clear that success is dependent on how one interacts with the environment. Structural aspects such as hierarchical layers were related to quantifiable contingency aspects.

THE MAIN MODELS

About Cross-Cultural Dimensions and Standards

There are two major strands in cross-cultural research: dimensions and standards.

---

23 Lawrence and Lorsch, 1967, "Differentiation and Integration in Complex Organizations" in Administrative Science Quarterly, 12,

In a general sense cultures and differences among cultures can be described and measured along culture dimensions[24].

In more detail and more descriptively, the cultural standard method deals with differences in the kinds of perceiving, norms of sensing, thinking, judging, and acting, which can cause critical incidents in cross-cultural encounters.[25]

The "dimensioners" set up and conducted quantitative studies with hundreds to thousands of participants, aiming at being able to measure cultural differences along certain dimensions, which are set up and defined ex ante. Their data are highly appreciated by the scientific community as well as by practitioners, and they are numerously cited.

The standard researchers' intention is completely different. Their main aim is to deal with differences in perception, actions, or judgment in cross-cultural encounters. Culture standard research is more context-related. Cultural dimensions regard a culture from "outside-in"—the so-called "etic" approach, while the cultural standard method regards a culture from "inside-out"—known as the "emic" approach[26].

Alexander Thomas (born in 1939, German)

The father of the cultural standard method is Professor Alexander Thomas from Regensburg, Germany. He was inspired by the work of Nancy Adler[27] and H.C. Triandis[28].

The cultural standard method was brought up as an answer to the early defined cultural dimensions, being presumably biased by characteristics of the researcher's own culture. From a quantitative method based on anonymous questionnaires, a qualitative research method was introduced. Through qualitative interviews, unexpected reactions to critical situations are identified. A cultural standard is defined when a

---

24 Hall/Hall 1990, 2000, Hofstede 1980, 1993, 2001, House/Hanges/Javidan/Dorfman/Gupta 2004, Kluckhohn/Strodtbeck 1961, Rokeach 1973, Schwartz 1992, Trompenaars/Hampden-Turner 1997
25 Thomas 1996, Fink/Meierewert 2001
26 Boitllehner / Hofstadler, 2008
27 Adler, 1983, Adler 1985
28 Triandis, 1984

number of individuals are reacting repeatedly to one critical situation the same way.[29]

PROS: One of the advantages of the cultural standard method is that it is more differentiated and more theoretically founded concerning the research methodology than cultural dimension approaches. Moreover, it *explains* the behavior of people living in a culture instead of just describing it.

CONS: On the other hand, using Thomas' cultural standard method might lead to imposing stereotypes, which is always a threat when trying to define "general" behavior for all people of a group.

Florence R. Kluckhohn (? - 1986, American) and Fred Strodtbeck's (1919-2005, American) Values Orientation Theory

One of the first attempts to analyze culture came in 1961 from Kluckhohn and Strodtbeck, who proposed categorizing culture in six dimensions:

- The nature of people
- The person's relationship to nature
- The person's relationship to others (social relations)
- The modality of human activity
- Temporal focus of human activity
- Conception of space (added later on)[30]

According to this concept of value orientation, cultural values shared by members of a group, defining what is important and desirable to them, guide the behavior of these group members and forms the basis for defining group norms. Kluckhohn and Strodtbeck's model has often been used in social science and counseling literature, including the development of new models and approaches and is, therefore, of significant importance in the context of cross-cultural management.[31]

---

29 Boitllehner / Hofstadler, 2007
30 Singh, 2004
31 Carter, 1991

PROS: Firstly, it aims at *understanding* core cultural differences by trying to find the reasons for a particular behavior in the values hidden behind it. Secondly, it has already been tested a lot and proven effective in many different research fields, including the analysis of organizational cultures. Thirdly, by just using five (six) dimensions, it nevertheless covers a wide range of values that can be seen as an explanation for acting in a certain way.

CONS: In spite of this, Kluckhohn and Strodtbeck's model is often criticized for its static structure, its limited options, and that it does not capture all aspects of cultural characteristics. Moreover, it should be taken into consideration that this model just analyzes values and no other levels, as, for example, in Schein's model.

Edward T. Hall (1914-2009, American)

Edward T. Hall (1914-2009) defined various concepts of space and demonstrated how people's use of it can affect cross-cultural behavior resulting in the concept of proxemics.

The book *Hidden Dimension* not only describes spatial dimensions but also polychronic and monochronic approaches to time, or the way in which cultures structure their time. A further dimension presented in the book *Beyond Culture* was identified as low-context and high-context culture. Low context refers to societies where directness, logical reasoning, and facts are appreciated, whereas high-context cultures focus on interpersonal relations, trust, and group harmony.

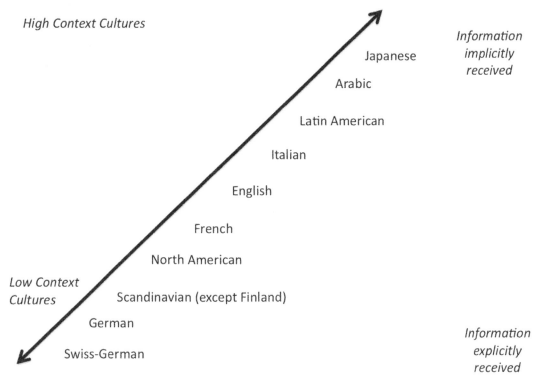

Fig. 2.1 – High and low context cultures model[32]

Hall's Cultural Matrix

Time	Context	Space
Monochronic ✓ Do one thing at a time ✓ Schedule/structure is important ✓ Time is useful tool to prioritize ✓ Identification with work	*High* ✓ Messages culturally coded ✓ Read between the lines ✓ Implicit context	*Close* ✓ Little need for much personal space ✓ Lower territoriality
Polychronic ✓ Do many things at once ✓ Relationship top priority ✓ Deadlines are not vital ✓ Identification with family/friends	*Low* ✓ Explicit, verbal messages ✓ Straight to the point ✓ Distinction content/relational level	*Far* ✓ Need for bigger space bubble ✓ Higher territoriality

Fig. 2.2 – Edward Hall Cultural Matrix model[33]

---

32 The Interpreter as Cultural Mediator, Giovanna Pistillo
33 Adapted from Hall 1976, 1982

PROS: The representative size of sample group (180 interviewees),

CONS: Survey only carried out among three countries (US, Western Germany, and France); therefore, the model is less operational.

Edgar Schein (born in 1928, American)

Edgar Schein, author of the introduction of this textbook, is a renowned professor of organizational psychology and management. He formerly worked at the MIT Sloan School of Management and has already made meaningful contributions in his area of expertise as a researcher, author, and consultant.

In 1992, Edgar Schein also developed one of the key models in the context of cross-cultural management, which is often referred to in scientific literature. According to this conceptual framework, organizational culture is divided into three levels:

1. Basic assumptions,
2. Espoused values,
3. Artifacts.

In this model, assumptions represent the lowest level as they are the core of culture, subconsciously fixed in our way of thinking and acting and, therefore, taken for granted by everyone in this culture. On the second, less abstract, level, values define what is important for us, leading to observable behavior and artifacts on the highest level of cultural manifestation. These artifacts include symbols, structures, procedures, and rules, openly visible for everyone.

PROS: Therefore, what can be mentioned positively about Schein's model is the fact that it helps to explain the behavior of people in an organization, although it could also be applied to analyzing the culture of a country. Moreover, since it just consists of three levels, it is relatively easy to understand and to remember.

CONS: However, it might not be so easy to define all three components and to define which aspects of a culture belong to which level.

Geert Hofstede (born in 1928, Dutch)

While working with IBM, Geert Hofstede noticed major cultural differences among staff from different countries despite a common corporate culture. These observations resulted in one of the most comprehensive studies conducted among 72 IBM subsidiaries in more than 40 countries. Armed with a vast database of cultural statistics, Hofstede analyzed the employee values scores collected between 1967 and 1973 and found clear patterns of similarities and differences. This survey covered 116,000 interviewees of 38 different professions in 20 different languages. In the 2010 edition of his book "Cultures and Organizations: Software of the Mind" there are scores for 76 countries available, party based on replications and extensions of his IBM study.

From the initial results and later editions, Hofstede developed a model identifying the following key dimensions of national cultures:

1. **Power distance** (PD) refers to the accepted degree of inequality among people with or without power. A high score in PD indicates that unequal distribution of power is acceptable within society.

2. **Individualism** (IDV) versus collectivism refers to the emotional dependence of an individual with respect to groups and organizations. A high score in IDV indicates a lack of interpersonal connections.

3. **Masculinity** (MAS) a high score in MAS indicates that a society values traditionally male qualities such as competition, assertiveness, ambition and concern for material possessions whereas the culture of femininity fosters equality and solidarity.

4. **Uncertainty Avoidance Index** (UAI) refers to the degree of anxiety individuals feel when being in an unfamiliar situation. A high score of UAI indicates a nation governed by rules and regulations.

5. **Long Term Orientation** (LTO) refers to the degree to which a society appreciates long-term-as opposed to short-term values and traditions. A high score of LTO indicates the fear of losing one's face. It is also known as Confucian dynamism.

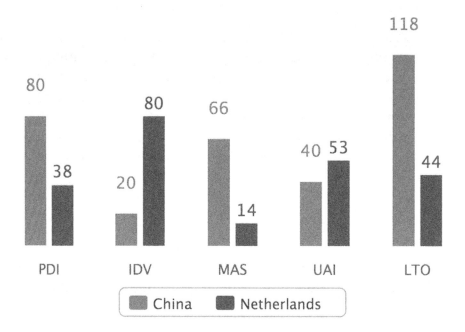

Fig. 2.3 – The Five dimensions of Prof. Geert Hofstede[34]

PROS: Hofstede's extensive survey was not only unique in size and structure; it could also prove the importance of cultural differences, providing managers with a cross-cultural understanding. The model shows that a single set of values cannot be applied universally and that managers from different national cultures approach work differently from those from related cultural backgrounds.

CONS: Hofstede's model only applies to employees from a specific professional group (IBM) and therefore lacks reference values with other groups, even if it has been updated. Another limit of this approach has to do with its practical use: terms like "uncertainty avoidance" are cumbersome to use in real life, and others are culturally loaded: a Dutch researcher has a very different understanding of the terms masculinity and femininity to a Japanese or Saudi colleague.

---

34 From http://geert-hofstede.com/countries.html

Fons Trompenaars (born in 1952, Dutch) and Charles Hampden-Turner (born in 1934, British)

Both contributing to this textbook (Chap. 4, 5 & 10), they identified 7 value orientations (called as the "7D") by classifying cultures as a mix of behavioral and value patterns. After using the dimensions developed by Talcott Parsons in his Social System, they added the two dimensions of Hall, Strodtbeck and Kluckhohn on time and nature that completed the seven dimensions.

Deriving their data from questionnaires completed by more than one hundred thousand executives from more than one hundred countries, they identified the following orientations that are described in detail later in the book:

1. **Universalism versus Particularism:** This dimension seeks to discover whether one's prime allegiance is to rules and rule-bound classifications, or to exceptional, unique circumstances.

2. **Individualism versus Communitarianism** measures the extent to which managers see the individual employee and shareholder as paramount, his or her development, enrichment, fulfillment, or to what extent the corporation, customers and the wider group should be the beneficiaries of all personal efforts.

3. **Specific versus Diffuse** measures the tendency to analyze, reduce and break down the field of experience, or to synthesize, augment and construct experience.

4. **Neutral versus Affective** concerns the legitimacy of showing or controlling emotions.

5. **Achievement versus Ascription** is about why status is conferred on people. Is this because they have achieved, or because of what they "are", i.e. human beings, male, of good background?

6. **Sequential versus Synchronous Time** has to do with whether one sees time as passing in a sequence, or coming around again and again. Cultures think of time as a sequence or as a synchronization or coordination.

7. **Inner versus outer directed** concerns the "locus of control". Is it inside each of us, or outside in our environments to which we must adapt?

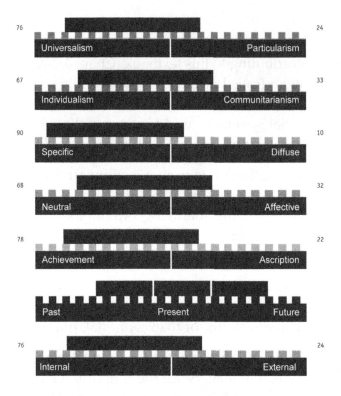

Fig. 2.4 – The seven dimensions model applied to the USA

PROS: Useful tool to explain differences in cultural behavior that provides managers with a better understanding of cross-cultural patterns. The model clearly demonstrates the importance of culture when doing business globally.

CONS: The model does not provide any recommendations of how to deal with cultural differences. The influence of personal behavior and character traits is not well taken into consideration.

The GLOBE project

GLOBE stands for Global Leadership and Organizational Behavior Effectiveness. It is a research project opting to studying leadership behavior from a cross-cultural perspective[35]. Findings from the GLOBE

---

35 House et al. 2010

study can be found in various monographies, journals, and book chapters[36].

The GLOBE idea emerged in the 1990s, when authors discussed whether and how leadership could be globally applied. In a first step, research instruments for assessing culture and leadership were developed. In a second phase, nine core attributes of societal and organizational cultures were assessed on a global basis. The final results constitute a ranking of sixty-two cultures according to their societal dimensions and findings from hypothesis testing "about the relationships between these dimensions and organizational practices and culturally endorsed implicit theories of leadership"[37].

Generally speaking, the GLOBE research is guided by an "overarching theory," suggesting that "(1) the characteristics of societal culture that distinguish cultures from each other are predictive of organizational practices, and (2) the leader attributes and behaviors that are most frequently enacted are considered most accepted and expected in that particular culture.[38]

The main objectives of GLOBE are finding answers to the following five fundamental questions[39]:

- Are there leader attributes and behaviors and organizational practices that are universally accepted and effective across cultures?
- Are there leader attributes and behaviors and organizational practices that are nation - or culture-specific?
- In what ways do cultural differences affect the kinds of leader and organizational practices that are effective?
- What is the relative standing of each of the nations studied on each of nine core dimensions of culture?
- Can the nation-specific and universal aspects of leadership and organizational practices be explained in terms of an underlying theory that accounts for systematic differences among cultures?

---

36 e.g., Koopman et al. 1999; Javidan et al. 2006a; House 2004
37 ibid
38 ibid
39 House, Hanges, and Ruiz-Quintanilla 1997a, p.125, as cited in Koopman et al. 1999

Societal Cluster	CLT Dimensions					
	Charismatic/ Value-Based	Team Oriented	Participative	Humane Oriented	Autonomous	Self-Protective
Eastern Europe	5.74	5.88	5.08	4.76	4.20	3.67
Latin America	5.99	5.96	5.42	4.85	3.51	3.62
Latin Europe	5.78	5.73	5.37	4.45	3.66	3.19
Confucian Asia	5.63	5.61	4.99	5.04	4.04	3.72
Nordic Europe	5.93	5.77	5.75	4.42	3.94	2.72
Anglo	6.05	5.74	5.73	5.08	3.82	3.08
Sub-Sahara Africa	5.79	5.70	5.31	5.16	3.63	3.55
Southern Asia	5.97	5.86	5.06	5.38	3.99	3.83
Germanic Europe	5.93	5.62	5.86	4.71	4.16	3.03
Middle East	5.35	5.47	4.97	4.80	3.68	3.79

NOTE: CLT leadership scores are absolute scores aggregated to the cluster level.

Fig. 2.5 – Example of CLT Scores for Societal Cluster[40]

CLT (Culturally Endorsed Implicit Leadership Theory) is an extended version of Hofstede's ILT (Implicit Leadership Theory). The individual level is translated into a more general, cultural level.

GLOBE empirically verified ten different clusters from the sixty-two-culture clusters, each differing with regard to the nine identified culture dimensions.

PROS: The most representative and biggest study of experts in the fields of societal and organizational culture currently available; combination of quantitative and qualitative data, elimination of common source and common method variance.[41]

CONS: GLOBE quantitative data do not allow for culture-specific, emic descriptions of cultural features.

The Etic/Emic perspectives

By using different dimensions for comparing countries, the GLOBE study applies an etic (or culture-general) perspective, which is in contrast to the emic perspective, an in-depth focus on a single national

---

40 Table taken from Javidan et al. 2006, p. 74
41 More about GLOBE at http://business.nmsu.edu/programs-centers/globe/

culture. According to some researchers[42], the etic approach presents some risks, like an easy linkage to stereotypes. This is why it is recommended to supplement the etic approach by emic dimensions and in-depth descriptions of a culture.

One method to do so is the usage of cultural metaphors, which means that one phenomenon is taken to describe another phenomenon of the culture. This might help to expand or modify the understanding that the etic dimensional approach provides. (see Workshop 2.1)

The Steyr Intercultural Management Model (SIMM)

The Steyr Intercultural Management Model (SIMM) has been developed at the University of Applied Sciences in Steyr and, in comparison to many cultural dimension approaches, it does not aim at just describing a culture, but finding out *why* a culture is the way it is in order to derive knowledge of *how* to (inter-) act in this culture. For this purpose, the relationship of two cultures (one's own and a foreign one), which is understood as cross-culture in this model, should be investigated step-by-step on three levels.

On the first level, the macro level, both cultures are examined objectively in terms of their history, philosophy, religion, society, politics, economics, and law. Subsequently, the results of these fields of research are compared, and the two cultures' differences and similarities are elaborated. On the second level, subjective perceptions are compared with the objective results of the first level, with the purpose of demonstrating that the point of view out of which a culture is seen plays an important role when describing this culture. Finally, on the third level, the SIMM deals with individual influence factors like status, origin, education, environment, stereotypes, or traditions, which are also included in the concept.[43]

---

42 Nielsen 2006 #9
43 Mayer / Hofstadler, 2007

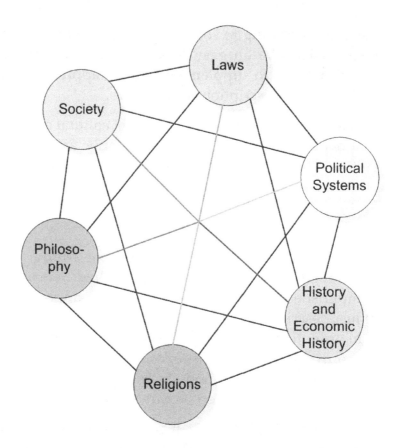

Fig. 2.6 – The Steyr Intercultural Management Model

PROS: Therefore, one argument in favor of using the SIMM is that it gives an holistic picture of a culture by not just analyzing all of the aforementioned fields of research but also displaying the connections between them. Furthermore, it "forces" you to also gain knowledge about your own culture instead of just dealing with a foreign one, and it combines objective and subjective aspects.

CONS: Nevertheless, it is still a relatively new approach that has not been tested a lot. It is also true that a thorough implementation of the SIMM takes much time and effort and can still never be completely up-to-date as culture and a country's history are constantly changing. Moreover, only assumptions can be made as to **why** a culture is as it is, and there is no guarantee that an assumed explanation is the correct one.

The Cultural Orientations Indicator®(COI)

The Cultural Orientations Indicator®[44] (COI) synthesizes the works of Hall, Hofstede, Trompenaars and Charles Hampden-Turner, Kluckhohn and Strodtbeck, Steward and Bennett, and Rhinesmith into a 10 dimensional model of cultural variability. It was developed by Danielle Walker, Tim Walker and Joerg Schmitz[45] (author of chapter 6).

Fig. 2.7 – The Cultural Orientation Model™

The COI is a description of general preferences restricted to work-related behaviors and situations highlighted through 10 cultural dimensions (with 17 cultural continua and 36 orientations) that form the basis for understanding the cultural basis of Thinking Style, Interaction Style, and Sense of Self.

Based on a series of 87 questions, it is considered by many practitioners as one of the most used models to compare an individual profile with a given culture (own or alien). With well over 150,000 users worldwide, it is used by certified practitioners to develop four key cultural skills, namely: cultural due diligence, style switching, cultural dialogue, and cultural mentoring.

The 10 dimensions of cultures presented are:

1. **Environment:** How individuals view and relate to the people, objects and issues in their sphere of influence. (Continuum: Control – (Harmony) - Constraint)

2. **Time:** How individuals perceive the nature of time and its use. (Continuum: Single-Multi focus / Fixed-Fluid / Past -(Present) - Future)

---

44 The COI® is owned and trademarked by TMC – a Berlitz Company. To learn more, visit: www.culturalorientations.com. Reproduced with authorization.
45 Walker & Walker, Schmitz, 2003, Doing Business Internationally, McGraw-Hill

3. **Action:** How individuals conceptualize actions and interactions. (Continuum: Being-Doing)

4. **Communication:** How individuals express themselves. (Continuum: High-Low Context / Direct-Indirect / Expressive-Instrumental / Formal-Informal)

5. **Space:** How individuals demarcate their physical and psychological space. (Continuum: Private-Public)

6. **Power:** How individuals view differential power relationships. (Continuum: Hierarchy-Equality)

7. **Individualism:** How individuals define their identity. (Continuum: Individualistic-Collectivistic / Universalistic-Particularistic)

8. **Competitiveness:** How individuals are motivated. (Continuum: Competitive-Cooperative)

9. **Structure:** How individuals approach change, risk, ambiguity and uncertainty. (Continuum: Order-Flexibility)

10. **Thinking:** How individuals conceptualize. (Continuum: Deductive-Inductive / Linear-Systemic)

PROS: The COI is a very practical tool to use in organizations. It is based on the classic cultural models developed by practitioners, synthesizing other models such as Hofstede's or Trompenaars'. The results are "filtered" in three relevant and easy-to-comprehend categories (Sense of Self, Interaction Style, and Thinking Style) which make the COI immanently usable. The COI also supports the analysis of culture at organization and team levels.

Cons: Surprisingly, only 65 countries are covered in this database, limiting seriously the scope of use of the tool for national culture based comparison. While the graphical presentation is attractive (10 dimensions in a wheel), some of these dimensions such as competitiveness are subject to discussion and there is some conceptual overlap and interdependencies between the discrete dimensions that are not explicitly recognized.

Conclusion

During the last decades, cross-cultural research was marked by profound changes, mainly determined by economic, social, cultural and politic context. The need for innovative ways of thinking and development of cross-cultural competencies has never been stronger and it is likely to become even more so as the process of globalization continues into the future.

Providing different and overlapping approaches, all models make a substantial contribution to developing cultural intelligence and cross-cultural competence. They all help to gain a better understanding of how cross-cultural dimensions impact management behavior and interpersonal interactions.

RECAP

- Cross-cultural management evolved from various fields of research: ethnology, ethology, semiotics, sociology and business management.

- Two major approaches have emerged: the cultural dimensions and the cultural standards.

- The cultural dimensions models are today the ones preferred by the practitioners, as they are less biased by the researchers' own culture. The main author(s) are:

  - Hall who identified the five key dimensions previously mentioned in the book.

  - Kluckhohn and Stodtbeck developed a concept of value orientations focusing on six cultural values with variations in each one: relation to nature, relationship among people, mode of human activity, belief about basic human nature, orientation to time and use of space.

  - Hofstede, one of the most prominent researchers in the field of cross-cultural research, identified the following key dimensions: individualism-collectivism, power distance, uncertainty avoidance, and masculinity-femininity—along with a fifth dimension subsequently identified as long-term orientation- also known as Confucian dynamism.

  - Schein's model of organizational culture where he identifies artifacts and behavior, espoused values and assumptions as three different layers that refer to corporate culture.

  - Trompenaars and Hampden-Turner extended Hofstede's classification with seven additional dimensions, which are explained in detail in this book.

WORKSHOP 2.1: MY METAPHOR:

Several models representing culture have been presented in Chapters 1 and 2, now it is your turn!

In small groups, discuss and exchange ideas to come up with your own model describing culture. Then, explain to the class your approach and logic.

Think about the foundation of a culture, its representative elements, its hidden norms and values, and so on.

After your presentation, you can upload and compare your model with others at www.crossculturaltextbook.org .

WORKSHOP 2.2: GENERATIONS OF ONIONS:

Cultures are also trans-generational. While we might live in the same area, we do not share with everyone the same understanding of what represent our culture.

Individually or in small groups, conduct a series of interviews with four generations coming from the same culture: your grandparents, your parents, your friends, your brothers & sisters or cousins.

Ask each of them about the Symbols, Characters/Heroes, Rituals/Traditions, and Values of their home culture.

Analyze what artifacts remain across generations, and the ones that are unique to a generation. If applicable, you can use the previous findings of Workshop 1.2 as a starting point.

Each participant (or small group) then presents to the class the findings and the difference of perception due to the generations' gap.

Chapter 3: Culture and communication

CHAPTER CONTENTS

Highlights
Introduction

WHAT IS COMMUNICATION?
Some models
The origins

VERBAL COMMUNICATION
PARALANGUAGE
The speed of speech
The volume, or loudness
The intonation, the accents
Turntaking: The timing of our verbal interactions
Intrturn pauses (silence) in conversation
Backchanneling across cultures

NON-LINGUISTIC COMMUNICATION
Gestures
Seeing
Haptics (Touching)
Tasting
Olfactics (Smelling)

Conclusion
Recap
Case study 3.1: Why do Japanese fall asleep in meetings?
Case study 3.2: Kissing across cultures

CHAPTER 3

CULTURE AND COMMUNICATION
By Jérôme Dumetz

Highlights:

After reading this chapter, you should be able to:

- Understand how culture is strongly revealed in communication
- Apprehend how our native language is influencing our way of communicating
- Be better prepared to notice verbal communication cultural misunderstandings
- Comprehend the importance of pauses when communicating
- Be familiar with non-linguistic communication involving our senses

Introduction

Cross-cultural management is influenced by many sources, from anthropology to sociology and of course business management. However, one field is particularly linked to it, communication.

For many, management is indeed all about communication [46]. Therefore, it is quite logical that communication across cultures differs greatly. While many expect verbal communication to reflect our cultural disparities, we will investigate how, more surprisingly, our paralinguistic

---

46 Blagg & Young, 2001, « What Makes a Good Leader? », Harvard Business School Bulletin

(we'll explain what it is) and our non-verbal communication tell us more about our culture, and the culture of others.

WHAT IS COMMUNICATION?

Some models

Whichever definition of culture you prefer (see chapter 1), culture is affecting us mostly when we communicate. If we use a caricature, one could say that a hermit in a cave shouldn't be much concerned with the topic of this book. It is only when we interact with others that culture becomes an issue. And it happens all the time for most of us. What we say, how we say it, what we mean, and even how we stand is communication. Everything we do is communication.

> The way you are reading this book is communication. Should someone film you reading, a world of information could be analyzed by observing you. Here are a few hints:
>
> - Where are you reading this book? At home with the book on the desk with a studious atmosphere around, on the living room sofa with the TV set on in the background, or on public transport with your headset on?
>
> - What time is it? If you read this chapter a week before the lecture in your bedroom, it tells something about you. If you read the same chapter only the day before the lecture, it tells about you something different. And of course, if you read through this text one hour before the exam, it definitely tells about you something else!
>
> - How do you treat your book? (Doesn't fully apply to e-books!) Did you cover it? Do you write notes? If you write notes in the margin, do you use permanent ink or a pencil?
>
> - In what language do you read this book? Is it your native tongue or your second one? How do you cope with unknown vocabulary? Do you leap over the word, try to guess its meaning, or check in a dictionary? How would it feel to listen to the book instead of reading it?

As you can see, communication is everywhere! Culture is also everywhere. Culture and communication fit well together. When analyzing communication, culture is at every step.

According to the most accepted model[47], communication is all about sending messages to others. An individual, the sender of the message, needs to choose several options when communicating. The message is coded into an acceptable format to fit the channel chosen. For instance, when you read this book the channel is written form. Should you listen to an audio book, it would be oral communication. The language you use, either in the written form or the oral form, is the code.

Extra information, called alternatively noise or contextual information, has an impact on the process but not a fundamental one.

So that the target of your message fully understands it, the receiver must share with you not only the same channel but also the same code. If you can't hear well, listening to an audio book isn't the best choice of channel. However, even if you can read well, but you decide to read the book in its printed form in Russian, you will need to master the Cyrillic alphabet and understand Russian to decode the message.

Finally, for the communication between several individuals to be complete, the receiver should send back some form of information, the feedback, to acknowledge having received the message. The feedback is essential in communication because only when you have the confirmation that your first message is understood can you send a new, different one.

Feedback may be of various forms. Most often it is a message of its own or sometimes a vague movement; sometimes there is none. If you forget to congratulate your beloved on a birthday, receiving no answer from your late text messages is a kind of feedback. Once again, everything we do is communication.

---

47 Shannon & Weaver (1949), *The Mathematical Theory of Communication*

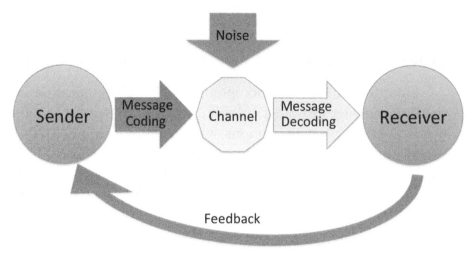

Fig. 3.1 – **A communication model inspired from Shannon & Weaver**

The origins

Linguistics tells us that all newborn babies "talk" (or better, babble!) the same way around the world. This lasts for about two months. After this period, it is possible to already distinguish differences of sounds from one culture to another. It is explained quite simply by the fact that during this period, babies hear their surroundings and the people around them. Variation in languages, tone of voice, and other verbally related elements influence the new sounds of a baby.

Languages are learned. It is true with the main language (mother tongue), but also with the minority ones (there rarely exists perfect equality of language; one is often the dominant[48]). Because language is a key component of culture, we can easily conclude that all other aspects of culture are learned.

During the first years of life, if our personality is shaped by the close contacts with others, it also has a cultural impact. How much we touch babies, kiss them, wash them, perfume them will influence their attitude toward such senses. How do we dress babies (or not): do we wrap them tight or let them loose, do we talk to them in whispers or with our normal voice, do we cuddle them or leave them alone, do we leave them in contact with animals—all those thousands of details will shape our communication type.

---

48 Cunningham-Andersson, (2004) *Growing Up with Two Languages*

CULTURE AND COMMUNICATION

VERBAL COMMUNICATION

It is difficult to know how much of our communication is verbal. Often, the studies of Albert Mehrabian[49] are quoted to justify an over-importance of nonverbal communication. His famous "7-38-55 percent rule" states that we convey most meaning through our nonverbal communication (words account for 7 percent, tone of voice accounts for 38 percent, and body language accounts for 55 percent). Yet, attentive students would know these studies have been repeatedly misunderstood, and if we may express different feelings with our facial expressions than with the words we utter, this applies to selected situations only.

In other words, words do matter in communication. In fact, most of our communication is verbal. Any workshop asking participants not to talk easily proves it.

Despite the increasing use of modern technology to exchange with others, verbal communication remains the main channel used to send a message from one individual to others. When you arrive in a foreign territory, despite all your skills in understanding facial expressions and moves, or, if you can't speak the local language or a common language with local people, you will have a hard time understanding what is being told to you!

Fig. 3.2 - Koori Mail #446

What would you associate with the heading above? Shouldn't the faces of the people pictured be concerned rather than happy because of the 'deadly' vibe that's impacting the town?

This is an example of how Aboriginal words can be mistaken by speakers of the English language. 'Deadly' is an Aboriginal slang word for 'fantastic', 'great' or 'awesome'. The article reports about the fun and joy people had at the two-day Aboriginal youth weekend Vibe 3on3.

---

[49] Mehrabian, Albert (1971). *Silent Messages*

We communicate with our five senses, but speech is the most direct, straightforward way to communicate in most of our daily interactions. Speaking is fast, almost instantaneous, and you can receive feedback (verbal or not) nearly immediately after you sent your message, sometimes even during.

Specialists count about seven thousand distinct languages in the world. Knowing foreign languages has always been a valued skill, and it is still true today. English has become the "hypercentral" language in many places around the word, just like Sumerian, Greek, Latin, or French used to be in the previous centuries. While it is impossible to know which language will become the next lingua franca, any globetrotter, businessperson, or simple tourist knows the usefulness of mastering a foreign language. Besides, most countries are actually multilingual territories (monolingual countries are indeed a rarity[50]), and as a consequence nearly 50 percent of the world population is bilingual.

It is also worth noting that a lot of various meanings can be conveyed within the same language. If we stick strictly to verbal communication (we'll deal with everything else in a moment), one can gather up much information from the quality of the language used (poor, average, or upscale), the semantic fields used, the range of vocabulary at our disposal, or, of course, local or community-related jargon. A Sevilla-born taxi driver, a literature teacher from Buenos Aires, or a policeman from San Jose in Costa Rica may all speak Spanish, yet they send verbal messages using a rather different code. The same is true in every language.

Besides, one "common" language may carry words with many various meanings depending on where it is spoken. International marketing often makes the headlines because of translation (see chapter 11) or misunderstanding issues.

As stated in the Koori Mail example, "Deadly" means "Fantastic" in Aboriginal English. In the French language, "Char" means "tank" (the armored vehicle) while in Québec it means a regular "car". Chinese is used in various areas in Asia and the same words can very easily mislead communication if used by people from different areas. For instance, consider Wo Xin (窝心). In northern China, Wo Xin means something that makes you upset and it is hard for you to relieve. While in Taiwan or

---

50 L-J Calvet (2011), *Il était une fois 7000 langues*, Fayard Ed.

Hong Kong, Wo Xin means something that makes you happy, delightful and moved or touched. Imagine the consequences of a Northerner coming to Hongkong…

Another example is Bao Gao (报告). In English it means "To report". China is a country high in hierarchy. Bao Gao are for leaders to use. In Mainland China, a leader is going to « Bao Gao » (report) some news to the subordinates, but never vice versa. When subordinates are supposed to report to leaders, they need to use the words Hui Bao (汇报). In Taiwan, Hong Kong or Singapore, Bao Gao is mutual. A subordinate can easily say Bao Gao to his/her leader in those areas, but it would be considered very disrespectful towards a leader from mainland China.

Words in one language may also sound similar to words in another language, leading to misunderstandings of variable amplitude. Czech people often confirm a statement by answering "Fakt yo", meaning something like "as a matter of fact"…

Verbal communication betrays many features of our personality but also elements of the cultures we belong to. A skilled listener is able to make a preliminary analysis of someone speaking. While such analysis is actually of little worth, we all do it unconsciously. Quite spontaneously, we tend to recognize others' cultures through such codes.

However, as we've seen earlier, because we communicate all the time, it means a sheer size of our communication is often unconscious. As far as verbal communication is concerned, we have an example of involuntary communication with lapses, mostly due to stress and fatigue, often to our embarrassment.

> **Lost in translation**
>
> Written communication is obviously also very much subject to cultural issues, mostly translation from one langue to another.
>
> Approximate translation is often the cause of much incomprehension and even misunderstanding. Consider this sign posted in a hotel room in Barcelona, Spain:
>
> « We send each wash towel, thrown into our rivers and seas more grams of detergent, if going to be several days with us and believes that his towel is able to use a second leave hanging, but put it in the ground. »
>
> Usually, all it takes to avoid such blunder is a better verification of a translated text!

But the other senses are also bringing their part in the communication. Just as we speak different languages in various cultures, our nonverbal communication is also closely related to culture. We can analyze the nonverbal communication through two categories: communication linked to language (not *what* we say—this is verbal communication—but *how* we say it), called paralanguage; and everything else we could call non-linguistic communication.

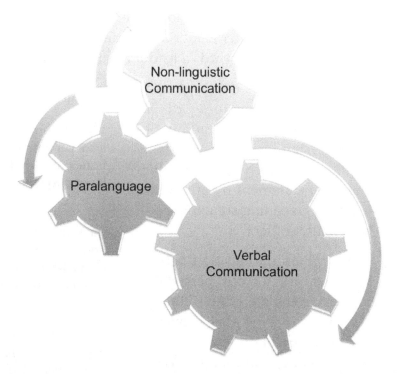

Fig. 3.3 – **Paralanguage and non-verbal communication**

PARALANGUAGE

Paralanguage refers to *how* we say things. It covers a wide scope of details that all reveal cultural influence. Paralanguage includes various types of acoustical elements that accompany language, as well as the vocalizations that replace or supplement speech. Both are carried on the vocal channels but are nonverbal[51]. Paralinguistic patterns do not only inform us about the emotional state of the speaker, but they also constitute cultural cues. Closely associated to paralanguage, the term prosody covers non-grammatical features such as loudness, tempo, intonation, rhythm, pausing, and accent placement.

How you say things bears little consequences when you speak with someone else in your mother tongue about topics all speakers understand with more or less the same quality. In such situations, the potential for cultural misunderstanding (or the cultural gap, if you prefer) is at the minimum.

Culture steps in when you cross the border and talk to people from other origins. Because we tend to export our paralinguistic characteristics when we speak another language, the gap will increase when you use a second language and is at its peak when both use a third language.

Most paralinguistic aspects carry distinctive cultural meanings and can vary greatly among cultures and languages, including:

- the speed with which we talk
- our volume or loudness
- the intonation or melody of the language
- our tone of voice
- the timing of our verbal interactions
- the use of pauses or silence
- sounds that are not really words

The speed of speech

When going to Spain, visitors who studied Spanish before are often taken aback by the speed at which people (often women) speak. They complain that people there speak too fast. One may also hear that people in Chile speak slower than the average. But once again, this depends entirely on what your standard is, and the first one is your own pace.

---

[51] Damen, Louise (1987). *Culture Learning: The Fifth Dimension in the Language Classroom*.

Yet, the speed of speech can create cumbersome situation when we speak foreign languages. Many people associate fast speech with stress and panic. Therefore, when they hear a foreigner speak fast in his or her own language, they may jump to the conclusion that this person is panicking when in reality an absolutely normal conversation is taking place.

As a rule, it is advised to slow the speed of speech when you use your native language with non-natives. This is pure politeness in order to let others understand your comments more easily. Learning a foreign language is already a challenge; adapting to the native flow is a step higher!

People may also speak deliberately slowly in order to concentrate on the content but also to prevent making mistakes. If a sound if new to you, chances are you'll be careful when pronouncing it to make sure others understand you, and you don't have to repeat yourself.

The volume, or loudness

Men tend to speak louder than women. In every family, village, or culture, some people tend to speak at a higher volume. There might be some physiological reasons (people who hear less tend to compensate by raising the volume of their own voices), but it is mostly linguistic and cultural.

One of the purposes of school is to teach children to control their voices. Young children easily alternate shouts and whispers during the same activity. Social pressure teaches us how to use our own voice volume. Such education differs from one culture to another; therefore, the volume of the speech is associated with clear meanings in every culture.

When cultural misunderstanding lead to abuse

One can observe the evolution of cultures when paying attention to the people's attitude to such elements. For instance, in Berlin, Germany, a "Department of Noise Protection" is making sure quietness is respected in the German capital. Only church bells, emergency sirens, snow ploughs and tractors are allowed to disturb Berliners. The (in)tolerance for noise reached such levels that several kindergartens have even been forced to close after local residents have gone to court! Finally, in Feb. 2011, German lawmakers adopted a new legislation allowing children to freely make noise…

A speaker who "declaims" is expected to either have a prepared speech, or, at the minimum, to be skilled speakers such as street vendors or politicians. In any case, in such cultures, speaking loud is a sign of self-confidence. Yet, in other cultures, this person might simply be loud, meaning impolite. Every culture has a tolerated limit of voice loudness, and it varies from one place to another.

When, in the opposite situation, you whisper in a low voice, some might think you are telling a secret, while others will believe you don't want to embarrass the listener in front of an audience. When a professor whispers into the ear of a student, it might mean, "I advise you to read carefully Chapter 5 for next week's exam", or "You mismatched your socks, but I won't tell in front of the class." The context will impact the meaning speech volume carries. Worshipers are expected to speak in low voices, or sometimes stay silent, in most religious sanctuaries, regardless of the religion. Meditation, connection with the deity, and respect toward other worshipers imply a relatively silent atmosphere. A loud tourist will immediately be shushed. In contrast, Bourses (stock markets) are places where participants, buyers and sellers, use their vocal capacities to the maximum, without any complex!

Speech loudness is also closely associated with emotions. Emotional people tolerate loud outbursts to display their emotions (of anger or sadness), while neutral ones expect others to keep a not-too-loud level in all circumstances.

Therefore, how loud we speak will be analyzed by others, mostly unconsciously, especially when we speak in a foreign culture. And the perception may be opposite to the original intention. A skilled negotiator will alternate the loudness of the speech to match the other speaker and use loudness to stress a nonnegotiable element. If the other negotiator is equally skilled, this maneuver should have no effect!

A safe bet is to speak after the host and to try to adjust to that level, at least at the beginning. This allows acknowledging the standard level of loudness without having to fundamentally change your speaking habits. In any case, it is advised to never speak louder than your host unless you wish to show strong feelings.

The intonation, the accents

Each language has its own intonation, and each voice its own tone; this leads to a multitude of possibilities. Regional accents can modify significantly how a language sounds, and those accents carry images that lead to specific representations of the group associated to them. Actually, accents will have a strong influence on our intonation. And once again, we transport this intonation onto our foreign language.

This can easily lead into unnecessary stereotypes. The French language has many speakers around the world and many more accents within France. Even if they have followed the same language course, a Parisian will display very different English skills than a speaker from Tunis or Montréal!

Living in a world where cultures mix more and more, intonations are no longer carriers of geographic location but they are still analyzed as such.

It is difficult to get rid of an accent, and one could wonder if it is at all needed. Our intonation is part of our identity, and what matters most is to be understood by others. The problem tends to be increasingly with native speakers who are confronted with the international version of their language. Languages are no longer "owned" by a territory, and accents are indeed equally shared.

In order to limit the risks of misunderstanding stemming from intonation, it is always advised to speak more slowly than usual and to repeat ideas in different forms. If someone did not understand you the first time, there is no need to shout.

The timing of our verbal interactions

Also called turntaking, once a topic is chosen and a conversation initiated, then matters of conversational timing arise. Knowing when it is acceptable or obligatory to take a turn in conversation is essential to the cooperative development of discourse.

This knowledge involves such factors as knowing how to recognize appropriate turn-exchange points and knowing how long the pauses between turns should be. It is also important to know how (and if) one may talk while someone else is talking—that is, if conversational overlap is allowed.

Cultural differences in matters of turntaking can lead to conversational breakdown, misinterpretation of intentions, and even conflict[52]. Some people are used to long pauses between turns, other prefer smooth transitions from one speaker to the next, and some even relish having several speakers talking at the same time!

Overlap is considered to be supportive by speakers who view a dialogue as an organic construction, sometimes separated from the discussion topic. Such cultures are called "high-involvement style." It is characterized by faster turntaking, a faster rate of speech, avoidance of interturn pauses, and participatory listenership [53]. This high-involvement style can also be found in a number of cultures, including French, Italian, Greek, Spanish, Russian, Arab, and some African cultures.

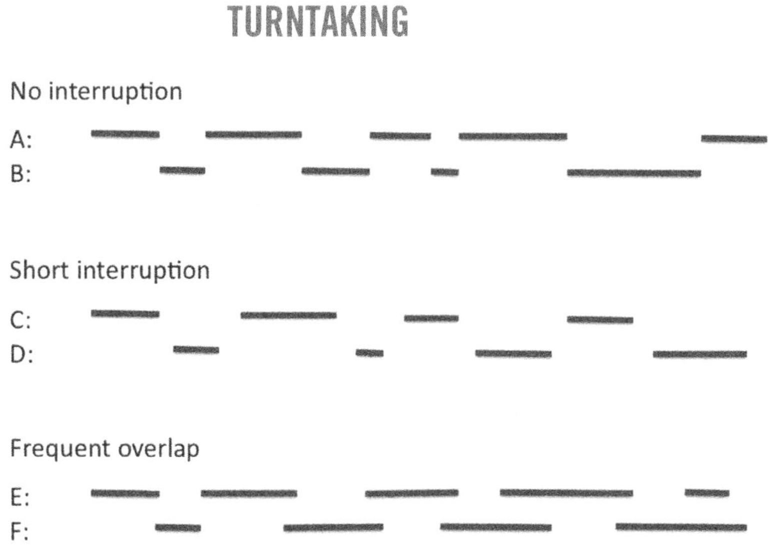

TURNTAKING

No interruption

A:
B:

Short interruption

C:
D:

Frequent overlap

E:
F:

Fig. 3.4 – Turntaking across cultures

---

52 Walt Wolfram, Natalie Schilling-Estes (1998). *American English: Dialects and Variation*
53 Tannen, Deborah (1981). *New York Jewish Conversational Style*

Intraturn pauses (silence) in conversation

An integral part of communication lies in our silences. The cultural weight is heavy and may result in misunderstandings galore.

You are sitting in front of a human resources manager of a company you wish to work for, and you've presented yourself and expressed enthusiasm in joining the firm. Yet, the human resources manager is sitting with the mouth shut, looking at you.

What does that mean? Does the manager expect you to continue talking, or are you supposed to keep quiet, too? Is it a good sign for your employment, or did you say something wrong that is spoiling the interview? With the silence lasting, how do you feel: relaxed or tense?

Such pauses may be due to "a variety of personal factors such as loss of words, search for a proper word, hesitation, absence of a script, empathic involvement, and temporary distraction.[54]" Long intraturn pauses (pauses a speaker creates for some private reason during his or her turn) on the part of the current turn-holder might encourage other participants to overlap the speaker's pause.

Irrelevant turntaking during intraturn spaces might even be associated with "silent, simultaneous talk," because the interruption might activate certain tacit ideas in the speaker's mind. Such feelings may include perceptions such as "I'm not finished yet," or "I'm thinking."

We can distinguish between three types of discontinuous talk in conversation: gaps, lapses, and pauses.

- A gap is "the silence between the end of one turn and some listener self-selecting for the next turn."

- If a current speaker stops and no speaker is willing to start or continue, the ensuing space of nontalk is called a lapse.

- If the current speaker has already selected a next speaker, the delay before the selected speaker's turn beginning will be perceived as a pause. A silence arising during the course of a participant's turn is also considered a pause.

---

54 Hayashi, (1996)

Among the factors contributing to the length of interturn pauses, interpersonal face relationships play an essential role. In general, "longer pauses are associated with independence politeness strategies, while shorter pauses are associated with involvement politeness strategies."[55]

In a hierarchical face system, persons in higher positions might use different pauses than persons in lower positions. In intercultural communication between English native speakers and Asians, the latter will often face considerable problems related to turn-exchange fluency. Firstly, as a second-language user, an Asian is likely to have a lower level of fluency. Secondly, the Westerner will prefer involvement politeness strategies and thus shorter interturn pauses, whereas the Asian will tend to assume a deference politeness system. Therefore, East Asian non-native speakers of English will often take longer to respond to a question. Americans who tend to get impatient with this silence will either repeat the question or simply change the topic.

Americans generally consider talk a means of accomplishing mutual understanding and a means of expressing their individuality. In contrast to Americans, Japanese value silence. As members of the Japanese culture, they emphasize group harmony and believe that one's feelings cannot be conveyed through talk. In other words, these differences can be associated with the dimension of individualism versus collectivism (see chapter #4).

In addition, Japanese business negotiators may favor silence as a means of avoiding a problem. Americans, trying to resolve conflict by talking even more, may, therefore, experience difficulties in cross-cultural communication.[56]

---

[55] Scollon/Scollon (1995)
[56] Yamada, Haru (1992). *American and Japanese Business Discourse: A Comparison of Interactional Styles*.

> ### CRAIG'S DIALOGUE: NEGOTIATIONS
>
> MARTHA: How did the negotiations go?
> JANET: Not so well. We were taken.
> MARTHA: What happened?
> JANET: Well, I proposed our starting price, and Maruoka didn't say anything.
> MARTHA: Nothing?
> JANET: He just sat there, looking very serious. So then I brought the price down.
> MARTHA: And?
> JANET: Still nothing. But he looked a little surprised. So I brought it down to our last offer and just waited. I couldn't go any lower.
> MARTHA: What did he say?
> JANET: Well, he was quiet for about a minute, and then he agreed.
> MARTHA: Well, at least we've got a deal. You should be pleased.
> JANET: I guess so. But later I learned that he thought our first price was very generous.

Backchanneling across cultures

The last part of the communication process is the feedback. In linguistics, this is also called backchanneling. It can either be:

- a spoken answer,
- a comment to the sender (a usual turntaking)
- one can use "sounds that are not really words"
- onomatopoeias (words that imitate a sound).

Often, using phrases or brief statements are meant to add one's token of attention in the discussion (for example, "Really?" or "Wow!" in English). However, as we have seen so far, this is already a misleading assumption.

In the USA, the word "great" is easily used to acknowledge the reception of an answer to a precise question:

The saleswoman: What color do you wish to choose for your new car?

The client: I was thinking of plain white…

The Saleswoman: Great. And do you take A/C ?

In many other cultures, such use of superlative can be either understood as praise, or, more likely, as irony. In both cases, unfortunately, the effect is very different from the one expected originally!

"Yes" is one of the most used verbal feedbacks around the world. That being said, the meaning behind "yes" may vary significantly across cultures. It depends on the importance played by the context in the culture (see chapters 1 & 4 for more details). Cultures that do not take into account much extra context when communicating are called "low context" cultures (or high content cultures). People from those cultures focus on what is being said, as literally as possible. Other cultures will analyze the meaning of a message with the help of as much extra information as possible, not only the content of the message: those are "high context" cultures.

Taking this into account, much information may lead to expressing ideas with a high level of un-said communication. In such cases, what is being said does not fully mean what the speaker wishes to transmit. Sometimes, it is simply the opposite: "Yes" means "No"!

> Research uncovered that Aboriginal people often answer 'yes' to advances by salespeople to appease the salesperson and politely end the conversation. Salespeople however took their 'yes' as agreement and sealed the contract with dire consequences.
>
> Hundreds of indigenous people entered unintentionally into exploitative, unfair contracts to buy, lease or lay-by products and services they couldn't afford and didn't understand. The North Queensland-based Indigenous Consumer Assistance Network (ICAN) cancelled more than 800 contracts, preventing an estimated $2 million of financial detriment, which they consider the 'tip of the iceberg'.
>
> Similarly, Aboriginal people 'agree' in everyday conversations with non-indigenous people. They try to politely tell the person that they do not want or can't answer their questions or request because they haven't built enough trust yet or it is not their call to reveal the answers.

---

57 'When 'Yeah Yeah Yeah' means no', Koori Mail 476 p.3

Non-lexical backchanneling is a variant when the turntaking exists thanks to sounds that are not really words such as "hmm", "err" or "uh-huh" in English. Those sounds are extremely culture related because they don't relate to precise definition, being not real words with an etymology as a guideline.

They are frequent sources of cross-cultural misunderstanding and should be avoided in such encounters to limit unnecessary frustrations. Negative questions ("You didn't lock the entrance door?) are also magnets to confusion as the same word ("Yes") can answer either the negation of the question (i.e. "Yes, I did not lock the door, it is still open") or the question itself (i.e. "Yes, I did lock the door, it now closed"). In doubt, it is always best to confirm what you understood.

NON-LINGUISTIC COMMUNICATION

What is left from our five senses? Verbal communication is linked to hearing. That leaves us with four senses to communicate:

- Seeing
- Touching
- Tasting
- Smelling

Gestures

A lot has been written about gestures across cultures, often with much approximation. This is probably the topic you are the most familiar when you meet representatives of other cultures.

Gestures are controlled expressions. Problems arise when the channel is understood (we can see the other) but the decoding is different; the meaning of the gestures is then different from the meaning carried at the beginning.

The OK hand gesture is one of the most common hand gestures. It is made by connecting the thumb and forefinger into a circle and holding the other fingers straight or relaxed in the air. The most common interpretation of this sign is OK, but there are some countries where it may be an insult or where it will not be understood.

Let's have a look at different countries and what the OK sign means there:

- *Australia* - Usually means zero rather than OK; not common
- *Canada* - OK, all right, good. You can use it to signify approval
- *China* - The OK sign is not used
- *France* - Zero, null
- *Finland* - Military conscripts use the sign to signal that they have zero days left in the military on their last day of national service
- *Germany* - Job well done or grave insult, depending on region
- *Greece* - OK (rarely used)
- *Ireland* - OK
- *Italy* - OK
- *Japan* - The general meaning is money, but for young people it means OK
- *New Zealand* - It's regarded as a cheesy way of saying OK. Not much used.
- *Russia* - Many people would understand this as OK, but they don't use this sign
- *Spain* - OK
- *Sweden* - OK
- *Turkey* - Homosexual
- *United Kingdom* - OK
- *Venezuela* - Homosexual
- *USA* - OK, all right, good. You can use it to signify approval

Please note that the meaning of gestures varies among various parts of countries and also among cultural groups and between generations.

Peter Siljerud
Hello Backpacker

Facial expressions apply here, too. Cultures differ greatly in their interpretation of such communication display.

Our relationship towards emotions comes again to play. Neutral cultures (see Chapter 4) tend to limit facial expressions to their minimum and might be shocked by a visitor making angry eyes, putting out the tongue or winking to the host! Other more emotional cultures are likely to better accept such mimics from a stranger but beware of the meaning they may carry! Whilein some cultures winking means a friendly "we understand each other, don't we?", in other cultures it might be understood as an invitation to an intimate relationship…

When in doubt, better keep a neutral expression in new situations.

> Blinis or not Blinis?
>
> "My mother is Russian and my father is Bulgarian, I was born and grew up in Bulgaria. As a child, we often visited our relatives in Moscow. I have a lot of memories of these trips but the first one that I have is a funny story: I was 3 or 4 years old, very shy and everyone tried to be extremely kind with me in order to gain my trust. My Russian aunt tried to "tame" me by offering me some delicious Russian chocolates. She asked me "Do you want some chocolates?" and I confirmed "Yes" by shaking my head from side to side (I was too shy to speak). She did not give me chocolates! Some minutes later the same thing happened: she asked me if I want some "blinis", I shook my head in order to say Yes. I did not get blinis! I started to cry and explained to my mother how bad my aunt was to me. My mother just laughed. Years later I understood that by shaking my head in the "Bulgarian" way in order to say Yes, my aunt was seeing the Russian way of shaking the head for No!
>
> Bulgarians nod their head to say no and shake their heads to say yes. When I speak with Bulgarians I try to make them always pronounce the word "Yes" (Да) or "No" (не) because a lot of Bulgarians travel a lot or study abroad and to confuse you even more they nod or shake heads in the western way, so I do not have a clue if they mean yes or no."
>
> Aliena Riminchan
Bulgaria/Russia
2011

Related to perception, oculesics (making eye contact) is also culturally related. Unfortunately, there isn't much completed research to use. Top-down or long consistent looks can be misinterpreted, especially if there is a hierarchical or gender relationship. Some cultures don't allow youngsters to look into the eyes of the elders.

Seeing

When we meet somebody, our appearance is the first message we send. While the message is usually not voluntary, each of us is carefully shaping our own appearance, hoping to send the appropriate meaning. Ignoring these messages (a seven-year-old wearing mum's high heels and heavy make-up will expect a reaction) can be as equally devastating as categorizing a person only on appearance (my neighbor wears goth-type clothes; he must be depressed and introvert). That being said, appearance is our first source of information when we try to analyze someone else. And this is very culturally loaded.

> A trip to Shanghai and Beijing with many different experiences also revealed a lot of cultural differences and therefore cultural misunderstandings. We had to learn that going out in China can be tricky. One of our colleagues was most of the time considered as chief due to his appearance and age, and therefore he was the one in charge for any order at a restaurant as well as any negotiation for our trips with the organizers. Different to what we were used to, Chinese waiters and waitresses only went to him for receiving the orders as well as for handing over the bill. This is due to the Chinese culture that the oldest or wealthiest person of the table orders the food and pays the bill for everyone. We indeed thought they were too lazy or even unqualified to divide the meals of the different people on the bill.
>
> Anna Mooser & Roland Pfeifhofer
> Austria
> 2010

Our physical appearance comes first. Gender, height, weight, skin color, hair color, and all the other physical attributes are understood differently across cultures.

The way we dress is also a key factor. While in some cultures nudity is a taboo, in others it is a mainstream attribute. The type of clothes is also prone to misunderstandings: while most men in south east Asia wear some long clothes covering their legs (called sampot, sarong, dhoti or lungi across the region) the same garment in Europe or North America would be understood as a women's dress!

Hair color is also often associated with cultural particularities: While blond children are likely to be photographed by Chinese or Japanese tourists because this is rare and curious where they come from, Irish are likely to associate closely with someone with ginger hair!

Superstitions and old wives' tales are full of examples when people are attributed some special characteristics (usually negative) linked to physical aspects. Just like stereotypes, the irony is that the same attributes can be positive in one place and negative elsewhere; having blue eyes will be looked on with suspicion in Greece but is considered a standard eye color for most people living around the Baltic Sea.

Gender can also be a strong source of cultural misunderstandings. This has often to do with the separation of roles in the society (if any) or the profession associated with gender. For example, regardless of the fact that medical faculties around the world increasingly enroll more female students than males, a doctor is often expected to be a man in cultures where women are not encouraged to study such a specialty. In opposition, a nurse is often expected to be a woman, much to the annoyance of male nurses. This is equally true for midwives who are increasingly men!

The skin can also bear extreme variation of cultural meanings. The tone of skin will be understood differently from one place to another. Most Western "fashion victims" will make sure to appear tanned after summer (thanks to exposure to sun or simply the use of creams), while many African women will not hesitate to use cosmetic creams (sometimes toxic ones) to whiten their skin. This is also changing throughout time, as European aristocrats in the eighteenth century would be careful to appear with skin as white as possible (using occasionally Asian rice power) to be certain not to be mistaken with working people, exposed to the sun.

Many more elements linked to appearance can be associated to culture. The essential factor is not necessarily to list them all but to be aware of their implication when we encounter others. Before reacting too strongly to artifacts that are extreme in your own culture, it is necessary to take a step back and to ponder their meaning in the original culture.

> ### CRAIG'S DIALOGUE: CHOICES
>
> ARABELLA: I liked the man from Liverpool.
> BOB: David Symes? Why is that?
> ARABELLA: I liked his style and his manners. He makes a very good first impression. He's also very well spoken.
> BOB: I guess you're right. But I wonder about his technical background. The man from Oxford seemed a bit stronger.
> ARABELLA: The one with the loud tie? Yes, he was stronger.

Haptics (Touching)

Our touching skills vary greatly from one culture to another. It has implications for our touching codes but also how we stand toward each other. This has been analyzed by Edward T. Hall (presented in the previous chapter and also in Chapter 6), who synthesized his founding under the term proxemics.[58]

As far as nonverbal communication across cultures is concerned, it has an impact on how we stand in a crowd (do we keep a certain distance of twenty to thirty centimeters when lining up at a cashier, or do we allow only a few centimeters?), how we stand face-to-face when discussing, or simply how we walk.

Actually, each of us has a unique way to move and walk. All of us have already experienced the situation when you are waiting for someone dear, and, from far away, you are able to recognize this person simply from the silhouette.

Not surprisingly, culture has its imprint, too. Taking the metro or the bus is, at the first sight, the same process around the world. Then, why is it that when you are a tourist you feel as though you are being pushed away by the unknown crowd? Crowd analysis shows that people move differently in a similar space, depending on their culture. This is useful to design public spaces such as airports, supermarkets, or religious centers. But touching triggers our awareness firstly when others don't share our touching codes.

---

58   Hall, Edward T. (1966). The Hidden Dimension

> Hugging Across Cultures
>
> On one of our classes we had to discuss cultural differences in groups. It was interesting what the Lithuanian girl said about private space. After the first semester when she arrived home at Christmas she gave a hug to her younger sister, as she had become use to a more touchy life here in the Czech Republic. That was the first time they met after four months. Her sister was embarrassed because of the hug. Touching is not acceptable even among the family members, she told us.
>
> Agnes Boda
> Czech Republic
> 2010

The French are notorious for kissing when meeting. But most foreigners (and French themselves, as a matter of fact) can be baffled by the regional differences of such touching codes. Below is a tentative map of regional differences, indicating the number of kisses people exchange when they meet.[59]

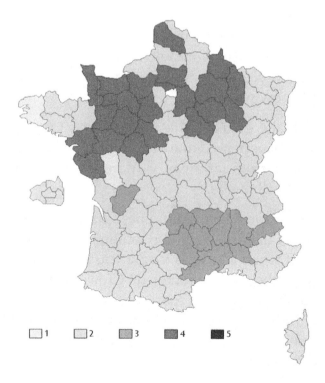

Fig. 3.5 – French kissing when greeting: mapping of number of kisses

---

59 http://combiendebises.free.fr/

Touching codes also have strong links with gender roles. Many Europeans are surprised to discover Iranian men, often stereotyped as macho, holding hands in the street.

In business relations, touching can provoke some real embarrassment if a person coming from a neutral region goes to a very kinesthetic culture. Holding one's arm, kissing, hugging, or patting the back can be understood as very intimate, sometimes intrusive, gestures.

Tasting

Out of the five senses, tasting is probably the least influenced by culture. Besides, to be fair, our use of tasting to communicate is limited! That being said, when encountering other cultures, food often represents the entry point into the discovery. And food has a lot to do with taste. Depending on where you come from, you may be used to certain tastes, while other tastes may make you feel bad.

> Did you know?
> "Bertie Bott's Every Flavor Beans," based on the invented treat from the Harry Potter world consist of a mixture of the original jellybean flavors, as well as some unique, less pleasant ones, like grass, vomit, and boogers. The Jelly Belly Candy Company manufactures them.

Some cultures feature very spicy recipes, usually out of tradition and for climate reasons. Some strong spices, such as red hot pepper, are thought to have some preservative and antiseptic qualities, very useful in areas where food cannot be refrigerated. Spices are also useful in bringing variety to staple food that would otherwise be plain and always the same.

A traveler, tasting Indian food for the first time will surely measure the cultural gap between his home and the host simply by the intensity of the pain in the mouth! But, once again, as culture is learned, it is actually quite accessible to alter our own perception of taste, and with time and a good dose of self-convincing, anyone can adapt to any food. Well, almost…

Olfactics (Smelling)

Smell is a powerful cultural element that is often ignored. In some aspects, it can be considered even stronger than taste because a smell cannot be prevented. If you walk across an open market in Ouagadougou in Mali and you are used to shopping in a local supermarket with refrigerated booths and temperature-controlled air, chances are you'll get a cultural shock, a shock carried by the smell. Your host from Mali, in return, is likely to feel very uncomfortable visiting your local shop, having the feeling of shopping in a sterile laboratory!

> My Cheese is Dead!
>
> French-American Clotaire Rapaille is famous for his analysis of cultural code in marketing. One of his studies had to do with sales of French cheese, Camembert, in the US -a successful commercial for cheese in France was a real flop in America. As a result, sales were absolutely disastrous.
>
> His findings showed that in France, a customer associates cheese with going to the farmer's market with his or her mother and watching her weigh, prod, and smell the cheese to ascertain its degree of ripeness. Alternatively, American mothers simply picked up the nearest package of the cheese they wanted and put it in their carts.
>
> The cultural differences shape behaviors as French people poke and smell the cheese and try not to place the cheese in the refrigerator. Meanwhile, Americans never poke or smell the cheese and always put the cheese in the refrigerator. In one case, the cheese is "alive" (like a flower), but it is "dead" (like chocolate) for others.
>
> The French cheese company changed its advertisements, focusing more on safety before pleasure. Sales went up immediately.
>
> Archetype Discoveries Worldwide
Case study #7
2002

The world is actually becoming less and less tolerant to smells. The ever-growing sales of deodorants and perfumes are the definite proof of this trend. However, differences are still very present. Such differences often have to do with the climate or access to water. People coming from the Caribbean islands don't mind taking several showers a day while nomadic peoples from cold places in Arctic territories such as the Inuits or the Nenets might feel perfectly comfortable washing once or twice a year!

Smell is a cultural element that may carry unfortunate consequences. Whether in business or dating, one can be put off by the odor of someone else. The outcome of the meeting is likely to be negative if the tolerance of the other's smell cannot be overcome.

Conclusion

Culture influences our behavior, and quite logically, the way we communicate with others and how we understand them. While it can be expected that verbal communication carries many cultural meanings, what we *don't* say also carries loads of information. Indeed, non-verbal communication is the vector of many misunderstandings across cultures.

More subtle but not less true, how we say things, especially when we speak a foreign language, is also interpreted through cultural spectacles. We transpose our cultural structure into the other languages.

Cultural awareness begins with acknowledging that our patterns might differ from the others. Observing our own preferences is the first step towards ethnorelativity, when we accept the validity of the other's opinion.

Paying more attention to our hosts' communication is also a safe way to limit awkward cultural blunders!

RECAP

A great deal of management of people is linked to communication; it is essential to understand how much culture influences both.

- We communicate all the time, with all our five senses.

- Our verbal communication is the easiest to control but it is still prone to cultural misunderstandings, even if we share the same language.

- Paralinguistic communication, how we say things, is strongly shaped by our native language and can be easily misunderstood by others.

- Non-verbal communication - our gestures, our posture, our facial expressions, is also sending signals to others, although its share in our communication has been greatly exaggerated in early research.

CASE STUDY 3.1: WHY DO JAPANESE FALL ASLEEP IN MEETINGS?

"One of the most common questions I receive from Americans who work with Japanese is, "Why do Japanese fall asleep in meetings?"

The fact is, when Japanese close their eyes in meetings, most of the time they aren't actually asleep! Often, closed eyes is a sign that a Japanese person is listening intensely. Japanese believe that by closing their eyes, they can hear more effectively, because they are screening out the visual stimulus and focusing only on the sound. Because Japanese find it challenging to listen to English conversations for long stretches of time, they are especially likely to use this technique in meetings with Americans.

Unlike Americans, Japanese don't have the custom of maintaining eye contact with the person who is talking. So the action of closing one's eyes, which appears to Americans to be extremely impolite, carries no such negative connotations for Japanese. And typically Japanese are unaware that closing one's eyes strikes Americans as being rude. Japanese typically don't realize how disconcerting, or even insulting, this habit can be to Americans.

Once, earlier in my career, I was giving an important speech. While talking, I looked over at a senior Japanese person in attendance, who I was hoping to make a good impression on. His eyes were closed, and his face wore a placid expression. He really looked like he was asleep! Even though intellectually I knew that Japanese often close their eyes when listening to English, on an emotional level I panicked, thinking, "Oh no, I'm so boring that this key person is sleeping!" Through the rest of the speech my eyes kept darting over to him, each time to find him with his eyes still closed. However, when the speech was over and it was the time for the question-and-answer session, his hand was the first one that darted up. He asked a very incisive question, the content of which indicated that he had indeed been listening to my talk very carefully. Phew!

In a meeting-type situation, if you see Japanese closing their eyes, it may be an indication that you need to slow down your speech and make sure you are speaking in a way that is not too complicated and doesn't use too many idioms. Be aware, however, that some Japanese will close their eyes almost no matter what—it's that ingrained a habit. You may also want to consider changing the format of your meeting, to encourage more discussion and interaction.

Another reason why Japanese close their eyes in meetings occurs in the case of senior executives. Typically this is limited to the one highest-ranking individual in the

CASE STUDY 3.1: WHY DO JAPANESE FALL ASLEEP IN MEETINGS?

meeting. They will sit with their eyes closed and their head tilted downward, looking for all the world like they are catching a catnap. However, this is merely a way for them to disguise their nonverbal signals—as if they had drawn a shade down in front of their face. Senior executives tend to do this as a way of keeping their cards close to them and not letting everyone know their reaction to what is being said. If they didn't do this, all the other Japanese in the meeting would be scanning their expression for clues as to what they are thinking.

Closing one's eyes and tilting one's head downward is also a way for a senior executive to demonstrate that they are not the one who is running the meeting. In Japan, senior people will often take a sideline role in order to give younger employees a chance to shine by taking center stage. It may also be the case that the younger employees speak better English and thus are better suited to the primary speaking role. Also, in Japanese culture being quiet is thought to be more dignified, and thus is more appropriate for a senior person than being talkative. Of course, this is the opposite of the American custom of having the most senior person take the lead in the meeting and do the most talking. So it's particularly unnerving to Americans when the senior-most person appears to be sleeping—it seems like a sure sign of failure! Just be sure to temper your emotional reaction with this logical information on why this is happening.

Recently I saw a senior American executive at one of my clients, a major Japanese firm. He had attended the shareholder's meeting of the parent company in Japan a short time prior to that. He said "Rochelle, I'm going to have to make you eat your words about Japanese really concentrating when they are closing their eyes in meetings, because at our shareholder's meeting there were several guys who really were sleeping, there was no doubt about it!" Of course, there are occasions when Japanese actually do fall asleep in meetings. (You can usually tell this is happening when someone's mouth falls open, their head nods, or they are snoring!) However, this is something that is typically overlooked in Japan, because their fatigue is usually a result of legitimate activities such as staying up late for overseas conference calls or entertaining customers. Furthermore, because in typical Japanese meetings large numbers of people are invited even if their connection to the topic is only indirect, meeting participants who are not at the center of the discussion may feel that they can safely catch a couple winks. It's not considered to be as rude as it would be in U.S. culture, because there is no norm like we have in the U.S. that requires all participants to make a contribution to the conversation. Often, just being present to show your support

CASE STUDY 3.1: WHY DO JAPANESE FALL ASLEEP IN MEETINGS?

for the topic is deemed to be sufficient. This would certainly be the case in the shareholder's meeting that my client attended—in Japan such meetings tend to be ceremonial, and would not require the board members to make any statements or participate in discussions. It's their presence alone that is required."

Rochelle Kopp
Managing Principal
Japan Intercultural Consulting[60]
2011

Discussion questions:

- How do you react when people stay silent after you speak?
- In your culture, how do senior managers display their authority?
- Can you think of other non-verbal communication displays that can be misinterpreted by other cultures?

---

[60] This article originally appeared in Japan Close-Up magazine.

CASE STUDY 3.2: KISSING ACROSS CULTURES

"Never shall I forget the first time I met my ex-boyfriend's mother – a 50 year old English lady with a well-kept perm, giving me a suspicious stare over the rim of her glasses. I briskly stepped out with my hand outstretched and ready to give her my Dutch three kisses – right, left, right. However, after my first kiss I noticed a considerable change in her body language – as I was nearing her enthusiastically, she all of a sudden froze, and I held a limp woman in my arms. Embarrassed, I stopped half-way through, my second kiss trailing in the air, trying to make up for the awkward situation by grasping her hand even more firmly, while trying to smile a reassuring smile that ended up not being seen by her averting eyes.

In sharp contrast with this situation, is the moment I met my husband's mother, years later – a small, cheerful and expressive Colombian woman. As I approached her with my outstretched hand, ready to shake hers firmly and plant three kisses on her cheeks, she swept me off my feet, embraced me passionately, held my face between her hands and placed a long lingering kiss on each cheek, while murmuring phrases I could not understand.

Why does an English woman freeze when a Dutch woman tries to kiss her? Why does a Dutch woman feel intimidated by a Colombian lady's passion? Why does the kiss have different meanings in different cultures? Kissing is one of the most intimate forms of communication – and communication, as Edward Hall argues "constitutes the core of culture and indeed of life." Whereas kissing prehistorically might have originated in a mother feeding her infant by transferring chewed food from mouth to mouth, nowadays, it is a form of communication that is acknowledged in most cultures, in one form or another. However, the context in which we kiss may differ: we can kiss because we love, because we respect, because we greet or say farewell – because we comfort or because we mate. Knowing when to kiss or when not to kiss – that's the question. Using kissing as a form of saying hello might be widely accepted in certain cultures but shivered upon in others. Hence I am sure most of us have been in situations where their kisses embarrassingly hovered in mid-air, or even worse, ended in someone's most intimate parts of the neck – or vice versa, where their "hello's" and formally outstretched hands were surprisingly met by passionate kisses. In a contemporary world where the meeting of people transcends nationalities, a certain 'kissing etiquette' could be useful – but, we have to ask ourselves, how accurate can such etiquette be?

There are certain cultures in which any type of physical contact in public is mostly frowned upon – hence kissing as a form of greeting someone is considered a taboo.

CASE STUDY 3.2: KISSING ACROSS CULTURES

Examples are countries like China or Japan. On the contrary, we'll find that in most western European cultures, kissing is so much accepted that it even has become a formality – examples are the Netherlands, Germany, Spain and of course France. The number of kisses, however, might differ across countries and depend on certain additional conditions like gender, age, relationship and context. In countries like the US or Australia, hugging might be more customary than kissing, however, a peck on the cheek is certainly not uncommon in Australia. Then there are Muslim cultures in which it is appropriate to kiss only within your gender – physical contact between males and females is not widely accepted. Lastly, there is a certain ambiguous category to which the English belong – known for being reserved, they shy away from kissing, however it has happened to me more often than not that I was kissed by an English person without having made previous acquaintance.

Hence, generalizations are there to be disputed. A culture averse to any form of physical contact in public – and hence to kissing – is the Chinese, as mentioned above. However, in 2004, a supermarket with the fascinating name "Everybody is Happy" in the Chinese municipality of Tianjin called out a kissing contest on Valentine's Day. This caused huge controversies between their more conservative, older customers and the younger ones – however, the kissing contest took place with great success. In Japan, the so-called western or Christian wedding ceremony has more and more commonly replaced the traditional Japanese wedding – and is thus sealed with a wedding kiss. However, in most of the cases, the kiss is planted on the cheek rather than on the lips.

In the Netherlands, as part of the "inburgerings-examen" or integration test (literally – civilization test) for future migrants into the country, a shot is shown of two gay men kissing. The exam includes a question on how to behave when witnessing two gay men kiss in a public place – next to questions on the Dutch colonial history, the nationality of the crown princess and public transport. This question has been met by a lot of protest among certain Arabic and Asian cultures, where even though kissing in public might be accepted by now, homosexual kissing is a taboo. So here, interestingly, the act of kissing is used as a tool to send out a certain message to future immigrants.

To kiss or not to kiss – it remains an ambivalent question where different layers of meaning disguise any straightforward attitude to the gesture of kissing. Taking a closer look establishes that in communication, nothing is as straightforward as it seems, however culturally determined it may be. Culture, as such, is in constant flux

CASE STUDY 3.2: KISSING ACROSS CULTURES

and human interaction, therefore, is continuously changing and adapting. Thus, the only thing we can do is to pay close attention to our surroundings wherever we are, and be prepared to kiss… or not."

Marielle van der Meer
Intercultural Development[61]
IOR Consulting
2011

Discussion questions:

- How do you great people in your culture?
- How do people tolerate physical contact in your culture?
- How does gender affect certain types of greeting?

---

61 Link to article: http://www.iorworld.com/blog/kissing-cultures

Chapter 4: Cultural dimensions relating to people

CHAPTER CONTENTS

Highlights
Introduction
Understanding the different meanings
Understanding the basic assumptions
Why the 7 dimensions?

UNIVERSALISTIC VS. PARTICULARISTIC
Identifying different cultural values
Did the pedestrian die?

INDIVIDUALISM VS. COMMUNITARIAN
How to measure
Some key findings

AFFECTIVE VS. NEUTRAL
How did we assess the difference in emotional expression across cultures?
Some key findings

SPECIFIC VS. DIFFUSE
How did we test the differences across cultures?
Some key findings
High/Low Context

ACHIEVED VS. ASCRIBED
How did we measure the status orientation in different cultures?
Hierarchy

Conclusion
Recap
Case study 4.1: Indians find it difficult to say no to their superiors
Case study 4.2: Japanese company's energy saving staff haircut

CHAPTER 4

CULTURAL DIMENSIONS RELATING TO PEOPLE
By Fons Trompenaars

Highlights:

After reading this chapter, you should be able to:

- Recognize the different aspects of human relationships that are affected by culture
- Effectively deal with those differences
- Practice your understanding of relational differences
- See how different cultures deal with different relational orientations

Introduction

It is remarkable how often cultural background is ignored in both business and scientific discourse. It is necessary to consider why this is often ignored not only in mergers and acquisitions, but also in change management processes, in spite of the fact that it seems to be one of the major reasons such alliances and change processes fail.

Organizations are cultural constructs and, at the end of the day, any social system is a set of relationships between actors. The essence of these relationships is communication. Communication is the exchange of information, and information is the carrier of meaning. Since culture is the system of shared meaning, the organization is essentially a cultural construct.

Understanding the different meanings

On arrival in your foreign destination to begin your professional assignment, you will immediately be aware of differences arising from the outer and the middle layers of culture. The importance of the inner layer of culture is that different cultures may give a different meaning to the same thing. You are likely to find differences in the following areas, among others:

- the status accorded to older people
- the relationship between men and women
- the respect given to the law (and even simple rules)
- the degree to which your working relationship is or becomes more personal.

It is very important that you do not make the mistake of assuming that cultural differences are just about such visible elements as clothes, food, and houses. You may embarrass yourself, or your host, because you give different meaning to the same things. If you have some understanding of these differences, and learn how to cope with them, your whole experience of working in a different culture can be enhanced and made much more effective—and enjoyable.

Understanding the basic assumptions

As explained in the previous chapters, every culture has developed its own set of basic assumptions, which can be categorized into different dimensions. In dealing with universal human problems, each cultural dimension can be seen as a continuum: at one end there is a basic value, which contrasts with the value at the other end. The continuum will cover every possible combination between the two contrasting basic values.

All cultures need to deal with the challenge of these extreme choices. They face a continuous series of dilemmas, because by itself each alternative is either unsatisfactory or insufficient. In business, for example, do we go only for the short -term or the long-term? For stability or change? For market-led or technology-led products? For rewarding individuals or teams? Transnational organizations respond to these dilemmas in different ways, according to how they stand on each separate dimension derived from their cultural heritage.

In short, culture is a dynamic process of human beings that are developing a set of behaviors and values that help them to survive as a group. If the solutions to the problems work, we see that the values become norms and the behaviors slip out of consciousness. These problems occur in three main areas:

❑ Relationships with people

❑ Orientations toward time

❑ Orientations toward the environment

In the first category we distinguish five aspects, the ones that Talcott Parsons developed in his *Social System*[62]. Together with his framework, we add the two dimensions of Edward Hall, Strodtbeck, and Kluckhohn on time and nature (See Chapter 2 for more details). This completes the seven dimensions.

Why the 7 dimensions?

In fact, the seven dimensions came about by accident. In 1980, I tried to defend my research proposal on the basis of Hofstede's four dimensions as he later described in *Culture's Consequences*. The exam committee asked me why I chose those four dimensions and not dimensions discussed in alternative work such as in the oeuvre of the authors just quoted. I had to go back to the library and combine the models of all authors. It gives a much more complete model. When discussing this with Hofstede, I didn't get a satisfactory answer[63].

This chapter presents five cultural dimensions in the way we deal with other human beings.

---

62 T. Parsons, 1970, The Social System, Routledge & Kegan Paul PLC
63 Look for more interesting debates about these models in Hampden-Turner et al. (Hampden-Turner, C. and F. Trompenaars (1997), "Response to Geert Hofstede," International Journal of Intercultural Relations, 21 (1).

UNIVERSALISTIC VS. PARTICULARISTIC

People in universalistic cultures share the belief that general rules, codes, values, and standards take precedence over particular needs and claims of friends and relations.

In such a society, the rules apply equally to the whole "universe" of members. Any exception weakens the rule. For example, the rule that you should bear truthful witness in a court of law, or give an honest account of an accident to an insurance company before it pays out, is more important here than particular ties of friendship or family obligations. This does not mean that, in universalistic cultures, particular ties are completely unimportant. But the universal truth—that is, the law—is considered logically more significant than these relationships. The United States is a notable example of a universalistic culture, which explains the high number of lawyers per head of population.

Conversely, particularistic cultures see the ideal culture in terms of human friendship, extraordinary achievements and situations, and a network of intimate relationships. The "spirit of the law" is deemed more important than the "letter of the law". Obviously, there are rules and laws in particularistic cultures, but these merely codify how people relate to each other. Rules are needed, if only so that people can make exceptions to them for particular cases, but generally individuals need to be able to count on the support of their friends. South America and parts of Africa are examples of cultures where, typically, relationships between friends and family members are deemed more important than the letter of the law.

CRAIG'S DIALOGUE: LUCKY FOR HASSAN

MS. ANDERSON:	Hassan was looking at your paper.
ABDULLAH:	He was?
MS. ANDERSON:	Yes. He copied some of your answers.
ABDULLAH:	Perhaps he didn't know the answers.
MS. ANDERSON:	I'm sure he didn't.
ABDULLAH:	Then it's lucky he was sitting next to me.

CULTURAL DIMENSIONS RELATING TO PEOPLE

Identifying different cultural values

A single incident can have different meanings in different cultures, depending on the prevailing values of the society concerned. You need to learn to distinguish these. As an example, imagine that you are a passenger in a car driven by your friend in an area of the city where there is a speed limit. Your friend drives too fast and hits a pedestrian, causing serious injuries. Your friend has to go to court, and you are the only witness. Do you tell the truth or adapt what you will say to help your friend? That is, do you choose for the law (impelled by universalism—everyone should be treated the same) or for friendship (where your particular relationship with your friend is more important)?

Implications for Business and Family resemblances		
Universalism	Vs.	Particularism
Consistency	*Vs.*	*Flexibility*
Systems, standards & rules	*Vs.*	*Pragmatism*
Uniform procedures	*Vs.*	*Make exceptions "it depends"*
Demanding of clarity	*Vs.*	*At ease with ambiguity*
Letter of the law	*Vs.*	*Spirit of the law*

Did the pedestrian die?

You are a passenger in a car driven by a close friend. He hits a pedestrian. You know he was going at least thirty-five miles per hour in an area of the city where the maximum allowed speed is twenty miles per hour. There are no witnesses. His lawyer says that if you testify under oath that he was only driving twenty miles per hour, it may save him from serious consequences.

What right has your friend to expect you to protect him?

a) My friend has a **definite** right as a friend to expect me to testify to the lower figure.

b) He has **some** right as a friend to expect me to testify to the lower figure.

c) He has **no** right as a friend to expect me to testify to the lower figure.

Would you help your friend in view of the obligations you feel toward society?

I will (d) or will not (e) testify to the lower figure.

This dilemma has been put to some ninety thousand managers in fifty-five countries. Obviously, one would expect the answers to vary considerably from country to country. In Switzerland and North America, more than 93 percent chose the combination c-e, while in China and Venezuela less than 35 percent showed preference for this answer. The results completely align with the expectations in the international business world where reliability and integrity are at stake. Germans, Dutch, British, and Americans are reliable and know how to behave in an ethically correct manner. Therefore they are considered more reliable than the Asians and South Americans. They always help their friends. They are not bothered in business and beyond by ethical principles. Up until here nobody will disagree.

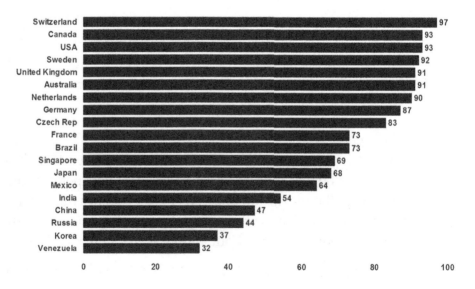

Fig. 4.1 – Universalism across selected cultures

The interpretation of results in the preceding paragraph is rather culturally biased. Look at the following Korean remark. A South Korean came to me in a break of a workshop and said, "I knew the Americans are corrupt but you gave it empirical evidence. Thank you." "Why"? "You can't trust the Americans. They do not even help their friends."

I have asked the question of the car accident to a large variety of people, and I have not met one that would like to participate in this experience. This type of dilemma is beyond culture. In all societies, this type of dilemma is seen as a dilemma because all people regardless of their culture would like to help friends in addition to respecting the truth and supporting laws that protect pedestrians. Culture is the way one solves dilemmas. The way one resolves dilemmas is culturally determined.

Talcott Parsons referred to this as the difference between universalism and particularism. The first is a value orientation quite popular in Protestant societies. Here order and authority prevails, codified in writing and checked by God and lawyers. On the other side of the spectrum, we find particularism, popular amongst the Catholics, who seem to be rather charmed by the exception. God wasn't looking during the accident, and a feeling of guilt is often ridiculed. We see that in universalistic countries there is often a need to look for standards (the hotel chain, ISO, basic business principles, how to get anything, McDonalds, Coca Cola). In particularistic countries, the exception and the unique are rather popular (Le Chateau, haute cuisine, haute couture).

International organizations are increasingly confronted with these types of value dilemmas. These dilemmas are quite easy to solve in multinational organizations in which Italians work in Italy and Dutch people work in the Netherlands. You just allow for different approaches in different cultures. It becomes more troublesome when the process of internationalization further develops. The quest for business principles in global organizations increases in order to enable the organization to superimpose similar ethical values.

Consider the following American organization that espouses two business principles: (1) uncompromising integrity (2) respect for diversity. After I had confronted its senior employees with the car accident dilemma, I asked them how they would approach this dilemma in practice when integrity was their leading value. A variety of answers drew my attention. The Chinese and Italians would lie for their friend (the unique part of any relationship), while the English, Dutch, and North Americans put the law (the universal truth) above anything. The introduction of the second principle, respect for diversity, made the consistent application of integrity even more complex than it was initially.

In universalistic cultures, the concept of integrity is often seen as a garbage can that is allowed in one's own environment and is laid down in legal writing. In particular, in dominant cultures such as in the US and Germany, integrity is nothing more than a natural extension of their own cultures. I was presenting this pedestrian dilemma to an international group of managers. An Englishman confessed that he would give his friend some right to expect him to lie, but it could have easily been a definite right or no right at all.

I presented the pedestrian dilemma, "Did the pedestrian die?" to an international group of managers. In an attempt to be amusing, I said that the pedestrian was very dead. "But why didn't you give us this information at the beginning?" asked a French woman with great irritation. "Why should I?" was my reply. "What's your problem?" "Like my English colleague, my answer was (b) somewhat right. But now that I know that my friend has killed a pedestrian, I realize I should have answered (a). He has a definite right to expect my help." You had to see the face of the Englishman! Again it confirms that in France friends are more important than pedestrians. If you know Paris, you know what I mean.

Last year I was invited to participate in a conference dealing with business ethics. The goal of the conference was to publish the result of large-scale research in a large number of European countries. One of the questions was, "If you have signed a contract, would you stick to it in all circumstances?" The answers had to be given on a five-point scale ranging from always to never. Interesting question. In great contrast to what lots of people would believe, the research was sponsored solely by the Dutch, and therefore the results and their interpretation were unfortunately very predictably Dutch. Italians, for example, scored at the lowest end of the scale of ethical behavior (if they answered truthfully) and the Germans highest. For the Italians, it is not always ethical to follow a contract through under circumstances that ask for a flexible approach. Amongst Germans, it seems to be expected that a contract be fulfilled even if one of the parties involved has to suffer. This research, in fact, measures how Dutch one is but not how ethical one is. The international manager needs a new logic. And the research on international ethics needs to be done by an international team. In fact, the logic should be based on the etymological meaning of the word integrity: unaffected condition, in a wholly integrated whole. Once one goes international, one needs this new logic to survive. I strongly believe that the international understanding of the concept of integrity should be the result of integrating seemingly opposing values.

A Japanese person came to me in a break. He said that in Japan we would test the strength of friendship by asking our friend to tell the truth in court. In the meantime we could go to the judge to lower the sentence for his courage and bad luck. Integrity deals with the question of how to reconcile the particular friendship with the universal truth. This integration makes it into a virgin unity. No culture will object to that.

Managing cultural differences is not about trying to emulate or denigrate what you find different. Doing business and managing across cultures **is** very much about integrating the strength of one culture with that of another.

INDIVIDUALISTIC VS. COMMUNITARIAN

In predominantly individualistic cultures, people place the individual before the community. The pace is set by individual happiness, welfare, and fulfillment. People are expected to decide matters largely on their own and to take care primarily of themselves and their immediate family. The quality of life for all members of society is seen as directly dependent on opportunities for individual freedom and development. The community is judged by the extent to which it serves the interest of individual members.

The United Kingdom and, to a greater extent, the United States, are examples of cultures that encourage the individual. Pay and performance systems in organizations are often based on this.

At the other end of the continuum, a predominantly communitarian culture places the community before the individual. It is the responsibility of the individual to act in ways that serve society. By doing so, individual needs will be taken care of naturally. The quality of life for the individual is seen as directly dependent on the degree to which he or she takes care of fellow members, even at the cost of individual freedom. People are judged by the extent to which they serve the interest of the community.

For example, in both China and Japan, working in a team and contributing to the group or society have a higher priority than individual performance.

CRAIG'S DIALOGUE: WEDDING BELLS	
ALICE:	I heard your son is getting married. Congratulations.
FATIMA:	Thank you. The wedding will be next spring.
ALICE:	How nice for you. How did they meet?
FATIMA:	Oh, they haven't actually met yet.

How to measure

The difference between an individual and a group orientation is about how we resolve the conflict between our individual interests and objectives, and those of the group to which we belong:

❑ Do we relate to others by determining what each one of us wants and then negotiating the differences? (individualism)

❑ Or do we relate to them by giving priority to a shared idea of what is good for the group? (collectivism)

Again, cultures differ in which orientation they primarily focus on, as can be shown by the following dilemma:

Two people were discussing ways in which individuals could improve the quality of life.

a) One said, "It is obvious that if individuals have as much freedom as possible and the maximum opportunity to develop themselves, the quality of their life will improve as a result."

b) The other said, "If individuals are continuously taking care of their fellow human beings, the quality of life will improve for everyone, even if it obstructs in1dividual freedom and individual development."

Which of the two ways of reasoning do you think is usually best—a or b?

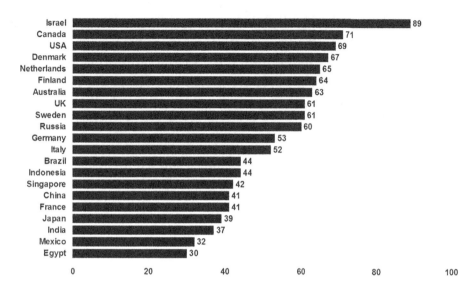

Fig. 4.2 - How to improve the quality of life
Percentage of respondents who think the quality of life improves with giving freedom to the individual.

Some key findings:

- Israelis score highest on this indicator of individual orientation (89 percent opting for individual freedom), followed by Canadians, Americans, and Danes, of whom more than 65 percent favor individual freedom.

- Among the French, 41 percent opt for individual freedom.

- In many Asian countries, including Singapore, Japan, and India, only about 40 percent or less opt for individual freedom.

This dimension is sometimes difficult to handle because the terms used are quite politically loaded. Regardless of their real behavior, people associate certain terms with concepts that have been used for a long time. For instance, "Individualism" in the United Kingdom is likely to mean "placing the individual at the center of the society", a laudable concept for many. Alternatively, many people in Russia might feel attracted by the echo surrounding the term "Collectivism", even if their actions are not particularly taking into account the well-being of their community.

Also, individualism is often regarded as characteristic of a modernizing society, and group orientation, in contrast, as reminiscent of more traditional societies and the failed communist experiment. However, the success of the "Five Dragons," Japan, Hong Kong, Singapore, South Korea, and Taiwan, raises questions as to whether it is the only and thus inevitable way toward modernization and affluence.

Implications for business and Family resemblances

Individualism	*Vs.*	*Communitarianism*
Use of "I"	*Vs.*	*Use of "we"*
Pay for performance	*Vs.*	*Team rewards*
Selection based on skills	*Vs.*	*Fitting the team*
Decide by voting	*Vs.*	*Decide by consensus*
Individual mandate	*Vs.*	*Group mandate*
One representative	*Vs.*	*Delegation*

Finally, it is worth knowing that the GLOBE research[64] (see Chapter 2) is separating collectivism in two categories: institutional and in-group collectivism.

Institutional collectivism is defined as "the degree to which organizational and societal institutional practices encourage and reward collective distribution of resources and collective action" while in-group collectivism is "the degree to which individuals express pride, loyalty, and cohesiveness in their organizations or families". When comparing several cultures, the distinction sometimes appears useful as people may display collectivism towards their immediate group and display disregard and disloyalty towards the larger group (such as civic behavior).

---

64 Robert J. House et al., 2004, *Culture, Leadership, and Organizations: The GLOBE Study of 62 Societies*, Sage Publications

AFFECTIVE VS. NEUTRAL

In relationships between people, reason and emotion both play a role. Which of these dominates will depend upon whether we are affective, i.e. show our emotions, in which case we probably get an emotional response in return, or whether we are emotionally neutral in our approach.

In an affective culture, people do not object to a display of emotions. It is not considered necessary to hide moods and feelings and to keep them bottled up. Affective cultures may interpret the less explicit signals of a neutral culture as less important. They may be ignored or even go unnoticed. For example, Italian and French cultures display their emotions—expressed, some would say, particularly in flamboyant driving! But this cultural bias is also revealed in their beautiful car designs and haute couture.

In a neutral culture, people are taught that it is incorrect to show one's feelings overtly. This does not mean they do not have feelings; it just means that the degree to which feelings may show is limited. They accept and are aware of feelings but are in control of them. Neutral cultures may think the louder signals of an affective culture are too excited and over-emotional. In neutral cultures, showing too much emotion may erode your power to interest people. For example, it may be difficult to tell what business partners in Japan are thinking, as they are likely to exhibit little body language.

Is a good manager an overtly passionate person, or rather a person who controls his or her display of emotions? Two extreme types can be recognized. Passionate managers without reason are seen as neurotics. Overly controlled managers without emotions are seen as robots or control freaks. Both these types are unsuccessful in a multi-cultural environment. Effective managers check passion with reason; conversely, they give meaning to control by showing their passion at specific, well-chosen moments.

Overly affective (expressive) or neutral cultures have problems in relating with each other. The neutral person is easily accused of being ice-cold with no heart; the affective person is seen as out of control and inconsistent. When such cultures meet, the first essential for the international manager is to recognize the differences and to refrain from making any judgments based on emotions or the lack of them.

This aspect of culture is quite clearly seen in the amount of emotionality people can stand across cultures. Kodak introduced an ad selling "memories," which Americans love, but which was seen by the British as overly sentimental. It was Michael Porter who said that Germans didn't know what marketing was about. In his American conception, marketing is about showing the qualities of your products without any inhibition.

Germans might see this as bragging. It is not accepted unless you sell secondhand cars. The degrees to which you express positive things in Germany need to be much subtler, with a subtlety that might escape Porter.

Implications for business and Family resemblances		
Neutral	Vs.	Affective
Business-like	*Vs.*	*Engaged*
Not speaking up	*Vs.*	*Speaking up*
Monotonous	*Vs.*	*Raising your voice*
Let someone finish speaking	*Vs.*	*Interrupting*
Keep a (physical) distance	*Vs.*	*Touching each other*

How did we assess the difference in emotional expression across cultures?

Participants were asked what they do when they feel upset about something at work. Would they express their feelings openly?

What do you think of the following statement? (1=strongly agree, 5=strongly disagree). In cases where one feels upset at work, one is inclined to express it.

CULTURAL DIMENSIONS RELATING TO PEOPLE

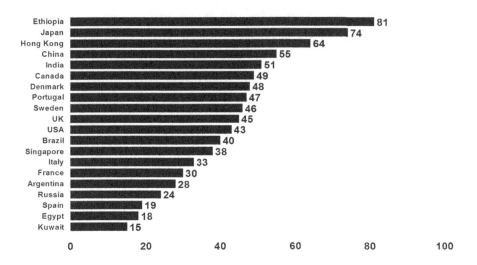

Fig. 4.3 - Would you show your emotions overtly?
Percentage of respondents who would not show their emotions overtly at work.

Some key findings:

- Culture differs clearly as to whether emotions can be expressed openly at work
- It is least acceptable in Japan (74 percent of respondents said they would not show emotions openly).
- It is somewhat more acceptable in India and Singapore.
- Within Europe, there are considerable differences.
- Sweden is the most controlled-oriented.
- Italy, Spain, and France are the least controlled-oriented.
- There does not seem to be a general pattern by continent.

SPECIFIC VS. DIFFUSE

This dimension concerns the degree of involvement in relationships. Closely related to whether we show emotions in dealing with other people is the degree to which we engage others in specific areas of life and single levels of personality, or diffusely in multiple areas of our lives and at several levels of personality at the same time. In specific-oriented cultures, a manager segregates out the task relationship she or he has with a subordinate and isolates this from other dealings. But in some countries every life space and every level of personality tends to permeate all others.

The specific personality can be represented as a peach. It is easy to access for a long time, but in the core you'll find a hard nut. The nut represents the privacy of the specific person, while the flesh is his or her public space. When specific types meet, we see that they quickly agree on the specific reasons for the relationship to exist. Human beings become human resources, and you are only Dr. Trompenaars in the university setting. Once you're met in the bar of a hotel, the same people might call you Mister or by your first name. Even the title is a specific label for a specific job at a specific time. Compare this with the more diffuse cultures, like the Germans or, in this case, the Austrians. You are called Herr Doctor in the university as well as at work. You buy a steak at the butcher shop, and they still call you Herr Doctor. Coming home, you greet your wife by "Hello, Frau Doctor, where are the little doctors?"

This more diffuse type could be compared to a coconut type of fruit. The initial encounter is taken with reservedness. You hit the hard outside. Why? Because there is some flesh of privacy that needs to be protected. But once you're in, you're in for life. They start calling you *Du* or *Tu* instead of *Sie* or *Vous*.

Implications for business and Family resemblances		
Specific	Vs.	Diffuse
Open & direct	*Vs.*	*Polite & implicit*
Analyzing	*Vs.*	*Connecting issues*
Easy contact	*Vs.*	*Personal involvement*
Letter of contract	*Vs.*	*Spirit of contract*
Hard selling	*Vs.*	*Client relationship*
Shareholders	*Vs.*	*Stakeholders*

CULTURAL DIMENSIONS RELATING TO PEOPLE

How did we test the differences across national cultures?

Our research shows pronounced differences on this dimension, as is illustrated by responses to the following situation (Question 38 of the cross-cultural questionnaire).

A boss asks a subordinate to help him paint his house. The subordinate, who does not feel like doing it, discusses the situation with a colleague.

a) *The colleague argues, "You don't have to paint if you don't feel like it. He is your boss at work. Outside he has little authority."*

b) *The subordinate argues, "Despite the fact that I don't feel like it, I will paint it. He is my boss and you can't ignore that outside work either."*

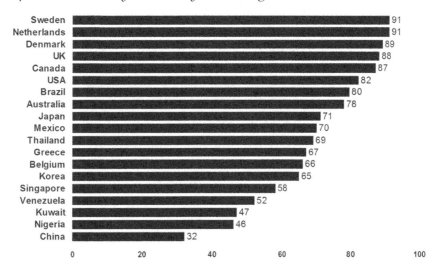

Fig. 4.4 - Painting the house of your boss
Percentage of respondents who would not paint the house of their boss if they did not feel like doing it.

In specific societies, with their sharp separation of work and private life, managers are not at all inclined to assist. As one Dutch respondent put it, "House painting is not in my collective labor agreement."

Some key findings:

- In the Netherlands and Sweden, and most of Northern Europe, more than 80 percent of employees would not paint the house.

- In China and Nigeria, the majority would paint the boss's house.

- More than 70 percent of Japanese employees would not help paint the house. Surprised by the Japanese score, we re-interviewed some Japanese respondents. They replied that in Japan, people hardly ever paint houses in the first place! Additional questions used in our research suggest that they tend toward the diffuse end of the dimension.

Implications of the different orientations for understanding cultural diversity

Another way to recognize specific versus diffuse cultures is the style in which they communicate. You see that specific cultures have a tendency to go straight to the core of the issue and are usually not hindered by any context. These low-context communicators are not known as most diplomatic but are very precise in what they say in whatever circumstance. Examples are the Australians and Dutch, who would call a spade a spade, while southern English and Japanese people have a tendency to say things in high context.

Context is about how much you need to know before you can communicate effectively and how much shared knowledge is taken for granted. In specific cultures there is a tendency toward low-context communication, meaning that people are straightforward in their communication regardless of in what context they are saying it. In diffuse cultures, there is a tendency toward high-context communication. Here, people have a tendency to say different things in different contexts, such as when the boss is there. Or they use one word where the meaning differs depending on the context in which it is said.

CRAIG'S DIALOGUE: A NUISANCE

BILL:	How did it go with Nigel?
MARY:	Much better than I expected. These English are hard to figure.
BILL:	What happened? Did you explain everything to him?
MARY:	Yes, completely. I said we were very sorry but we simply weren't going to be able to meet the deadline.
BILL:	And?
MARY:	He just said, "That's a bit of a nuisance" and changed the subject.
BILL:	That's great!

High-context people tend to "circle around" new business partners. It is important to get to know them diffusely. However, it takes time to establish trust. One is, therefore, advised to come down to the specifics of the business only later. Strangers must be filled in before business can be properly discussed. They are rich and subtle in their meanings and may carry a lot of "baggage." Foreigners may never really feel comfortable or fully integrated.

CRAIG'S DIALOGUE: THE DELIVERY DATE	
MR. CARPENTER:	I'd like to come back to the question of the delivery date again. We seem to have skipped over that one.
MR. SATO:	Yes. This issue is slightly complicated. It will take some thought.
MR. CARPENTER:	Not really. It's just a matter of choosing a date all of us here can agree on.
MR. SATO:	Yes, choosing a date.
MR. CARPENTER:	I think three months after the start of production is reasonable. What do you think?
MR. SATO:	Yes. Three months; very reasonable. Perhaps we can take a break now.
MR. CARPENTER:	A break? Right now? We only have this one item left and then we'll be finished. If we could just decide.
MR. SATO:	Yes, we need to decide. If we could just have a break.
MR. CARPENTER:	OK. But let's make it quick.

In **low-context** cultures, one can get straight to the point by quickly addressing the neutral, objective aspects of the business deal. If the other maintains interest, then it is time to learn more about him or her (circle outside) in order to facilitate the deal. One believes that relative strangers can quickly share in rule-making. Systematic steps to get strangers involved and up-to-date should be minimized. One tends to be adaptable and flexible. You don't waste time wining and dining a person who is not fully committed to the deal in the first place.

Consider Linux's creator, Linus Torvalds. Although an I.T. guru, he doesn't really even like to talk about technology. He'd rather *write*. "I think it's so much easier to be very precise in what you write and give code examples and stuff like that," he said in an interview for Wired.com . "I actually think it's very annoying to talk technology face-to-face. You can't write down the code."

Obviously the main problems are raised when the specific peach meets the diffuse coconut. Consider the following graph when having a critical discussion.

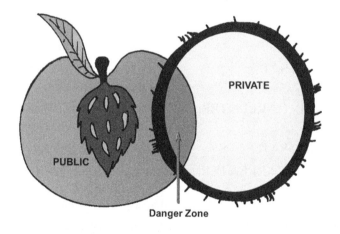

Fig. 4.5 – Specific Vs. Diffuse cultures as peaches and coconuts

We see that the arrow of criticism for the specific personality on the right is perceived as something that can be discussed in public, like in a meeting. The diffuse personality on the left feels that the criticism is something private and should not be discussed in the meeting. When I was working for the Royal Dutch Shell oil company, it was obvious that the high-context English had a tendency to discuss important things before or after the meeting. The Dutch often waited for the meeting to get things discussed. The misunderstandings were obvious. You can't trust the English—they always want to keep options open. Conversely, the Dutch were seen as pushy, wanting to force issues on the English. The graph is a very good symbolic expression of what is known as "loss of face." One loses face when private things are discussed publicly.

CRAIG'S DIALOGUE: THE FLU	
SARAH:	I was hoping we could have that meeting of the sales team tomorrow morning.
FELICE:	Actually, my daughter has some kind of flu and I was going to take her to the doctor tomorrow morning.
SARAH:	I see. Well, let me check with Bob and see if he can sit in for you. Shouldn't be any problem. I'll let you know.
FELICE:	Thank you.
SARAH:	Don't mention it.

ACHIEVED VS ASCRIBED

Achieved status is a reflection of what an individual does and has accomplished. In cultures that are achievement-oriented, individuals derive their status from what they have accomplished. An individual with achieved status has to prove what he or she is worth over and over again; status is accorded and maintained on the basis of his or her actions. The Dutch culture is a good example of one that encourages people to achieve results, while family background is less important. It is what the individual does that is significant.

Ascribed status is a reflection of what an individual is and how others relate to his or her position in the community, in society as a whole, or in an organization. In ascriptive cultures, people derive their status from birth, age, gender, or wealth. People with ascribed status do not have to achieve results to retain status; it is accorded to them on the basis of their being. In the Middle East and Far East, for example, who you are has to be taken very much into consideration.

> **Implications for business and Family resemblances**
>
> | Achievement | Vs. | Ascription |
> |---|---|---|
> | *More egalitarian structure* | *Vs.* | *More hierarchical structure* |
> | *Short-term contract* | *Vs.* | *Job on recommendation* |
> | *Budget based on last year's* | *Vs.* | *Budget based on past achievements* |
> | *Bonuses* | *Vs.* | *Fixed salary with regular rises* |
> | *Promotion based on bottom line Contribution* | *Vs.* | *Promotion based on reputation or seniority* |

How did we measure the status orientation in different cultures?

We collected responses to the following statements, using a 5-point scale (1=strongly agree, 5=strongly disagree).

The most important thing in life is to think and act in the ways that best suit the way you really are, even if you do not get things done.

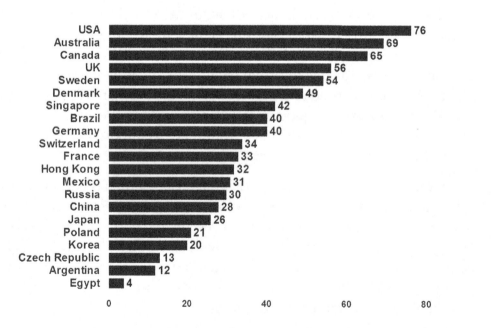

Fig. 4.6 - Doing vs Being—Quality of life is acting as suits you
Percentage of respondents who disagree that one should always act in the way that best suits the way one is

CULTURAL DIMENSIONS RELATING TO PEOPLE

- Countries in which only a minority disagrees with "getting things done" are, broadly speaking, being-oriented cultures

- In the US, Australia, and Canada, a majority opted for the doing approach—deciding in favor of getting things done at the expense of acting the way that best suits you

- The US is clearly a culture in which status is mainly based on doing: 76 percent of US Americans disagree that status depends on family background.

- Both figures indicate that achievement orientation and type of religion correlate.

CRAIG'S DIALOGUE: DR DE LEON	
MS. PORTER:	I heard the board has chosen a new CEO.
MR. DOMINGO:	Yes, they've appointed Dr. Manuel Cabeza de Leon of the de Leon family.
MS. PORTER:	Who is he?
MR. DOMINGO:	It's an old family with large landholdings in Guadalajara province.
MS. PORTER:	But what's his background?
MR. DOMINGO:	I just told you.
MS. PORTER:	I mean does he know anything about the textile industry.
MR. DOMINGO:	I don't know.
MS. PORTER:	Do you think he's a good choice?
MR. DOMINGO:	Dr. de Leon? I'm sure.

Hierarchy

Social environments can be categorized by the way they structure power relationship. Several dimensions presented here encounter the concept of hierarchy. For instance, Specific cultures and Ascribed cultures are likely to feature higher hierarchical structures. But hierarchy isn't only about those dimensions, other models might use different terms (Hofstede call it Power Distance, others simply High/Low Hierarchy) but all acknowledge its influence in management.

A hierarchy orientation is indicated by having a high degree of acceptability of

different power relationships and social stratification. An Equality orientation is indicated by showing little tolerance for differential power relationships and a minimization of social stratification.

Key questions are: How acceptable are hierarchical relationships? How does the value on equality or hierarchy guide behavior, business practices and processes?

CRAIG'S DIALOGUE: DINNER ON WEDNESDAY	
MR. SOGO:	Mr. Collins! Good to hear your voice again. What brings you to Osaka?
MR. COLLINS:	Good to hear you too, Sogo-san. I'm here on business with my new company. I'd like to invite you and Ozawa-san to dinner on Wednesday.
MR. SOGO:	Thank you very much. I'll tell Ozawa-san. Did you hear his good news?
MR. COLLINS:	No.
MR. SOGO:	He's been made president of the company.
MR. COLLINS:	That's wonderful. Please give him my congratulations. I look forward to seeing you both on Wednesday.
MR. SOGO:	I'm sure Ozawa-san will be very pleased to see you again. Where shall I tell him to meet you?

Conclusion

When doing international business it is important that you understand more deeply the underlying aspects of human relationships.

Are they dictated by rules or do you settle for exceptions? Do you start with yourself or rather the team you are part of? Do you control or express emotions and are you specifically or diffusely engaged? And finally is the status of your counterpart based on what he or she does or rather on where he/she is coming from?

And with understanding the importance of those aspects one can work on the most effective ways of dealing with them

RECAP

You are likely to find differences in the following areas:

- the status accorded to older people
- the relationship between men and women
- the role of a contract
- the degree to which your working relationship is or becomes more personal.
- The importance of showing passion in what you do
- The role of the surrounding team

CASE STUDY 4.1: INDIANS FIND IT DIFFICULT TO SAY NO TO THEIR SUPERIORS

"Saloni is a friend of mine who works in the Bangalore office of a big multinational company working in the I.T. sector. An incident happened in her office around mid-August. As their team performance was good, a senior manager asked if they were able to provide resources for more cases. Despite an already heavy workload, the team leader of the branch said "Yes" without hesitation. With extra efforts by each team member, the September release was made on time.

However, the significant increase of workload had affected the team severely. Most team members started their workday at 8:30 in the morning and ended at 02:00 at night! Whenever the onshore (i.e. foreigner) manager called the team leader, he would always be answered to his requests in a positive way. With extreme hard work, they managed to meet all the expectations. With all the positive signs given by the Team Leader of the Bangalore branch, the October release was made on time.

The team leader felt incapable of explaining the capacities and limits of the team to the senior manager abroad. Saying "no" to a superior is extremely difficult to do.

But something happened during the following month: productivity dropped all of a sudden. The team members began to feel too squeezed and were resentful towards the company and the project. A high turnover took place. Up to 50 people requested to be assigned to another project. By November, down to 20 members, the team comprised only 3 of the original members and the rest were new. The team leader was now reduced to a mere normal leader of an underperformed team. The new team never managed to performed as before."

Jeta Prakash & Lalzarzova
Bangalore, India
2010

CASE STUDY 4.1: INDIANS FIND IT DIFFICULT TO SAY NO TO THEIR SUPERIORS

Discussion Questions:

- What cultural dimensions are featured in this case?

- What parallels can you make between this case and the way your relationship with your professor?

- In your culture, how do you say "no" to the request of a senior manager that cannot be answered favorably?

- How are managers from hierarchical cultures perceived in equalitarian ones?

CASE STUDY 4.2: JAPANESE COMPANY'S 'ENERGY SAVING' STAFF HAIRCUT

A Japanese company has ordered all of its 2,700 employees to get identical hairstyles. This unusual request is its efforts to help the country save energy. The Tokyo-based construction firm Maeda Corporation has requested that men have a short back-and-sides and women have a "cute" bob with a longer fringe that can be swept to one side.

Company spokeswoman Chizuru Inoue explained: "Our company is very keen on protecting the environment and we encourage our staff to adopt many environment-friendly actions." She added: "We are not sure of the data yet, but we believe if people have short hair, they do not need to use their hair driers for so long and they will use less water." Some staff are confused about which style they must have and have been asking which salons give the best cut.

There is another advantage for employees of the construction firm, Ms Inoue added, as it is easier to make short hair neat again after staff have been wearing hard hats.

Some other Japanese companies are redefining the workweek in order to stagger energy consumption peaks and troughs. Environmental Leaders report that "Casio Computer Co. will redefine employee weekends as Sundays and Wednesdays in order to stagger its energy consumption peaks and troughs. Candy maker Morinaga & Co. has asked workers to start and end their day an hour earlier, so they work in cooler weather."

Many government institutions have taken measures to save power, including a reduced use of air-conditioning in offices and schools. Many employees cannot turn down the air-con below 27 degrees in the hottest summer months. Instead, the campaign encourages professionals to save electricity by wearing Hawaiian shirts, T-shirts and sandals to work instead of the usual stuffy three-piece suits.

CULTURAL DIMENSIONS RELATING TO PEOPLE

CASE STUDY 4.2: JAPANESE COMPANY'S 'ENERGY SAVING' STAFF HAIRCUT

The energy-saving initiatives are part of a national campaign to reduce energy consumption following the Fukushima nuclear disaster in March 2011. Japan has been struggling to produce enough electricity since the tsunami ended production at the Fukushima plants. The disaster resulted in a review of the country's energy policy that now means less than a quarter of its remaining nuclear plants are in use.

Masahiro Kobayashi
From various media sources
Japan
2011

Discussion Questions:

- What cultural dimension(s) is illustrated here?
- Would you be ready to change your hair style to save energy for your country?
- How would you react if your manager asks you to change your hair cut, or to wear a special uniform?
- Do you know other ways to save energy by changing individual behaviors?

Chapter 5: Cultural dimensions relating to time

CHAPTER CONTENTS

Highlights
Introduction

CULTURES WITH OR WITHOUT TIME
Cultures without time
Cultures run by time

TYPES OF TIME ACROSS CULTURES
Clock time
Development time
Calendrical time
National time
Religious time
Bureaucratic time
Social relationship time
Symbolic rebirths

SEQUENTIAL VS. SYNCHRONIC

PAST, PRESENT AND FUTURE ORIENTATION

SHORT TERM VS. LONG TERM ORIENTATION

Conclusion
Recap
Case study 5.1: Touareg time
Case study 5.2: A bag's time

CHAPTER 5

CULTURAL DIMENSIONS RELATING TO TIME
By Fons Trompenaars and Jérôme Dumetz

Highlights:

After reading this chapter, you should be able to:

- Recognize the different aspects of time that are affected by culture
- Effectively deal with those differences
- Practice your understanding of differences in time-orientation
- See how different cultures deal with different time-orientations

Introduction

Often, when we are immersed in our own culture, it is difficult to understand how those from other ethnicities perceive our culture, customs, and way of life. In addition, some aspects of our culture are so ingrained in our minds and so commonplace to us that we begin to feel they are universally accepted.

One of these cultural variables is a person's perception of time. Most people have their own idea of what time is and give little thought to the possibility that their definition could be different from anyone else's. For instance, it would not occur to someone living in most parts of the world today that the future couldn't possibly exist. However, the people of Piraha heritage living in the Amazon have no concept of time beyond the present, so the concept of future for them doesn't exist. They don't even have a word for "future" in their vocabulary. Similarly, most humans on earth find it nearly impossible to picture an extraterrestrial culture of some sort where the arrow of time—the direction of its flow from past to future—is reversed. Because we can't envision it, does that mean it cannot be?

Time also has a huge effect on interpersonal relations within a society. Would you want to be late for your wedding or an important job interview? Think of the problems that would result if you thought nothing of showing up to work two hours late each day. Or think of how aggravated your employees would be if you regularly held committee meetings hours longer than scheduled. Our understanding of and attitude toward time affects us and those around us. To fully understand the fascinating dynamics of the abstract, concrete, relative, and universal properties of time that govern the way we live, we must first examine the ways in which people around the world view and use their time within their lives each day.

Not everyone in the world views the concept of time in the same way. In fact, some cultures don't even make time a part of their lives. Some cultures are wary of time passing by, while others run their lives by the clock. Imagine for a moment what would happen if you took someone living in a hectic society controlled by time and let them switch lives with a second person living in a culture without time. How do you think the two individuals would react? Would the first person be able to function without a schedule? Would the second be able to function with one?

CULTURES WITH OR WITHOUT TIME

Cultures without time

The Pirahã Tribe. This small native tribe of the Amazon rainforest has an extremely limited language of humming and whistling.[65] They use no numbers, letters, or art, and—more importantly—they have no concept of time. Despite attempts by linguists visiting the tribe, to even consider introducing the concept of time to this tribe would be foolish, as their

---

65 Davies (2006). *Unlocking the Secret Sounds of Language: Life without Time or Numbers.*

concept of numbers is nonexistent. They have no specific religious beliefs—no reverence to ancestors or heroes of the past.

> There is no past tense...because everything exists for them in the present. When it can no longer be perceived, it ceases, to all intents, to exist. The linguistic limitations of this "carpe diem" culture explain why the Pirahã have no desire to remember where they come from and why they tell no stories. So, although it may be difficult for many people in time-dependent cultures to understand the ways of the Pirahã tribe, there is an important lesson in their relaxed lifestyle—encouraging people to live every moment for what it's worth.

The Hopi Tribe. The Hopi tribe is a small Native American group located in Arizona. Since the first research by Edward T. Hall[66] (see Chapter 2), the tribe is known for their interesting language due to its lack of verb tenses and resulting omission of any conception of time. The closest that the Hopi language comes to a sense of time are two words in the entire language: one meaning "sooner" and another meaning "later."[67] The Hopi tribes live, for the most part, in northeast Arizona. They make their homes atop flattened sections of hills called mesas, in villages called pueblos. The Hopi Indians are also well-known for being a very peaceful tribe.

Cultures run by time

The United States of America. It would be safe to say that, very often, the cultures that are run by time are those that appear to have the fastest pace. The United States—as one of the fastest paced societies of the world—fits this idea completely. (To learn more about the pace of life in different cultures, see our article on pace). Most people from the United States can honestly say that they often feel rushed. This may be partly due to the fact that many Americans strive for the "American Dream,"—the epitome of success, luxury, and happiness. The concept is often regarded as an illusion; yet by pressuring its citizens to constantly do more, earn more, and consume more—in order to achieve more—the ideals of American society drive people to constantly be in a hurried state of mind. Time decides

---

66 Hall (1994). *West of the Thirties*
67 Le Lionnais (1960). *The Orion Book of Time*

when Americans make their appointments, when they do their work, and even how they spend their leisure time. "For many Americans the 'free moments' that once glued a busy life together have almost disappeared."[68] In the United States, time is undoubtedly in control of the everyday lives of most people.

Japan. The Japanese live lives that are run by time, as do the Americans. Still, the Japanese tend to feel less rushed and frustrated with this fact than the Americans do; they seem to have achieved a greater handle on time management and extremely efficient lifestyles. The Japanese run on time because of their extremely low tolerance for tardiness and delay. If American deadlines and meeting times are said to be strict, then the same aspects in Japanese culture would be even stricter. A great example of this rigid view toward promptness can be seen in the Japanese train system.

> "In most European railway systems, a 'delay' is defined as 'ten to fifteen minutes behind schedule.' In other words, for example, 'fourteen minutes behind schedule' is still counted as 'on time.' This is how European railway companies are able to obtain high punctuality. On the other hand, the definition of 'delay' in Japan is more severe; only trains with less than a minute's delay are defined as 'on time.'"[69]

Examples of cultures with unique views on time

Nomadic tribes of Afghanistan and Iran. The peoples of nomadic tribes do not feel tied down by time in any other form than the seasons. In the spring, they migrate from the valleys to the mountains, where they will find richer and more abundant grasslands for their animals.[70] When the warm days of summer have passed, the nomads head back to the valleys from which they came in spring. Often this is a fairly long journey. This cycle continues throughout their entire lives.

Asian Buddhist Culture. Although the system of months that so many people live by today is a lunar concept, the strictly lunar aspect is sometimes given little thought. Buddhists have a stricter lunar calendar

---

68 Whybrow (2006). *American Mania: When More is Not Enough*
69 Mito, Yuko (2007). *Corporate Culture as a Strong Driving Force for Punctuality*
70 Goudsmit & Claiborne. Time. Life Science Library

because the moon has always been to them "...an object of wonder and veneration." Buddhist monks meet for prayer twice in one lunar month, at the beginning and end of the lunar cycle. The Buddhist calendar consists of twelve months. Throughout the year, the days in each month alternate from twenty-nine to thirty—making each month shorter, on average, than the months that many other modern societies are used to.

TYPES OF TIME ACROSS CULTURES

Prof. Cecil G. Helman was Associate Professor of Medical Anthropology at Brunel University in London. Probably one of the founders of this unusual specialty, Prof. Helman studied various fields involved in the cultural aspects of time and ageing[71].

His approach to time is interesting from a cross-cultural perspective because he proposed several "types" of time, that can be found in any culture. Each of these may have major effects on an individual's physiology and psychology, as well as on behavior.

Clock time

Clock time is the twenty-four-hour cycle that is regulated by clocks and other timepieces. Exposure begins at birth, with the timing of infant feeding and mealtimes, and then continues throughout life. Later, it is reinforced on a daily basis by environmental time cues such as the background sound of alarm clocks ringing, traffic rush hour, children leaving for school, or news bulletins every hour on the radio.

Developmental time

Developmental time is the linear model of human development that is imposed on the life path of children and adolescents. It is intrinsic to the concepts of developmental psychology and "age-appropriate" behavior and to definitions of maturity and immaturity. This model dictates the timing of children's developmental milestones, such as the ages at which they ought to walk, talk, or learn to read. It also determines when

---

71   Helman, 2005, *European Molecular Biology Organization, EMBO reports, Vol. 6*

children get immunized and when they start school. Later on, it defines when young people are considered developed enough to vote legally, drive cars, inherit money, or have sexual relations. It also defines at what age people are considered to be old. These linear concepts, in some cases, may take little account of individual variations in development.

Calendrical time

Calendrical time describes the division of the year, based on the natural world—usually the lunar or solar cycles—into days, weeks, and months, which includes its recurrent spring, summer, harvest, and winter festivals. Modern calendars usually include the year's division into work time and vacation time, and into festivals or special days such as New Year's Day or the summer equinox.

National time

National time is specific to an individual nation state and includes its annual public holidays and celebrations, such as Bastille Day in France, or special occasions like the Queen's birthday in the UK. With newly independent nation states, national time—and history—may be seen as beginning on their first day of independence. Significant periods in a nation's history are often coalesced into large blocks of time, such as "the second Elizabethan Age" or "the Third Republic."

Religious time

Religious time is linked to the weekly cycles of Sabbaths and workdays, as well as to annual feasts, fasts, and festivals such as Saints' Days, Christmas, Easter, Ramadan, Yom Kippur, or Diwali. It also includes the spiritual time of religious rituals, prayer, meditation, and contemplation, events that are experienced by their participants as being "timeless" or as "time out of time." Religions such as Christianity, Judaism, and Islam all have their own specific calendars that date from their birth.

Bureaucratic time

Bureaucratic time encompasses the time cycle of workplaces and educational institutions, such as the cycle of the academic year and the dates of vacations, as well as clocking-in times at work, the prescribed length of the working day, and the dates of annual reports, annual general meetings, tax returns, and office parties. At the individual level, it includes the age at which one can legally begin to work and the age at which one is expected to retire.

Social relationship time

Social relationship time is linked to the specific events of an individual's personal social network, such as the dates of birthdays, weddings, anniversaries, or memorial days—times when these social relationships must be reinforced by gifts and personal contact.

Symbolic rebirths

Symbolic rebirths can occur after major points of transition or crises in the life cycle, such as religious conversions—when one is "born again"— major illnesses or traumatic experiences; major social transitions, such as giving birth or getting divorced; or migration to another country. In each case, individuals may have the sense of a "second life" or a "second biography" within their lifespan, and time may therefore be experienced as time before and time after that major event.

Every culture has developed its own response to time. The time-orientation dimension has three aspects: a culture's approach to structuring time, time horizon, and the relative importance it gives to the past, present, and future.

SEQUENTIAL VS SYNCHRONIC

Time can be structured in two ways. In the sequentialist approach, also called monochronic time (see chapter 2) time moves forward, second by second, minute by minute, hour by hour, in a straight line. In the synchronistic approach, also called polychromic time, time moves round in cycles of minutes, hours, days, weeks, months, and years.

People structuring time sequentially tend to do one thing at a time. They view time as a narrow line of distinct, consecutive segments. Sequential people view time as tangible and divisible. They strongly prefer planning and keeping plans once they have been made, rather than extemporizing and adapting. Time commitments are taken seriously, and staying on schedule is a must. Sequential cultures include Canada, Australia, and Switzerland.

Conversely, people structuring time synchronically usually do several things at a time. To them, time is a wide ribbon, allowing many things to take place simultaneously. Time is intangible and flexible. Time commitments are desirable rather than absolute. Plans are easily changed. Synchronic people especially value the satisfactory completion of interactions with others. Promptness depends on the type of relationship. The whole philosophy of "just in time" management is derived from the highly synchronic Japanese.

CRAIG'S DIALOGUE: HELPING MISS THOMAS

ROBERTO:	Miss Thomas! How nice to see you.
MISS THOMAS:	How are you, Roberto?
ROBERTO:	Fine, fine. Thank you. What can I get for you?
MISS THOMAS:	Well, to start with I'd like half a dozen eggs.
ROBERTO:	Yes.
MISS THOMAS:	And then I'd like 500 grams of butter.
ROBERTO:	Yes. Ah, Octavio! Good to see you. Como estas?
OCTAVIO:	Bien, gracias. And you?
ROBERTO:	Bien. How can I help you?
OCTAVIO:	I need some bananas.
ROBERTO:	Of course. Rosita! Como estas? I haven't seen you in a long time. How is that little boy of yours?
ROSITA:	He's very well.
ROBERTO:	What can I do for you?
MISS THOMAS:	Roberto, I thought you were helping me.
ROBERTO:	But I am helping you, Miss Thomas.

The way that people in different societies interact with each other has important repercussions for business practice. To take an everyday example, consider buying food at a delicatessen. If you are in, for example, the United States, the United Kingdom, or the Netherlands, you might collect a numbered ticket that shows your place in the queue. You patiently wait your turn in the orderly, sequential queue. The sales assistant serves you with everything you need before the next customer, and this is an efficient system. But if you are in, say, Italy, and you ask the assistant for salami, he or she will serve you and then shout, "Who else wants salami?" Other customers will then be served accordingly, before the assistant again asks you what else you want. This is also an efficient system. The salami is unwrapped just once, and the knife does not have to be washed again. This process also promotes social interaction between the cluster of customers who have a common bond (in this case, a need for salami).

Now imagine that you are running the computer services for a global hotel chain. You commission a computerized database for the check-out system, which has been written by a US-based software house employing programmers with an Indian ethnic/cultural background. The desk clerk asks guests for their room number and retrieves their accounts from the database. This is a sequential system that works well in the United States, the United Kingdom, Germany, and other countries.

But this system is not customer-friendly in the synchronic cultures of South America, Spain, or Italy. Here, the desk clerk and one guest expect to examine the account for extras (telephone, mini bar, and so on) while the guest in front is paying and the guest behind is shouting his or her room number. Sequential culture is actually built into the internal architecture of database software that originates in sequential cultures. It is difficult to make such a database work in synchronic contexts.

> **Implications for business**
>
> | | | |
> |---|---|---|
> | Sequential | Vs. | Synchronic |
> | *Cut time in pieces* | *Vs.* | *Cyclical time* |
> | *One activity at a time* | *Vs.* | *Parallel activities* |
> | *Universalistic time* | *Vs.* | *Particularistic time* |
> | *Situations are subject to planning* | *Vs.* | *More paths to the goal* |
> | *I manage my time to get the best of my actions* | *Vs.* | *I manage my actions to get the best of my time* |

PAST, PRESENT AND FUTURE

Saint Augustine pointed out in his *Declarations* that time as a subjective phenomenon can vary considerably from time in abstract conception. In its abstract form we cannot know the future because it is not yet here, and the past is also unknowable. We may have memories, partial and selective, but the past has gone. The only thing that exists is the present, which is our sole access to past or future. Augustine wrote, "The present has, therefore, three dimensions…the present of past things, the present of present things, and the present of future things."

Past-oriented cultures. If a culture is predominantly oriented toward the past, the future is seen as a repetition of past experiences. Respect for ancestors and collective historical experiences are characteristic of a past-oriented culture.

Present-oriented cultures. A culture that is predominantly oriented toward the present will not attach much value to common past experiences nor to future prospects. Rather, day-by-day experiences tend to direct people's thinking and action.

Future-oriented cultures. In a future-oriented culture, most human activities are directed toward future prospects. Generally, the past is not

CULTURAL DIMENSIONS RELATING TO TIME

considered to be vitally significant to a future state of affairs. Detailed planning constitutes a major activity in future-oriented cultures.

CRAIG'S DIALOGUE: CLASS OF 2015	
KAREN:	How did you make out at registration?
CARMEN:	Quite well. I got into every course I wanted. But one thing confused me.
KAREN:	What was that?
CARMEN:	They said I was in the class of 2015. I don't understand what that means.
KAREN:	That's easy. You'll graduate in 2015, four years from now.
CARMEN:	But that's just what confused me.

Measuring cultural differences in relation to time

The methodology used to measure approaches to time in this book comes from Tom Cottle, who created the Circle Test[72]. The question asked was as follows: Think of the past, present and future as being in the shape of circles. Please draw three circles on the space available, representing past, present, and future. Arrange these circles in any way you want that best shows how you feel about the relationship of the past, present, and future. You may use different size circles. When you have finished, label each circle to show which one is the past, which one the present, and which one the future.

Cottle ended up with four possible configurations:

- First, he found absence of zone relatedness. Figure 5.1 shows that on our measurements this is a typically Russian approach to time; there is no connection between past, present, or future, though in their view

---

[72] Cottle T., 1967, «*The Circles Test; an investigation of perception of temporal relatedness and dominance* », Journal of Projective Technique and Personality Assessment, No. 31

the future is much more important than the present and more important than the past.

- The second Cottle configuration was temporal integration,
- The third a partial overlap of zones, and,
- The fourth, zones touching but not overlapping, hence not "sharing" regions of time between them.

Figure 5.1 shows that this last approach is characteristic of the Belgians, who see a very small overlap between present and past but the present and future as just touching. In this they are not dissimilar to the British, who have a rather stronger link with the past but see it as relatively unimportant, whereas the Belgians view all three aspects of time as equally important. Both are quite different from the French, for whom all three aspects overlap considerably; they share this view with the Malaysians. The Germans think the present and the future are very strongly interrelated. What the figure does not show is that half the Japanese see the three circles as concentric.

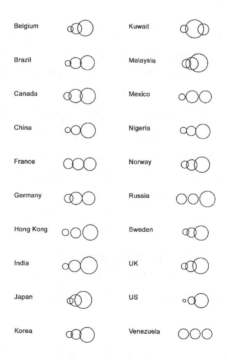

Fig. 5.1 – Past, present and future orientated cultures

CULTURAL DIMENSIONS RELATING TO TIME

SHORT TERM VS LONG TERM ORIENTATION

This aspect of time deals with an orientation to focusing on either short-term results or long-term results. The short-term view supports maximizing performance currently as the key to success, while the long-term view supports achieving optimal performance over an extended timeframe. Countries with cultures that have a short-term focus include those in North America, while those with a longer-term focus include most in Asia.

Consider the following question:

My past started …… ago and ended …… ago.

My present started …… ago and ended …… from now.

My future started …… from now and ended …… from now.

7= years

6= months

5= weeks

4= days

3= hours

2= minutes

1= seconds

We have taken the average of each of the six scores and calculated an average score per country, for which very significant differences can be found (see Figure 5.2). The longest horizon is found in Hong Kong and the shortest in the Philippines.

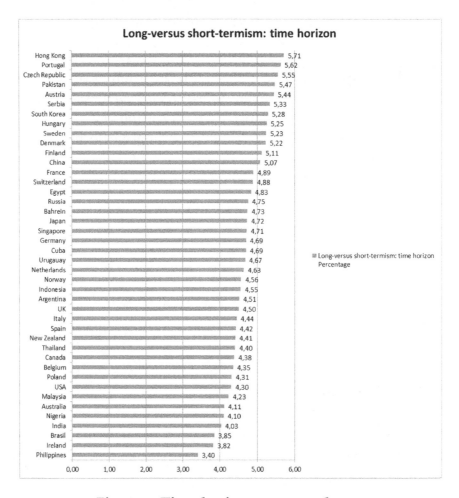

Fig. 5.2 – Time horizon across cultures

Our time horizon significantly affects how we do business. It is obvious that the relatively long-term vision of the Japanese contrasts with the "quarterly thinking" of the Americans. This was shown in a striking way when the Japanese were trying to buy the operations of Yosemite National Park in California. The first thing they submitted was a 250-year business plan. Imagine the reactions of the Californian authorities, "Gee, that is a thousand quarterly reports."

CRAIG'S DIALOGUE: HOME FROM OSAKA	
HIROSHI:	I understand Bob's coming back from Osaka.
CHRISTINE:	Yes, we're reassigning him to New York. It's too bad, too; he's been pulling out all the stops ever since he got there last year.
HIROSHI:	Is there something wrong? With his family or his health, maybe?
CHRISTINE:	No. Nothing's wrong. It just hasn't worked out over there.
HIROSHI:	I heard he had made some good contacts and even got a few feelers.
CHRISTINE:	There's been some interest, but he says the Japanese are just being polite. There's been no real business.

Conclusion

When doing international business it is important that you understand more deeply the underlying aspects of how time is experienced.

Are people dictated by rules as in sequential cultures or by exceptions like in synchronic ones? Do you plan in the short or long term perspective? And finally are your actions more focused on the past, present of future things?

And with understanding the importance of those aspects one can work on the most effective ways of dealing with them across cultures?

RECAP

You are likely to find differences in the following areas:

- Do we plan one thing or more things at one time?
- Are we rather focused on the end or on the process of getting there?
- Is history an important aspect to explain present situations, or rather, future plans?
- Do we plan in quarters or in years or even decades?

CASE STUDY 5.1: TOUAREG TIME

"My name is Fatiha, I was born in France from Moroccan parents. I have been used, from birth, to a bi-cultural life where my immediate environment and nationality interwove with the roots of my ancestries. This is why I decided to make some personal genealogical research on the other side of the Mediterranean Sea to find out more about who I am.

My family comes from the Moroccan Sahara. They were nomads from generation to generation. I come from the nomads known as 'Touareg", sometimes called the "Blue People" although their "cheche" (veil) can be also black or white. The social organization of the Touaregs is divided into tribes and villages spread throughout the entire Sahara, beyond the Southern Morocco.

Their life is one of perpetual travelers, with no settled home, moving from one area to another, using elders' wisdom to decide their way. They travel with their belongings and live among their animals and crops. My family has settled only recently, in 1984 for my father's family, and early 1990's for my mother's side.

I went on a quest to find out where I came from, digging information from the past about my parents, grandparents and maybe before them. Although I didn't expect the same level of detail as in my own birth certificate (where the date and time of the birth is noted), I wasn't prepared for what I found: there were simply no records of my great-grandparents and other ancestors. We are talking of people born about a century ago, not prehistoric times!

But the surprise continued when I heard from my grandfather that he has documents about him only because he needed some to go and work to France in 1961. This was actually the first trace of my family history. Most probably, people of his generation who stayed in Morocco have little evidence of their birth.

The surprises didn't stop here. When asked about his own birth and my father's, he was unable to give me precise birth dates (forget about time of the day…). I then realized their understanding of time was very different from mine.

I subsequently found out that birth dates are related to everyday events, not calendar time. For instance, I discovered that my mother was born during a cold period, but her birth certificate, written in Arabic, bears only one date: the year of birth! And a wrong one even! My father, meanwhile, was born during a drought period when the harvest was very bad, and information was carried verbally across generations.

CASE STUDY 5.1: TOUAREG TIME

Today, even if they had to adapt to this European calendar time relation, they still have an understanding of time linked to external events in their daily life."

Fatiha Badouh
2012

Discussion Questions:

- Fatiha's family comes from the Moroccan desert; what other cultures are likely to share the same understanding of time?
- What kind of time is in use in your region?
- How was the relationship to time in your region a few generations ago?

CASE STUDY 5.2: A BAG'S TIME

" San Francisco is a fantastic town, on the west coast of the USA. It is known for many features, such as its proximity to the Silicon Valley, it's tolerance towards minorities and illicit products (San Francisco is the birth place of the beat generation), but also its cable cars (tramways pulled by an underground cable) and its steep roads.

San Francisco is also famous for its bicycle messengers, also called couriers. Since the end of the Second World War, thousands of daredevils have rushed down the steep roads of the city. They carry their parcels in a messenger bag, designed with a single strap that wraps diagonally across the chest so it can be swung around the messenger's body to allow access without removing the bag.

While working in the city in the late 90's, I fancied cycling to go to work during the warm days. I equipped myself with basic, second-hand equipment (helmet!) and bought a bag from a company specializing in such product. The company, called Timbuk2, is based in San Francisco, and is proud to assemble those bags in the USA. They are made of Cordura water resistant nylon, a very tough material. Not too cheap, they are very good quality bags. Under the nametag, you can read "Made in USA - lifetime warranty".

I left the Bay Area and my bicycle behind but kept the bag. It has become my "bag-where-I-stuff-everything" for about 15 years. It accompanied me in the hot sands of Egypt, in the humid forests of Costa Rica or in the cold winters of Russia: a tough life for a tough bag!

The bag is nearly intact save for the plastic buckles that close the strap. They broke, one by one, giving up to the extreme temperatures and the use put to by the bag.

"Lifelong warranty" usually means a product is fixed or exchanged as long as it is still produced and it has been used normally. Some manufacturers of quality tools and hardware are famous for such policy and exchange broken tools often without questions. I was in the same situation so, around 2008, I decided to contact the company, back in San Francisco.

I did it for the fun of it. Glad to tell them how their product had become my companion for the last 10 years. I asked about the buckles, whether they could send me some new ones. I was ready to pay for the delivery of course.

I received an enthusiastic and vibrant answer from their sales department: "Thank you so much for your loyalty. Ten years using the bag, whoah! Isn't it time to change it and to buy a one? ".

CASE STUDY 5.2: A BAG'S TIME

Speechless, but amused, I decided to look for the buckles nearby and bought a pair of them, in Germany, for 50 cents each. Indeed, the concept of *Lifetime* warranty isn't shared equally around the world! »

Jerome Dumetz
2012

Discussion Questions:

- What does lifetime warranty means to you?
- What time dimension is involved in this story?
- How are you influenced by the past reputation of a company?
- Do you often return products under a warrant for exchange? How can you relate that to time?

Chapter 6: Cultural dimensions relating to the world

CHAPTER CONTENTS

Highlights
Introduction

THE VARIABLE OF CONTROL
    Some key findings

THE SPACE VARIABLE
    Physical space and distance
    Space in business
    The psychological dimension of space
    Charting new territories
    Mapping cultural space

THE VARIABLE OF UNCERTAINTY AVOIDANCE
    Uncertainty avoidance and global competitiveness
    Uncertainty avoidance at work

    Conclusion
    Recap
    Case study 6.1: Locus of control in a Korean-US leadership team
    Case study 6.2: Re-coding the hidden language of space

CHAPTER 6

CULTURAL DIMENSIONS RELATING TO THE WORLD
By Joerg Schmitz

Highlights:

After reading this chapter, you should be able to:

- Describe the role of the cultural dimensions of *locus of control*, *space*, and *uncertainty avoidance* in relating to the external world.
- Assess the impact of these classic dimensions of cultural variability on a variety of interactions, including business and management.
- Recognize their relevance for contemporary challenges related to sense making, technological development and competitiveness.

Introduction

How we perceive, create, and express our relationship to the external world is an aspect of cultural conditioning that reaches deeply into the individual and collective human psyche. In *Nature Loves to Hiden*, physicist Shimon Malin observes, "The human mind abhors a vacuum. When an explicit, coherent world-view is absent, it functions on the basis of a tacit one. A tacit world-view is not subject to a critical evaluation; it can easily harbor inconsistencies. And, indeed, our tacit set of beliefs about the nature of reality is made of contradictory bits and pieces."[73]

---

[73] Shimon Malin (2003). *Nature Loves to Hide: Quantum Physics and Reality, a Western Perspective.* New York: Oxford University Press.

While Malin writes this as an introduction to an ambitious work on physics, his words are a perfect beginning to a chapter on the cultural underpinnings of how we see ourselves in the world and structure our relationship to our external reality. Our individual and collective sense of self, of otherness, and of our purpose and ethical conduct are made up of inconsistent bits and pieces of explicit and tacit views of reality.

Three classic dimensions of cultural variability help us explore the deep connection between these large and small aspects of our daily worldview:

- control
- space
- uncertainty avoidance

They recognize that the invisible hand of culture regulates existential conditions that impact each of our lives: how empowered we feel and act within our environment (control), how we create and maintain boundaries and context for interactions (space), and how we manage and react to the invariable uncertainty and unpredictability of life (uncertainty avoidance). In this chapter, we will review each briefly and discuss their relevance to today's social, business, and management challenges.

WHO IS IN CHARGE HERE? THE VARIABLE OF CONTROL

Locus of control has been widely recognized in the academic literature across a number of fields as a key underpinning of human behavior. Its origin can be traced to social psychologist Julian Rotter, who recognized that individuals and groups operate with different beliefs and assumptions about their ability and responsibility to control the events that affect their lives[74]. A key variable is whether decisions and actions are based on their

---

74 Rotter, J.B. (1954). *Social Learning and Clinical Psychology*. NY: Prentice-Hall. Rotter, J.B. (1966). "Generalized Expectancies of Internal Versus External Control of Reinforcements." *Psychological Monographs* 80 (609). Rotter, J.B. (1975). "Some Problems and Misconceptions Related to the Construct of Internal Versus External Control of Reinforcement." *Journal of Consulting and Clinical Psychology*

own (internal) drive, judgment, vision and responsibility or whether, and to what degree, they take external factors into account.

Internal control is expressed by beliefs that individuals and groups are the masters of their own destiny by controlling the circumstances, context, and conditions of their actions; that is, control over the environment emanates from the inside out and is a function of will, intention, and determination. By contrast, external control is expressed by beliefs that see destiny as determined (or predetermined) by external forces, including chance, luck, or supernatural forces.

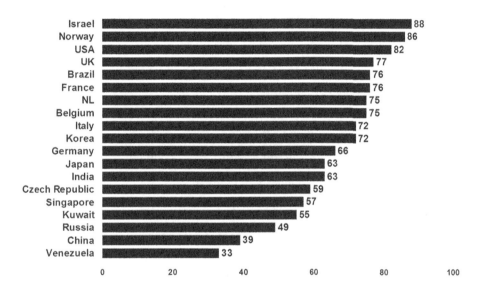

Fig. 6.1 Internal vs External control – Making your plans work
Percentage of respondents who think that they can make their plans work

This dimension captures a foundational attitude toward the world and our role, purpose, and limitations as we perceive and experience them. Its importance in cross-cultural interactions has been recognized by a number of social psychologists and anthropologists who have explored the cultural variation related to locus of control. Some models of cultural differences, including those of Trompenaars and Hampden-Turner and Walker, Walker, and Schmitz explicitly highlight this variable[75].

---

75 Trompenaars, Fons and Hampden-Turner, Charles (1998). *Riding the Waves of Culture*, McGraw-Hill, New York. Walker, D., Walker T, and Schmitz J. (2003) *Doing Business Internationally*. McGraw-Hill.

Some key findings

- Most Western countries score high on internal control
- In the US, 82 percent of managers believe they control their own destinies
- Of the Dutch, 75 percent believe they control their own destiny
- In Asia, the score is more diverse: 39 percent of Chinese respondents agree with Statement A, and 63 percent of Japanese respondents agree with Statement A

Implications for business		
Internal Control	Vs.	External control
Pushing a product	*Vs.*	*Client satisfaction surveys*
Planning and control	*Vs.*	*Options and scenarios*
Preventive maintenance	*Vs.*	*Trouble shooting*
Sticking to what you planned	*Vs.*	*Going with the flow*

In cultures that operate with an internal locus of control, the following types of messages and themes predominate: *Life is what you make of it. Don't let anything stand in your way. You are the master of your destiny. Your future is in your hands. Where there is a will, there is a way. God helps those who help themselves.* According to this perspective, external conditions, including other people, can and should be molded to fit human needs. There is a driving belief that goals and desired transformations can be accomplished only if the right tools, sufficient resources, and proper planning and focus are applied. The future we envision is within our reach, and even aggressive or remote objectives and goals can be achieved. From this perspective, there are few real obstacles in life, only challenges that can be overcome or opportunities that are waiting for solutions. Initiating change is positive and desirable, signaling progress.

In cultures that operate with an external locus of control, the following types of messages and themes predominate: *It's a matter of luck. It's fate. You take what life gives you. It's destiny. If God wishes it to be so.* From this perspective, it is presumptuous to claim control over the circumstances and conditions of one's life. Cultures that stress an external locus of control tend to be fatalistic and ready to accept limitations, events, and their consequences without attempting to interfere. They may emphasize time as cyclical and events as predetermined and accept limitations and barriers. From this perspective, initiating change and assuming that visions, goals, or objectives can be realized seems unrealistic, presumptuous, and improper.

Some cultures have cultivated a belief system that recognizes a balance between internal and external loci of control, also referred to as a harmony-orientation.[76] This is a perspective of creating a balanced relationship between external forces and internal will and determination. Predominant messages and themes are: *Go with the flow. We need to adjust.* In this view, people are an integral and responsible part of and deeply connected with their environment, the steward rather than the master of nature. The goal and purpose of human action is to establish and maintain harmonious relations among the various forces in the world.

The predominant orientation regarding locus of control of a given cultural group is often an adaptive response to history, including economic and material circumstances. For example, we can easily see how the history and colonial experience of the United States would reinforce an internal locus of control in the European American population and not in the African American or Native American populations. For peoples with a history of colonial subjugation, a balanced perspective of locus of control is an adaptive response ensuring a certain level of social stability. Persistent experiences of resource deprivation or limited opportunities, unpredictable conditions, such as hyperinflation or a great depression, make a balanced locus of control a functional part of a belief system, permitting groups to survive psychologically and emotionally.

Religious traditions, with their historical imprint on societies and civilizations, can be seen as reinforcing a specific locus theme. As Walker, Walker, and Schmitz write, "Through their interpretation of the world and human life, and through the specific practices they command, religions are perhaps the single most important source of these core orientations

---

[76] Walker, D., Walker T, and Schmitz J. (2003) *Doing Business Internationally*, McGraw-Hill. The Cultural Orientations Model recognizes the orientations of control as internal locus of control, constraint as external locus of control, and harmony as a state of equilibrium between the two.

in our formative social groups. It is a most powerful reinforcement and reward mechanism for the value systems and their behavioral expression that define a particular social group or cultural community."[77]

They recognize that this interpretation of religious belief systems echoes sociologist Max Weber, who "demonstrated a relationship between systems of religious and ethical belief and economic outcomes." They associate the Asian belief systems of Confucianism, Taoism, and Buddhism with a balanced harmonious theme regarding relations with the natural and social world. They attribute the themes of external locus of control to varying degrees with Islam, Hinduism, and Catholicism.

Locus of control can be found to tacitly influence business practices, specifically those related to risk management, planning, goal setting, marketing, and change. An internal locus of control is reflected in many US American management and leadership notions where risk management is routinely based upon forecasts and modeling, and on scenario planning aimed at predicting events and proactively determining strategies to overcome obstacles to reaching performance objectives. The objectives themselves are often a result of "stretch goals" that assume that higher performance of individuals, teams, and entire organizations is mostly a function of focus, commitment, and resources. The vision of an ideal employee is one who acts in an empowered way, showing initiative, taking charge, and achieving ambitious goals. There is a pervasive belief that ambitious visions of change can and should be realized if only the right tools and skills are applied. This belief is echoed in the separation of marketing (to create the market) and sales and talent management practices in which the employee participates in goal setting and development planning based on aligning his or her "inner drive" with organizational goals and priorities.

In cultures with a more external locus of control, risk forecasting is certainly part of the planning process, but it is understood that not all risks can or should be controlled and flexibility will be required. The idea that markets can be created may not seem realistic, and the emphasis will be on selling to meet existing needs in the marketplace rather than systematic and proactive demand generation. In such cultures, employees have little, if any, control in setting their own goals. The company

---

[77] Walker, D., Walker T, and Schmitz J. (2003) *Doing Business Internationally*, McGraw-Hill.

determines development and career trajectories. The ideal employee is one who reliably performs predetermined tasks and procedures. Figure 6.1 provides some generalization of national cultures regarding locus of control as operationalized by Trompenaars and Hampden-Turner.

CRAIG'S DIALOGUE: OUT OF ORDER	
NATASHA:	Excuse me, but the elevator is out of order.
SHARON:	Really? Whom should we talk to?
NATASHA:	Talk to?
SHARON:	To report it.
NATASHA:	I have no idea.
SHARON:	Oh, I'm sorry; I thought you lived here too.
NATASHA:	But I do.

TERRITORIALITY RULES! THE SPACE VARIABLE

Space is a complex and important dimension of culture. After all, space is not only a critical condition for human interaction, but the primal need to structure and control it is deeply anchored into our shared humanity and evolutionary past[78]. In *Communicating across Cultures*, Ting-Toomey aptly describes space (and time) as, "[…] boundary-regulation and identity-protection issues because we, as humans, are territorial animals. Our primary identities are tied closely with our claimed territories. When our territories (e.g. extending from our home down to our personal space) are 'invaded,' our identities perceive threats and experience emotional vulnerability. Protective territory or sacred space satisfies our needs for human security, trust, inclusion, connection, and stability."[79]

---

78 See: Ardrey, Robert (1966). *The Territorial Imperative. A Personal Inquiry into the Animal Origin of Property and Nations* or DeWaal, Frans (2009). *Our Inner Ape*.
79 Ting-Toomey, Stella (1999). *Communicating across Cultures*. Contributors: author. New York: Guilford Press.

However, how we perceive, mark, and behave in space is culturally conditioned. Every day, each of us shapes, observes, (re-)interprets and modifies the rules of space and territorial behavior. These rules, like other cultural rules, are mostly learned and applied unconsciously, but determine significantly how comfort and security/safety are experienced. Space is linked to place and territoriality in both physical and psychological/symbolic forms.

Physical space and distance

Anthropologist Edward Hall deserves credit for highlighting this key dimension and its hidden influence on communication and interaction processes. He focused his observations primarily on the meaning and patterns of physical space in human interactions. He was among a group of researchers who speculated that in interaction among humans, unlike in other animals, spatial boundaries for flight (triggering escape behavior) and fight (triggering attack behavior) were culturally mitigated.[80] In 1966, Hall introduced proxemics as the study of measurable distance between humans in interaction. He specifically discerned four fields of distance in human interaction:

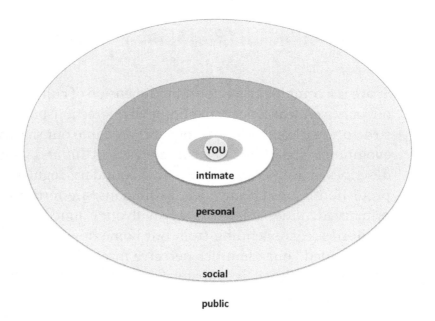

Fig. 6.2 - The foundation of proxemics: categories of distance.

---

[80] Hall, E.T. (1959 to 1985). *The Silent Language, The Hidden Dimension, Beyond Culture, The Dance of Life, The Other Dimension of Time*, New York: Doubleday. Hall, E.T. (1985). *Hidden Differences: Studies in International Communication*, Hamburg: Grunder and Jahr

- **Intimate-space** demarcating an area at which physical contact as well as heat and smell perceptions are most intense. It is a space used for interpersonal comfort, protection, and sexual intimacy. Hall measured this space spanning from skin contact to about forty-five centimeters (1.5 feet).

- **Personal-distance** demarcating a space that is used to indicate relative closeness and at which people are perceived to possess a "space bubble" that surrounds the person. Hall defined this space spans from approximately 45 centimeters to 1.2 meters (1.5 to 4 feet).

- **Social-distance** demarcating a space at which acquaintants and strangers recognize each other and at which formal or official and often group-related interactions take place. Hall defines this space at 1.2 to 3.6 meters (4 to 12 feet).

- **Public-distance** demarcating a space of interaction at which recognition of those present is not mandatory and subtle forms of expression and communication are lost, such as facial expression or voice-tone (4 to 25 feet).

The perceived boundaries of these spaces vary across cultures and with it the size and observance of personal space. The notion of personal space is particularly important. It is the zone that surrounds a person like a bubble, and transgressing its psychological boundaries often leads to discomfort, anger, or anxiety. Hall, for example, notes that the middle class North American norm for distance in normal conversation is approximately twenty inches; this distance is significantly less in Latin or Middle Eastern cultures and more in Nordic cultures. Such differences in proxemic patterns were established and validated for a variety of cultural groups.[81]

What makes these findings significant is their impact on the subjective experience, cognition, and interactive choices of individual. For example, in a conversation with a new colleague, a Swede may *feel* crowded and *perceive* a Moroccan colleague as pushy, invasive, and aggressive. The Moroccan, on the other hand may *feel* rejected and *perceive* the Swedish colleague as unapproachable, reserved, and exuding a sense of superiority. Since an individual's sense of personal space tends to be

---

[81] Little, K.B. (1968) "Cultural Variation in Social Schemata." *Journal of Personality and Social Psychology*, 10:1-7.

shared within a cultural group, the predictability of these experiences in cross-cultural interaction contributes significantly to the formation and seeming validation of stereotypes (and therefore their persistence).

Alongside these proxemic notions of space and boundaries are the perception, demarcation, and use of physical places, including the objects they contain, and respective threshold (or liminal) behavior. Examples of this are public spaces, as found in cities and towns, such as most streets, pedestrian areas, or squares or parks. Their public-ness enables people who are not personally acquainted with each other but are attributed use-rights based on some basic criteria of their identity or behavior to access and use this space according to explicit and implicit social norms and rules. For example, I may not pitch and live in a tent or hang pictures of my family on Lord Nelson's column on London's Trafalgar Square, even though as a visitor to London, I am perfectly entitled to walk across the square or linger on its steps.

In some cultures, the use of public places at particular times is associated with a sense of formality or informality. Either sense is communicated by attire, posture, and speech. This behavior is accompanied by a normative desire and expectation to present oneself in a manner assumed to be most socially desirable to a community at large. This concern influences the choice of the dressed-up Mexican family to stroll along the *zocalo* on a Sunday afternoon as much as a U.S. family in torn jeans and t-shirts barbecuing in a community park at the same time. We present ourselves in public places in a way that we perceive as most favorable and desirable. The relaxedness, down-to-earth-ness, or honesty associated with casual dress or the respect, sincerity, and propriety associated with formal dress trigger feelings of comfort and well-being for exactly the same reason.

The same is true for the structure and use of space in many homes. There are rooms or areas that are associated with intimate, personal, and social uses. We guard their boundaries carefully and are sensitive to their transgression. For example, many homes demarcate an area for social use, where impersonal and official interactions and affairs are conducted. This may be an area in front of the building, the threshold of the front door or entrance, a hallway, foyer or antechamber, or a formal dining or sitting room. The objects displayed and contained in these spaces are frequently guided by social desirability as well. We frequently display what is valued by the social context at large. We display objects of widely recognized significance, value, status, or prestige. Entering this space is frequently accompanied by specific ritualized behaviors to announce oneself, acknowledge or greet each other, and an often-ritualistic seeking or granting of permission to enter. Other notions of appropriate host and guest behavior are deeply connected with entering and interacting in such spaces, such as the presentation of gifts, admiration of objects displayed and serving of drinks and food, including the kind of drink and food.

This is similar for other areas, such as those intended for personal use of the owner, family, and close friends. These may include an informal family room, kitchen, patio, or backyard. The objects contained in these areas often have more personal significance, and the space is often marked by clear boundaries. Admitting persons into this space is frequently associated with a change from a more distant, formal, or functional to a closer, more familiar relationship. Similarly, there are areas associated with intimate use, including spaces for washing, grooming, or sleeping.

Since the exact boundaries and associated behaviors are culturally determined, the use and interpretation of physical spaces can create disorienting and embarrassing moments in cross-cultural interactions. For example, a German exchange student in the United States reported shock and disbelief when an invited acquaintance freely walked into her kitchen and opened the refrigerator to help himself to something to drink. In an instant, she recognized how much she regarded her kitchen as personal space and how almost intimate she felt about her refrigerator and its contents. She did not see acquaintances privileged or "close enough" to find this behavior appropriate. She reported a similar impropriety and awkwardness whenever she found herself standing in the bed- and bathrooms of U.S. American hosts during many, and quite common, U.S. hosting ritual: the house tour that included spaces she regarded as personal, private, even intimate.

Another example also relates to the use of bedrooms and highlights the complex intersection between space and social identity. A British couple being hosted by Indian friends on their visit to southern India recounted their profound confusion when the six men were seated around the dining table, while the six women took their plates with food into the bedroom and ate there while lying on two large beds. Being served by servants and eating with hands rather than cutlery had already caused disorientation enough, but the assignment of space by gender and specifically the use of the bedroom for eating made the entire experience utterly disconcerting and uncomfortable for the couple. Their dinner experience turned so many culturally based assumptions, including those of the appropriate use of space, upside down. Most importantly though, it heightened their awareness of the profound force of cultural conditioning that governs most of our assumptions, behaviors, habits, and expectations.

CRAIG'S DIALOGUE: NEIGHBORS

HELGA:	I'm glad you could come by.
TONY:	Thanks. Nice place you've got.
HELGA:	Let's sit here on the balcony. Can I get you something?
TONY:	I'll take some juice if you've got it. Say, who's that guy in the blue Volkswagen?
HELGA:	That's my neighbor.
TONY:	Really? I've got a car just like that. Volkswagen doesn't make them anymore; it's really hard to find parts. I wonder where he gets his serviced? Could you introduce me?
HELGA:	Sorry. I don't know his name.
TONY:	I thought you said he was your neighbor.
HELGA:	He is.

Space in business

In business, cultural conditioning regarding the use and meaning of space is no less profound. For example, in U.S. or British business culture, a semi-private cubicle is frequently associated with low status. And, while there is status difference based on the location and size of the cubicle, a private office, even if small, is much preferred and associated with higher status. A corner office with a window on a high floor, on the other hand, indicates high status. Offices or cubicles are rarely shared among employees. When they are, it is usually due to temporary space constraints. While greater levels and area of private space seem to be more desired and associated with status, one finds office doors rarely closed. Open doors project the value of reducing the open display of power and status differentials and for increasing the display of transparency and accessibility in business interactions.

In German office environments, doors are frequently closed to clearly demarcate the private nature of the workspace. While it is common at lower levels to share an office with a colleague, or even a team, the space remains closed off to others. This is correlated with the value of clearly demarcated and managed boundaries, as well as a separation by accountability and responsibility among individuals.

In Japan, work is frequently performed in an open space environment with the supervisor at every level seated at the head of his or her work unit or team. Seating arrangements will reflect the role and status of the individuals with the higher ranked, more senior individuals seated in closer proximity to the supervisor. This pattern is correlated with a strong team orientation and accessibility and sharing of information among the members of a given work unit.

The above are just a few examples of cultural variance, but they reflect significant differences. In the beginning of this section, we described space as both a condition and context for interactions. In business, space configurations and their meaning create important conditions and context for business interactions and processes. Spatial arrangements reflect basic assumptions about work, empowerment of individuals, information sharing and accessibility, and decision-making.

The U.S. spatial arrangement reinforces the individual as the basic unit of work and enshrines individual empowerment as the hallmark of status. At the same time, the value of ad hoc access to each other, even across rank, is an important factor in day-to-day information exchange, decision-making, and overall responsiveness.

The German spatial pattern also reinforces the individual or small group as the basic unit of work but emphasizes clearly defined boundaries. This goes hand-in-hand with formal and structured processes for information access, exchange, and decision-making based on clear recognition of rank and authority. Information, in this cultural configuration, is shared on a "need to know" basis.

The Japanese spatial pattern reinforces the group or functional team as the basic unit of work. Work units and teams share space with little spatial dividers. In this context, information is most frequently shared on a "good to know" basis and travels easily among team members and across units.

The psychological dimension of space

Just as Hall considered personal space a "bubble" around an individual, span of responsibility and control is a form of spatial demarcation or territory in business. This psychological extension of space is expressed in notions of decision-making authority over resources, strategies, priorities, and projects. Providing a general navigational framework of cultural differences, several approaches recognize a cultural continuum related to space and define opposing cultural orientations.

Trompenaars and Hampden-Turner refer to "specific" and "diffuse" cultures while the Cultural Orientations Approach™ refers to "public and private."[82] In the latter approach, cultures are indicated as public (or diffuse) when a value for open access and accessibility predominates, and ownership of space and boundaries are less important. This definition entails a low level of territoriality, or a cultural configuration in which the sharing of territory, shared ownership, and permeable boundaries are expected, reinforced, and rewarded. Physical proximity, a relationship orientation, and high-context communication are often correlated with this pattern. Also in a public (or diffuse) culture, information is shared freely and on a "good to know" basis. However, there is no direct correlation to power-distance. As the authors[1] point out, "On one hand, a public space orientation allows more personal and informal interaction between managers and employees. On the other hand, it also facilitates centralized authority, more authoritarian monitoring and control systems, and line-of-sight management."

Conversely, cultures are indicated as private when the value for clear demarcation of ownership and boundaries and their respectful treatment predominates. This definition entails a high level of territoriality, that is, a cultural configuration in which marking borders, boundaries, and ownership, and safe-guarding of boundaries are expected, reinforced, and rewarded. Private cultures may experience a high frequency of boundary-related friction and conflict. Security and protection from undesirable intrusion become key concerns in private-oriented cultures. Their members tend to value interpersonal distance (both physically and socially) and information sharing on a "need-to-know" basis. Discretion and following established processes and procedures for information sharing and decision-making are highly valued in interpersonal and organizational interactions.

---

82 Trompenaars, Fons and Charles Hampden-Turner *Riding the Waves of Culture*
Walker, D., Walker T, and Schmitz J. (2003) *Doing Business Internationally*, New York, NY: McGraw-Hill.

Charting new territories

The current globalized experience is a profound transformation of the human condition. Its enormity remains obscured by its mundane manifestations in everyday life. Interactive marketing agencies collect information on my most ordinary purchases at the grocery store, Internet browsers stream advertisements to me through monitoring the traffic and content of my emails, millions of strangers share seemingly personal and private information and experiences on blogs, YouTube, Twitter, Myspace, and Facebook walls. They publish personal information, events, likes, dislikes, pictures, and videos of experiences and life events for others to see, download and use.

However, it is well worth to behold consciously the significance of the information and communication revolution. In a relatively short span of time, the initial modification of the space-time relationship in human experience has led to a radical and profound transformation. While the inventions of radio, telephone, rail, automobiles, air travel, television, and various recording and storage technologies have changed the space-time experience, the advent of cyberspace and new media have profoundly reconfigured the physical-material and spatial aspects of human interaction. But even as the shared abstractness increasingly shapes our daily interactive experiences, we do so with the conceptual and linguistic foundation of our temporal-spatial experience as the basic template. After all, the new media exist and function in cyber*space*—a created virtuality with roots in our temporal-spatial condition. And, virtual territory is carefully marked and mapped over the real territory of political, social, and economic power.[83]

In the daily lives of "connected" individuals, cyberspace and new media reconfigure the basic private-public duality around which interactions are structured. We blur and redraw the boundaries between public and private in the way information is used and shared on Facebook, YouTube, and Twitter.

The changing attitudes and behaviors related to telephone calls are a good example of the shift of public-private boundaries. Readers of a certain age may remember their use of the phone booth or phone box—a small, enclosed space that allowed the user to conduct a *private* telephone conversation, or conduct a conversation with clear separation from third parties. Until the early 1990s, a phone conversation in public

---

[83] Bills, Scott (2001). "Cyberspace And The Territorial Imperative: Colonization, Identity, and the Evolution of Peace Cultures," *International Journal of Peace Studies*, Volume 6 (2). Dodge, Martin, and Kitchin (2001) *Mapping Cyberspace*, Routledge.

spaces and away from one's private home phone was spatially confined, creating a "privacy bubble" that kept the telephone conversation private. Mobile technology has transformed the telephone from a fixture to a portable device and moved phone conversation into a public domain in which third parties and bystanders become recipients of once-personal and private information. Technological advance and convenience have shifted cultural norms within a relatively short time span—attesting to the essential malleability of culture.

Mapping cultural space

Not only have the boundaries of communities, identities and culture shifted as a result of the globalization effect of cyberspace, but they have also led to a rethinking of the very discourse of the relationship between locality, culture, and community. The most common is the idea of national culture or, in its simplest form, the assumed and perceived relative cultural homogeneity within a specific geographic boundary, such as provinces and regions, but more frequently nationality. The national culture paradigm is pervasive in the study of culture, and much of the existing empirical work is grounded in it. And, while the root of the word, "natio," suggests the much smaller locality of one's birthplace, it is frequently equated with the boundaries of the modern nation state. Only about 10 percent of nation states, however, can be considered culturally homogeneous. And in 50 percent does a single ethnic majority predominate (up to 75 percent of the population)[84] These figures suggest that cultural heterogeneity is the norm among nation states when ethnic identity is applied as a definition of cultural difference.

Erich Wolf poignantly warned against this reductionist tendency: "By endowing nations, societies, or cultures with the qualities of internally homogeneous and externally distinctive and bounded objects, we create a model of the world as a global pool hall in which the entities spin off each other like so many hard and round billiard balls. Thus it becomes easy to sort the world into differently colored balls."[85] He is echoed by Francis Fukuyama: "It is a typical way to divide the world in regions, but it is not significant, because it does not take into consideration the different cultural

---

84 Barber, Benjamin. (1996). *Jihad vs. McWorld: How Capitalism and Tribalism are Reshaping the World*, New York, NY: Ballentine Books

85 Wolf, Eric (1982). *Europe and the People without History*, London: University of California Press.

attributes of those regions, especially from Asia and Europe. I think that, for example, family customs from Hong Kong or Taiwan have more common characteristics with Italy than with Japan. Also, the German cultural capacity to self-organize the society beyond family bindings, with no help from the government, makes them more like Americans than French people... Some countries—especially Japan, USA, and Germany—have a greater capacity to generate new forms of voluntary association, a so-called spontaneous sociability."[86]

Our current global and connected experience may indeed expose the tendency to spatially define and circumscribe cultural identity through national boundaries as oversimplified and inherently limited. And so, too, may be the ethnicity-focused definition of culture. Upon a comprehensive analysis of shifting community and identity boundaries in our transnational, global context, Kennedy and Roudometof comment, "Within anthropological discourse in particular, this revision has led to the open questioning of the connection between culture and locality. In the new revisions, anthropologists have raised a twofold argument. First, they have argued that the traditional anthropological notion of 'culture'—as essentially localized and moored to a particular place while existing as a self-contained, internally coherent, all-inclusive package with clearly defined borders—is misguided. Second, the idea of 'culture' as fixed through childhood socialization—to be later reinforced by unchanging and uncontested external social pressures—fails to take into account the social actor's reflexivity."[87]

These insights serve nothing more than to call into our consciousness the intricate connection between culture and space (or locality) that pervades our thinking about culture and diversity and informs entire research programs. The ideas of cultural space—defined by demarcated areas, regions, and spheres of influence—is an engrained paradigm that may well require refinement and redefinition.

The brief survey of the space variable cautions us to neither underestimate nor trivialize its role in human behavior, cognitions, and interactions. In its physical, psychological, and virtual manifestations,

---

86 Fukuyama, Francis (1995). *Trust: The Social Virtues and The Creation of Prosperity*, New York, NY: The Free Press.
87 Kennedy, Paul, and Roudomet, Victor (editors). (2002). *Communities across Borders: New Immigrants and Transnational Cultures*. London: Routledge.

space *is* context. It is perhaps the most critical element to give meaning and perceived coherence to our behaviors and cognitions. It guides and structures our expectations and interactions in profound ways on both micro- and macro-levels and in real and virtual ways.

ARE YOU SURE? THE VARIABLE OF UNCERTAINTY AVOIDANCE

Let's turn to the third existential condition culture helps us regulate, namely uncertainty. Uncertainty may be a fundamental property of reality. Heisenberg's uncertainty principle, at least, seems to say so. A helpful summary of its meaning for non-physicists reads, "The act of measuring one magnitude of a particle, be it its mass, its velocity, or its position, causes the other magnitudes to blur. This is not due to imprecise measurements. Technology is advanced enough to hypothetically yield correct measurements. The blurring of these magnitudes is a fundamental property of nature."[88]

CRAIG'S DIALOGUE: MORE STUDY

MR. JOHNSON:	What did you think of the new plan?
MR. TRUDEAU:	Seems OK, but I'm still studying it. I want to be sure.
MR. JOHNSON:	Still studying it after three weeks? It's not that complicated.
MR. TRUDEAU:	There are one or two aspects that might be a problem.
MR. JOHNSON:	Oh, I know that. But we should put it in place and work the bugs out later.
MR. TRUDEAU:	Seriously?

Uncertainty avoidance, recognized as a fundamental cultural variable, relates to different levels of tolerance for and acceptance of this fundamental uncertainty. Hofstede defines this dimension of culture as "the degree

---

88 Knierim, Thomas (2005-2011) TheBigView.com at http://www.thebigview.com/spacetime/uncertainty.html

to which members of society feel uncomfortable with uncertainty and ambiguity."[89] The degree of uncertainty avoidance indicates the degree to which a group is conditioned to feel either uncomfortable or comfortable with ambiguous and unstructured situations and in approaching the novel and unknown. High levels of uncertainty avoidance are expressed and reinforced by beliefs and practices that increase predictability of outcomes and therefore provide a sense of safety. These may include tightly articulated agendas, processes, and procedures, strict and detailed rules and laws controlled by recognized authorities, and unambiguous belief in the absolute truth-value of existing knowledge at the philosophical, scientific, or religious level. They will also strive towards the "correct" answer, solution, or decision.

Members of cultures with relatively high levels of uncertainty avoidance, such as Greece, Portugal, Guatemala, Uruguay, and Belgium, may experience a profound sense of anxiety or "diffuse state of being uneasy or worried about what may happen," according to Hofstede. This anxiety is particularly related to an unpredictable future and is correlated with impulse expression, particularly in reaction to anything that is perceived as threatening the certainty of the established "order."

On the other hand, cultures with a low level of uncertainty avoidance, such as Singapore, Jamaica, Denmark, Sweden, and Hong Kong, tend to be relatively more open to uncertainty and ambiguity. They value flexibility and agility in response to changing circumstances, embrace change and ambiguity as sources of innovation, and experience lower levels of anxiety about the future. They also tend to prefer fewer rules and formalities and have a pragmatic outlook on actions and decisions. Figure 3 provides a relative ranking of national cultures generated on the basis of Hofstede's Uncertainty Avoidance Index (UAI).

---

89   Hofstede, G. (1983). "Dimensions of National Cultures in Fifty Countries and Three Regions." In J. B. Deregowski , S. Dziurawiec, & R. C. Annis (Eds.), Expiscations in Cross-cultural Psychology. Lisse, Netherlands: Swets and Zeitlinger.

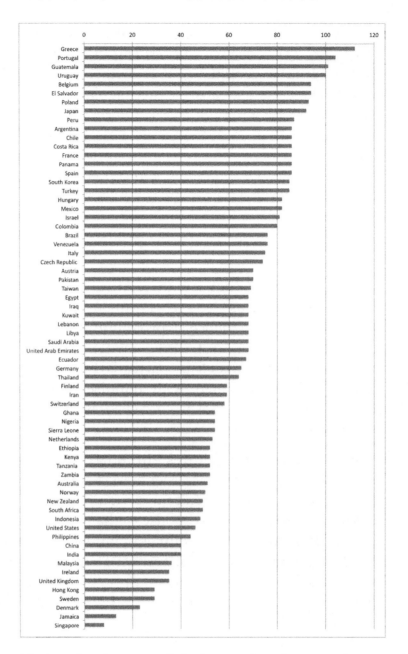

Fig. 6.3 - National cultures and their associated uncertainty avoidance index (UAI), based on Hofstede [90]

Note: The higher the number, the higher the uncertainty avoidance. According to these data, Denmark, Singapore and Jamaica have the lowest levels of uncertainty avoidance index, whereas, Greece, Portugal and Guatemala have the highest.

---

90 Hofstede, G. (1983). *Dimensions of National Cultures in Fifty Countries and Three Regions.* In J. B. Deregowski

If uncertainty avoidance is understood as the extent to which the members of a culture feel threatened by uncertain or unknown situations and try to avoid such situations, it plays an important role in the relative competitiveness of a society in an environment of increasing economic, social, and political interconnectedness that is the essential hallmarks of globalization. The dynamic complexity that characterizes the global environment introduces new levels of ambiguity and uncertainty. The financial crisis of 2008 and its worldwide impact is a very recent example. Others are the SARS crisis, the feared swine flu pandemic, and concerns over food safety that spread through the globally interconnected and increasingly integrated system, as much as revolutionary potential spread through the globally connected youth of the "Arab spring" uprisings.

Uncertainty avoidance and global competitiveness

Dynamic complexity[91] is characterized by:

- Information ambiguity (i.e. we do cannot clearly and easily make sense out of things)

- Long time lags between cause and effects (i.e. we are unsure about how to best impact the system)

- Multiple interacting and nonlinear feedback loops (i.e. we lose the ability to reliably predict future outcomes).

Most individuals, organizations, and societies lack the capacity to deal effectively with dynamic complexity, but the degree of uncertainty avoidance will influence competitive strategies and response patterns. Global competitiveness can be broadly defined as the capability to efficiently seize the opportunities of the dynamically complex international marketplace and to gain and sustain economic advantages from this.

This understanding of global competitiveness is more easily measured and assessed at the level of company/organization than the level of country/nation. However, leading analyses suggest a correlation between

---

91   Senge, Peter (1990) *The Fifth Discipline: The Art and Practice of The Learning Organization*. New York. Doubleday. For a discussion of how dynamic complexity can be applied to the phenomenon of globalization, see Nicholas C Georgantzas, Evangelos Katsamakas, and Dominik Solowiej, "Exploring dynamics of Giddens' globalization" in Systems Research and Behavioral Science, Vol. 7, Issue 6, 2010, or Dominik Solowiej and Nicholas C. Georgantzas, *"Toward a Validation of Anthony Giddens' Globalization,"* The Global Studies Journal, Volume 2, Issue 1

key cultural variables and global competitiveness, notably the dimensions of power-distance, individualism, and uncertainty avoidance. In general, countries with a small power distance, predominant individualism, while low levels of uncertainty avoidance show a significantly higher level of competitiveness over countries with comparatively high levels of power distance, collectivism, and uncertainty avoidance.[92]

In business, management, and organizational contexts, the level of uncertainty avoidance has equally important ramifications. High uncertainty-avoidant organizations are more likely to focus on operational excellence and incremental process improvement leading to reliable, consistent, and replicable results. Employees will value stable employment and low job mobility. Roles and responsibilities will be clearly and unambiguously defined. Fear of failure, avoidance and mitigating of perceived risks, and conforming to relatively narrow cultural norms are pervasive motivators of behavior and highly valued attributes. Loyalty, seniority, and "fitting in" will be the main criteria for promotion. Surprises will be avoided or kept to a minimum through the practice of informal meetings before the formal meetings. Precise guidelines and instructions will be expected, as much as detailed agendas and plans.

Low uncertainty-avoidant organizations are more likely to lead through innovation or embrace radical transformation priorities in response to changing conditions. They are more tolerant of novel situations and open to a diversity of people, thoughts, and ideas. Deviation from established procedure tends to be tolerated—in fact, it is often expected and valued. Conflict and calculated risk taking are considered desirable. Such organizations will be comfortable learning from mistakes, tolerant of conflict and dissent. Improvisation and a broad and adaptable outlining of goals, roles, and responsibilities will be the norm.

Uncertainty avoidance at work

The following are verbatim comments made during separate conversations with the author. They were recorded as part of a consulting project for a large global IT organization in 2005. Names and minor details have been changed to protect the privacy of the individuals and company. Bert L. is from the US and has been with the company for thirteen years, working at

---

[92] Herciu Mihaela, Ogrean Claudia, and Belascu Lucian, (2011). *"Culture and National Competitiveness"* in African Journal of Business Management, Vol.5 (8).

their global headquarters. He is responsible for the timely implementation of an "on demand" IT solution that is a global project. Frederika S. is part of Bert's project team. She is from Germany and a ten-year employee with the German subsidiary. On this project she reports to Bert, but otherwise has a straight-line reporting relationship to her manager in Germany. Both worked as colleagues on the same global project team in charge of launching a global IT solution for a multinational technology corporation headquartered in the United States. The perspectives about each other reflect typical experiences related to differences in uncertainty avoidance. Both were relatively inexperienced working in a global team.

> **Frederika S:** *You know, this is so typical! I cannot believe Bert's attitude. We have this tight release deadline, and you know how nervous I have been getting because not all components are thoroughly tested and some features are not even in place or developed. With only one more week to go, and so much to do, I am not sure how we will get things done. Even if all of us worked through the nights, it is simply impossible to get a high-quality solution released. We need more resources and time to do this job right, but he does not seem to be concerned at all. He wants to release whatever we have. He told me: "In the context of the on-demand strategy, the 80:20 rule is good enough. We need to get things out fast. When we are 80 percent there, it's good enough. We can always fix and upgrade later." I simply do not understand this attitude. It seems so foolish. Why should I compromise my professional standards and integrity and that of our company just to be quick? I simply do not understand Bert. What is so great about meeting an unrealistic deadline and creating an unsatisfied client? I tried to talk to him about this many times, but he just gets upset and repeats the 80:20 story."*
>
> **Bert L:** *You know, they just don't get it! I don't understand why it is so hard for them to understand. We are in the on-demand era and that just means change for all of us. But this teammate of mine is determined to resist change. She constantly points out that we should not release this product on time because not everything is in place and properly tested. You know, how can we compete in the on-demand world if we do not apply the 80:20 rule. We need to get things out fast. Eighty percent is good enough. We can always fix and upgrade later. We are 80 percent there with this product, so we need to release it—that's quick and on-demand. Frederika talks about professional standards and integrity, but it is really a matter of survival in a very competitive market. Speed and responsiveness are key. She doesn't get that. This is why we need the right people to win; we cannot afford to hesitate or linger. We need to be aggressive and get things out if we want to dominate the on-demand era. Frankly, I think that she does not want to understand this. She is not a team player!*

Conclusion:

The dimensions of control, space, and uncertainty avoidance make up an important part of the tacit worldview, which, as Malin reminded us in the very beginning, is frequently inconsistent and not usually subject to critical evaluation. Bringing them into our consciousness and exploring their role in individual, organizational, and societal behavior gives us more than a level of cultural self- and other-awareness. It grounds a critical evaluation of how we perceive the nature of our relation with the external world and pursue our agency within it.

Globalization (whether understood as a dynamically complex system or a technology-enabled new frontier of human interconnectedness) both privileges and challenges us to discover the invisible hand of culture that conditions our cognition and behavior. Key dimensions of cultural differences, such as those discussed in this chapter, help us call into consciousness the fundamental relativity of this conditioning and afford us a glimpse of alternative ways of being in and relating to the world. These discoveries can serve to formulate new and adaptive responses to contemporary challenges for individuals, organizations, and entire societies alike.

CULTURAL DIMENSIONS RELATING TO THE WORLD

···
RECAP:

In this chapter, we reviewed and discussed three classic dimensions of cultural variability—control, space, and uncertainty avoidance. They are part of an invisible hand of culture that shapes how we perceive, create, and express our relationship to the external world.

- **Locus of control** is a cultural variable that recognizes different beliefs and assumptions about the ability and responsibility to control events that affect one's life. Internal control is expressed by beliefs that individuals and groups are the masters of their own destiny by controlling the circumstances, context, and conditions of their actions. External control is expressed by beliefs that see destiny as determined (or predetermined) by external forces, including chance, luck, or supernatural forces. Assumptions about control can be found in business practices as much as in religious belief systems.
- **Space** is a variable that significantly regulates and structures human interaction at micro- and macro-levels. The structure of space establishes culturally regulated senses of boundaries, associated with corresponding rules for use, display, and disclosure of information, and presentation of self. In its physical, psychological, and virtual manifestations, space *is* context. It is perhaps the most critical element to give meaning and perceived coherence to our behaviors and cognitions.
- **Uncertainty avoidance** is a variable that relates to different levels of tolerance for, and acceptance of, uncertainty and ambiguity. National cultures have been found to differ significantly in their tolerance for uncertainty and ambiguity. This has been demonstrated to impact competitiveness, particularly in a global context in which uncertainty is an escalating byproduct of increasing complexity.

···

CASE STUDY 6.1: LOCUS OF CONTROL IN A KOREAN-US LEADERSHIP TEAM

In the mid-1990s, I was asked to facilitate an executive teambuilding session with a team of twenty-six leaders in a Korean electronics company in their US headquarters in New Jersey. The participants were evenly divided between managers from the US and expatriate managers from Korea. In general, the Korean expatriates occupied the higher-level positions, with the US managers reporting to them. The reluctance to admit non-Koreans into key leadership roles was only one of the reasons the human resources department sought to discuss, explore, and bridge cultural differences and build effective and cohesive teams.

As always, when asked to provide impact and improvement in a short period of time, it is important to demonstrate the reality of fundamental cultural differences to the participants and leverage the awareness generated by engaging participants in a process of constructive reconciliation. I chose to engage the participant groups in a survival simulation. The participants were assigned to one of five teams. Each team was provided with the same instructions: each group was stranded in the desert with their mini-bus on a road that was rarely traveled and without hope to reach a gas station. Besides a map and description of the geographic environment, each group was given a set of materials, food and drink items, tools and equipment (*no mobile phones!*) in their possession. The groups were then instructed to decide and agree on a suitable survival strategy within a given period of time.

The participants were divided into five teams: two mono-cultural teams, one with five Korean participants and one with five US participants; two teams with only one member from a different cultural background each (i.e., one team of four Koreans and one US manager, and one team of four US Americans and one Korean manager); one team of six participants evenly split between the Korean and US managers.

The difference in survival strategies between the two mono-cultural groups illustrates significantly different assumptions about locus of control. The all-US team generated a very detailed and differentiated plan to enhance their chance of survival:

- Rationing of available food and water sources that accounted for the likely spoilage of the various items

- A schedule for rest and wake periods for each team member to guarantee twenty-four-hour monitoring of any movements and opportunities for attracting help

- A division of roles and responsibilities among the team members, including a rotation among various geographic lookout positions

CASE STUDY 6.1: LOCUS OF CONTROL IN A KOREAN-US LEADERSHIP TEAM

- Detailed action paths accounting for a variety of possible contingencies

- A plan for converting the various components of the mini-bus into new and improvised tools and implements that would aid in the survival. Among these:

  - A mechanism to reflect sunlight and send emergency messages to airplanes

  - Plans to convert the radio of the mini-bus into a communication device

  - A sequence for burning all flammable materials to send clearly visible emergency signals that could be recognized from the largest possible distance

  - A communication and signaling system that allows the team members to split up, scout the area, and send messages to coordinate activities

  - Hunting and digging devices that allow the team to look for additional food sources and construct a safer, warmer, and more conducive base

In the same period of time, the all-Korean team developed a very different strategy. The group assessed their overall chances of survival and determined that unless a vehicle was to pass by within a carefully calculated period of time, there would be no chance of survival; i.e., the "point of no survival." They calculated the point in time at which survival was extremely unlikely. They agreed to a plan to monitor their surroundings and signal potential vehicles up to that point of time.

Most of the time, the team discussed and planned the events after the "point of no survival." They agreed to reserve a specific quantity of food items for that event and planned a ritual to share their anticipated communal demise. The team presented specific ways and roles in which they would share their last moments and support each other through the final moments of their lives.

Discussion questions

- How are different attitudes and perspectives toward locus of control reflected in the two survival solutions?

- What kind of team processes, dynamics, and outcomes would you expect of the other three teams?

CASE STUDY 6.2: RE-CODING THE HIDDEN LANGUAGE OF SPACE

The organization's global headquarters (GHQ) with its small team of twenty-five executives was located in the Jinbōchō area of Tokyo. The head office of its Japan subsidiary (JHQ) was located a good twenty-minute subway ride away in the Aoyama district. The global executives at GHQ were all Japanese, while the 125 employees of the Japan subsidiary also contained a small group of *gaikokujin*, or non-Japanese, concentrated in a separate business unit.

From the perspective of the global executives, the physical distance between these two headquarters was less than ideal. In the face-to-face business culture, managerial oversight and communication was difficult, particularly in this period of time where a number of innovation- and efficiency-oriented change projects were underway. A small group of employees in the JHQ frequently traveled to the GHQ for meetings to plan and coordinate a variety of change projects and align processes.

The decision to move GHQ into the JHQ building was motivated to enable closer managerial oversight and allow for more efficient communication and coordination. However, it was not an easy decision, since the only space available in the building was located one floor below JHQ. In this high-power distance and high-context culture, for GHQ executives to be located below the country organization would certainly send an awkward message. The decision was taken nevertheless and set in motion a number of interesting and unforeseen dynamics.

During the first three months, the JHQ staff collectively struggled to adjust their linguist references and frame of reference to this counter-cultural setup. With considerable amusement, the "higher ups" became "those down below." "Running things upstairs" became "passing things downstairs" or "checking with downstairs." And, someone being "called downstairs" would set in motion some stress and anxiety.

The move did not change the visibility of GHQ executives at JHQ, however. In the traditional office set up where "higher ups" also occupy the offices on higher floors, they would frequently be seen in the offices below for informal chats. Sometimes, executives would pass through the lower offices on their way to their office in the morning, for lunch, or upon leaving the office in the evening. In this case, however, a sense of avoidance of the JHQ floor by the global executives became very noticeable.

CASE STUDY 6.2: RE-CODING THE HIDDEN LANGUAGE OF SPACE

While the move certainly shortened the commute by JHQ staff, saving both time and money, it also had a rather unforeseen effect: the offices used a different security and access system. While JHQ used a biometric entry system that required placing a hand on a reader, GHQ used a card access system. This created a visible split among the JHQ staff population in two groups: those with their own access card and therefore "easy access," and those without. Those without access could be seen waiting in front of the GHQ door to be admitted for meetings or predetermined appointments. Those with access could freely come and go and also admit their JHQ colleagues to GHQ space.

Those with access could be seen wearing their access cards around their necks, visibly displaying their privilege. This would not have been meaningful if this privilege were bestowed by formal rank of the JHQ staff. However, the formal rank had little to do with the assignment of access privilege. Those deemed as more critical and important to GHQ projects received these access privileges—and this list did not follow the formal hierarchies of JHQ. This led to the situation where sometimes significantly lower ranked individuals flaunted their GHQ access card, and therefore their connectedness to the center of power, in front of their JHQ supervisors and managers without such connectedness.

Discussion questions

- What would you anticipate the impact of this situation to be on the work environment and work relationships?
- What (if any) might be the impact on the foreign (non-Japanese) staff?

Chapter 7: Trust as a cultural dimension

CHAPTER CONTENTS

Highlights
Introduction

WHAT IS TRUST? HOW CAN WE LINK CULTURE WITH TRUST?
    Trust issues affect everyone
    Getting a handle on trust

A CRISIS OF TRUST AROUND THE WORLD
    Trust in the world

THE ECONOMICS OF TRUST
    The trust tax
    The trust dividend

THE HIDDEN VARIABLE
    Trust myths

    Conclusion
    Recap
    Case study 7.1: Trust in the supermarket
    Case study 7.2: International finance and trust

CHAPTER 7

TRUST AS A CULTURAL DIMENSION
By Stephen M.R. Covey

Highlights:

After reading this chapter, you should be able to:

- Realize how trust is key in management
- Explain why trust can be understood as a cultural dimension
- Recognize the costs and benefits of trust
- Correlate the current financial crisis with the change of trust around the world

Introduction

While not a cultural dimension per se, trust is more and more associated with cross-cultural management by practitioners.

As we will see, the perception of trust varies greatly from one culture to another. Also, its mechanism follows very similar patterns to the previously presented cultural dimensions.

WHAT IS TRUST? HOW CAN WE LINK CULTURE WITH TRUST?

Here is a story: I'll never forget an experience I had several years ago when I worked for a short stint with a major investment banking firm in New York City. We had just come out of a very exhausting meeting, during which it had become evident that there were serious internal trust issues. These issues were slowing things down and negatively affecting execution. The senior leader said to me privately, "These meetings are dysfunctional and a waste of time. I just don't trust Mike. I don't trust Ellen. In fact, I find it hard to trust anyone in this group."

I said, "Well, why don't you work on increasing trust?"

He turned to me and replied seriously, "Look, Stephen, you need to understand something. Either you have trust or you don't. We don't have it, and there's nothing we can do about it."

I strongly disagree. In fact, both my personal life and my work as a business practitioner over the past twenty years have convinced me that there is a lot we can do about it. Just like we reach out often across cultures, we can increase trust—much faster than we might think—and doing so will have a huge impact, both in the quality of our lives and in the results we're able to achieve.

Trust issues affect everyone

As I speak to audiences around the world about the Speed of Trust, I repeatedly hear expressions of frustration and discouragement such as these:

- I can't stand the politics at work. I feel sabotaged by my peers. It seems like everyone is out for himself and will do anything to get ahead.

- I've really been burned in the past. How can I ever trust anyone enough to have a real relationship?

- I work in an organization that's bogged down with bureaucracy. It takes forever to get anything done. I have to get authorization to buy a pencil!

- The older my children get, the less they listen to me. What can I do?

- I feel like my contributions at work are hardly ever recognized or valued.

- I foolishly violated the trust of someone who was supremely important to me. If I could hit "rewind" and make the decision differently, I would do it in a heartbeat. But I can't. Will I ever be able to rebuild the relationship?

- I have to walk on eggshells at work. If I say what I really think, I'll get fired…or at least made irrelevant.

- My boss micromanages me and everyone else at work. He treats us all like we can't be trusted.

- With all the scandals, corruption, and ethical violations in our society today, I feel like someone has pulled the rug out from under me. I don't know what—or who—to trust anymore.

All those comments are also heard from people experiencing cross-cultural situations.

So what do you do if you're in a situation like one of these or in any situation where a lack of trust creates politics and bureaucracy, or simply slows things down? Do you merely accept this as the cost of doing business? Or can you do something to counteract or even reverse it?

I affirm that you can do something about it. In fact, by learning how to establish, grow, extend, and restore trust, you can positively and significantly alter the trajectory of this and every future moment of your life.

Getting a handle on trust

So what is trust? Rather than giving a complex definition, I prefer to use the words of Jack Welch, former CEO of General Electric. He said, "You know it when you feel it."

It sounds like culture, doesn't it? Or you can also say you feel it when it's not here anymore, like oxygen.

Simply put, trust means confidence. The opposite of trust—distrust—is suspicion. When you trust people, you have confidence in them, in their integrity, and in their abilities. When you distrust people, you are suspicious of them—of their integrity, their agenda, their capabilities, or their track record. It's that simple. We have all had experiences that validate the difference between relationships that are built on trust and those that are not. These experiences clearly tell us the difference is not small; it is dramatic.

So we could indeed create a continuum Trust—Distrust, like the other cultural dimensions.

Trust   Distrust

Fig. 7.1 Trust Vs. Distrust Dimension

Implication for business		
Trust		Distrust
Faster negotiations	Vs.	Need time to "get to know each other"
Little bureaucracy	Vs.	Heavy bureaucracy, replacing trust
Many medium-size companies	Vs.	Few medium-size companies
NGO exist to be the link between the State and the population	Vs.	Few NGOs, the State intervene in people's life
Efficiency gains		Vs. Bureaucracy costs

Take a minute right now and think of a person with whom you have a high-trust relationship—perhaps a boss, coworker, customer, spouse, parent, sibling, child, or friend. Describe this relationship. What's it like? How does it feel? How well do you communicate? How quickly can you get things done? How much do you enjoy this relationship?

Now think of a person with whom you have a low-trust relationship. Again, this person could be anyone at work or at home. Describe this relationship. What's it like? How does it feel?

How is the communication? Does it flow quickly and freely or do you feel like you're constantly walking on land mines and being misunderstood? Do you work together to get things done quickly or does it take a disproportionate amount of time and energy to finally reach agreement and execution? Do you enjoy this relationship or do you find it tedious, cumbersome, and draining?

The difference between a high- and low-trust relationship is palpable!

Take cross-cultural communication. In a high-trust relationship, you can say the wrong thing, and people will still get your meaning. In a low-trust relationship, you can be very measured, even precise, and they'll still misinterpret you.

Can you even begin to imagine the difference it would make if you were able to increase the amount of trust in the important personal and professional relationships in your life?

Though I eventually left FranklinCovey to start my own company and write this book, I am happy to report that they have weathered the storms created by the merger and are now doing very well. On a personal basis, the whole experience helped me to understand trust far more clearly than in premerger times when trust was high and things were good.

First, I learned that I had assumed way too much. I assumed I had trust with people, when in fact I didn't. I assumed that people were aware of my track record and Covey Leadership Center's track record, which they were not. I assumed that because I was teeing up the tough issues in my private meetings and making decisions based on objective business criteria, this was being reported down line, but it was not.

I also learned that I had been politically naïve. Yes, I made mistakes.

But I didn't make the mistakes I was being accused of making. The most significant mistake I made was in not being more proactive in establishing and increasing trust. As a result, I experienced firsthand both the social and the hard, bottom-line economic consequences of low trust.

In addition, I learned that trust truly does change everything. Once you create trust, genuine character-based and competence-based trust, almost everything else falls into place.

A CRISIS OF TRUST AROUND THE WORLD

You don't need to look far to realize that, as a global society, we have a crisis of trust on our hands. Consider recent newspaper headlines:

- Employees' New Motto: Trust No One
- Companies Urged to Rebuild Trust
- Both Sides Betray the Other's Trust
- 20 NYSE Traders Indicted
- Ethics Must Be Strengthened to Rebuild People's Trust
- Relationships Fall Apart as Trust Dwindles
- Now Who Do You Trust?

News headlines reveal the symptoms of the compelling truth: low trust is everywhere. It permeates our global society, our marketplace, our organizations, our relationships, our personal lives. It breeds suspicion and cynicism, which become self-perpetuating, resulting in a costly, downward cycle.

Consider our society at large. Trust in almost every societal institution (government, media, business, health care, churches, political parties, etc.) is significantly lower than a generation ago, and in many cases, sits at historic lows. In the United States, for example, a 2005 Harris poll revealed that only 22 percent of those surveyed tend to trust the media, only 8 percent trust political parties, only 27 percent trust the government, and only 12 percent trust big companies.

According to the 2009 Edelman Trust Barometer[93], 62% of 25-to-64-year-olds surveyed in 20 countries say they trust corporations less now than they did a year ago. When people do not trust companies they:

- Refuse to buy their products or use their services
- Refuse to work for them
- Refuse to invest in them

---

[93] www.edelman.com

TRUST AS A CULTURAL DIMENSION

- Refuse to do business with them
- Share their distrust with people whom they know, and,
- Actively demonstrate or protest against them.

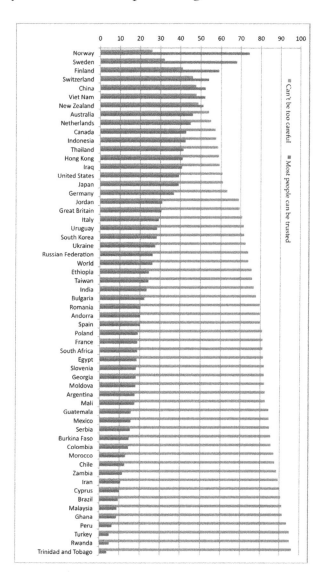

Fig. 7.2 – Trust across cultures[94]

In blue, percent of respondents who agree, "Most people can be trusted", in red, percent who think "You can't be too careful".

---

94   Values Surveys Databank (2004-2008)

Perhaps even more telling is the loss of trust with regard to people trusting other people. Figures clearly show that a majority of people in the world doesn't trust each other, and this is rather worrying. The "good" news of such study, relatively speaking, is that nearly 70 percent of Scandinavians (Norway, Sweden, and Finland) and more than 50 percent of the people in New Zealand and China believe others can be trusted, indicating that there are some higher-trust societies. Yet, when working with intercultural teams, it is a major challenge to overcome.

CRAIG'S DIALOGUE: AT THE WINDOW	
CAROL:	I have some great news for supervisors.
MICHELE:	What is it?
CAROL:	I've found some new software that puts customer account information right at the window, at the teller's fingertips.
MICHELE:	You mean tellers will be able to access customer accounts directly, without calling in a supervisor?
CAROL:	Exactly. It's really efficient. I'm sure customers will be very impressed with how fast they get answers.
MICHELE:	No doubt.

On the organizational level, trust within companies has also sharply declined. The subprime crisis in 2008 followed by the sovereign debt crisis in 2010 didn't help, either. Just look at what the research shows:

- Only 51 percent of employees have trust and confidence in senior management.

- Only 36 percent of employees believe their leaders act with honesty and integrity.

- Over the past twelve months, 76 percent of employees have observed illegal or unethical conduct on the job—conduct that, if exposed, would seriously violate public trust.

What about trust at the personal relationship level? While this naturally varies with regard to particular relationships, trust is a major issue for most people in at least some relationships (and too often with their most significant relationships, such as with a boss or coworker or a spouse or child at home).

Consider the following:

- The number one reason people leave their jobs is a bad relationship with their boss.
- One out of every two marriages ends in divorce.

Relationships of all kinds are built on and sustained by trust. They can also be broken and destroyed by lack of trust. Try to imagine any meaningful relationship without trust. In fact, low trust is the very definition of a bad relationship.

What about trust at the individual level? Consider the percentage of students who acknowledged that they cheated in order to improve their odds of getting into graduate school.

- Liberal arts students—43 percent
- Education students—52 percent
- Medical students—63 percent
- Law students—63 percent
- Business students—75 percent

How does it make you feel to know that there's more than a 50 percent chance that the doctor who's going to perform surgery on you cheated in school? Or a 75 percent chance that the company you're going to work for is being led by someone who didn't consider honesty important?

Recently, when I presented these data to a group of attorneys, they were thrilled to find out that they were not in last place! And they chided me because—with my MBA—I was! (It didn't help when I further pointed out that 76 percent of MBAs were willing to understate expenses that cut into their profits, and that convicts in minimum-security prisons scored as high as MBA students on their ethical dilemma exams.)

Trust in the World

Trust also varies by geography, there's no question that trust issues are global issues. There's also a country tax. The Edelman Trust Barometer tells us, for example, that trust is often based on country of origin. US companies are being taxed in Europe, in Germany, France and England, for example. Yet, trust can be rebuilt thanks to your behavior.

We've identified 13 behaviors which build trust:

1. Talk Straight
2. Demonstrate Respect
3. Create Transparency
4. Right Wrongs
5. Show Loyalty
6. Deliver Results
7. Get Better
8. Confront Reality
9. Clarify Expectations
10. Practice Accountability
11. Listen First
12. Keep Commitments
13. Extend Trust

Companies need to have a strong promise, because the promise builds hope. Keeping the promise is what builds trust.

My father has an expression: "You can't talk yourself out of a problem you behaved yourself into." So it is with trust.

Sometimes it takes a little time, but you can accelerate the process by declaring your intent and signaling your behavior, so others can see it.

People and companies can learn these behaviors. It's not a simple process which happens overnight. But it is a systemic, cultural process which can happen one leader at a time, one division at a time, one company at a time, and you can see the behavior shifting toward authentic, real trust-building behaviors as opposed to the more common counterfeit behavior of spin and hidden agendas and the like which tend to dissipate and diminish trust.

How do you know if you are dealing with a culture of Trust or of Distrust? Well, usually you feel it quite fast! When people don't trust you, it doesn't feel very good does it? But there can be other elements that reveal the actual level of trust the environment you are confronted with.

Bureaucracy is an easy element to spot. When trust is lacking, it has to be replaced by something. If you borrow $10 from a friend, there is no need for any document stating it: it's a matter of trust. But if you borrow $1.000 from a bank, then the institution is likely to ask you for some kind of "documents" such as I.D., salary pay checks and so on.

In societies with little trust as a natural element, bureaucracy is meant to replace the trust between people. When your request cannot be approved because of procedural reasons, you usually cannot beat the bureaucracy… unless you have a relation of trust with a person involved in the process. Another way is to ask to talk to the manager, who, hopefully, will be convinced by your situation and will agree to create a derogation: The manager then takes responsibility based on the trust in you.

Thus, we can also state that people avoiding responsibility are more likely to live in low-trust cultures. Does it sound like your local Post Office? Think about certified letters. A postman will never leave a certified letter to anyone else than the official recipient… unless the postman knows personally this third person!

The size of companies can also tell us a lot. The same logic applies to management in companies. Most companies are started as family ones, where everyone knows each other. Usually, through time, three outcomes are possible: The company grows, stagnates or dies. When the founder leaves, the company can either be taken over by the second generation, or some specialists form outside are called-in to manage it. They are "strangers" to be trusted… or not! If the children of the founder are competent, all will go well. Unfortunately, this is not always the case. Companies with stewards from outside are more likely to grow into robust family-owned companies, taking advantage of the outsiders' skills and the family members' experience. Germany and Austria are known to feature many such companies; both countries scoring high in all trust indexes. Low trust cultures also have large companies, usually very large ones, often closely linked to the State even if the ownership is private, like in France or in Russia.

A last detectable element of trust is efficiency, although it is hard to measure. Productivity can be achieved in any system, with high or low trust: Scientific management of the early 20th century was all about that. Efficiency needs trust. One aspect of efficiency at a country level is innovation, or easier to measure, the number of patents filed by residents, per million population[95]. Consider this ranking of countries:

1. Japan
2. South Korea
3. USA
4. Germany
5. Australia
6. New Zealand
7. Finland
8. Denmark

---

95 World Intellectual Property Organization

9. United Kingdom

10. Sweden

The correlation between high trust and innovation is quite striking and should not really surprise us as all of these countries are scoring higher than the world average in trust indexes.

Creativity thrives when freedom and trust reign. In the USA companies can even get a tax break if they donate they unused patent!

THE ECONOMICS OF TRUST

A cynic might ask, "So what? Is trust really more than a nice-to-have social virtue, a so-called hygiene factor? Can you measurably illustrate that trust is a hard-edged economic driver?"

Here's a simple formula that will enable you to take trust from an intangible and unquantifiable variable to an indispensable factor that is both tangible and quantifiable. The formula is based on this critical insight: trust always affects two outcomes—speed and cost. When trust goes down, speed will also go down and costs will go up.

$$\downarrow \text{Trust} = \downarrow \text{Speed} \uparrow \text{Cost}$$

When trust goes up, speed will also go up and costs will go down.

$$\uparrow \text{Trust} = \uparrow \text{Speed} \downarrow \text{Cost}$$

It's that simple, that real, and that predictable. Let me share a couple of examples.

Immediately following the 9/11 terrorist attacks, our trust in flying in the US went down dramatically. We recognized that there were terrorists bent on harming us and that our system of ensuring passenger safety was not as strong as it needed to be.

Prior to 9/11, I used to arrive at my home airport approximately half an hour before takeoff, and I was quickly able to go through security. But after 9/11, more robust procedures and systems were put in place to increase safety and trust in flying. While these procedures have had their desired effect, now it takes me longer and costs me more to travel. I generally arrive an hour and a half before a domestic flight and two to three hours before an international flight to make sure I have enough time to clear security. I also pay a new 9/11 security tax with every ticket I buy. So, as trust went down, speed also went down and cost went up.

Recently, I flew out of a major city in a high-risk area in the Middle East. For geopolitical reasons, the trust in that region was extremely low. I had to arrive at the airport four hours before my flight. I went through several screenings, and my bag was unpacked and searched multiple times by multiple people. And every other passenger was treated the same.

Clearly, extra security measures were necessary, and in this instance I was grateful for them, but the point remains the same: because trust was low, speed went down and cost went up.

Consider another example. The Sarbanes-Oxley Act was passed in response to the Enron, WorldCom, and other corporate scandals. While it appears that Sarbanes-Oxley may be having a positive effect in improving or at least sustaining trust in the public markets, it is also clear that this has come at a substantial price. Ask any CEO, CFO, or financial person in a company subject to Sarbanes-Oxley rules about the amount of time it takes to follow its regulations, as well as the added cost of doing so; it's enormous on both fronts. In fact, a recent study pegged the costs of implementing one section alone at thirty-five billion dollars—exceeding the original Securities and Exchange Commission estimate by twenty-eight times! Compliance regulations have become prosthesis for the lack of trust, and a slow-moving and costly prosthesis at that. Again, we come back to the key learning: when trust is low, speed goes down and cost goes up.

On the other hand, when trust is high, speed goes up and cost goes down. Consider the example of Warren Buffett, CEO of Berkshire Hathaway (and generally considered one of the most trusted leaders in the world), who recently completed a major acquisition of McLane Distribution (a twenty-three-billion-dollar company) from Walmart. As public companies, both Berkshire Hathaway and Walmart are subject to all kinds of market and regulatory scrutiny. Typically, a merger of this size would take several months to complete and cost several million dollars to pay for accountants, auditors, and attorneys to verify and validate all kinds of information. But in this instance, because both parties operated with high trust, the deal was made with one two-hour meeting and a handshake. In less than a month, it was completed.

In a management letter that accompanied his 2004 annual report, Warren Buffett wrote, "We did no due diligence. We knew everything would be exactly as Walmart said it would be—and it was." Imagine—less than one month (instead of six months or longer), and no due diligence costs (instead of the millions typically spent)! High trust, high speed, low cost.

Consider the example of another legendary leader, Herb Kelleher, chairman and former CEO of Southwest Airlines. In the book *Executive E.Q.*, the authors[96] share a remarkable story. Walking down the hall one day, Gary Barron—then executive vice president of the seven-hundred-million-dollar maintenance organization for all Southwest—presented a three-page summary memo to Kelleher outlining a proposal for a massive reorganization. On the spot, Kelleher read the memo. He asked one question, to which Barron responded that he shared the concern and was dealing with it. Kelleher then replied, "Then it's fine by me. Go ahead." The whole interaction took about four minutes.

Not only was Kelleher a trusted leader, but he also extended trust to others. He trusted Barron's character and his competence. And because he trusted that Barron knew what he was doing, the company could move with incredible speed.

---

96   Cooper & Sawaf, 1998, Executive E.Q., Perigee Trade

> Here's another example on a much smaller scale. Jim, a vendor in New York City, set up shop and sold donuts and coffee to passersby as they went in and out of their office buildings. During the breakfast and lunch hours, Jim always had long lines of customers waiting. He noticed that the wait time discouraged many customers, who left and went elsewhere. He also noticed that, as he was a one-man show, the biggest bottleneck preventing him from selling more donuts and coffee was the disproportionate amount of time it took to make change for his customers.
>
> Finally, Jim simply put a small basket on the side of his stand filled with dollar bills and coins, trusting his customers to make their own change. Now you might think that customers would accidentally count wrong or intentionally take extra quarters from the basket, but what Jim found was the opposite. Most customers responded by being completely honest, often leaving him larger-than-normal tips. Also, he was able to move customers through at twice the pace because he didn't have to make change. In addition, he found that his customers liked being trusted and kept coming back. By extending trust in this way, Jim was able to double his revenues without adding any new cost.
>
> Again, when trust is low, speed goes down and cost goes up. When trust is high, speed goes up and cost goes down.

Recently, as I was teaching this concept, a CFO who deals with numbers all the time came up to me and said, "This is fascinating! I've always seen trust as a nice thing to have, but I never, ever, thought of it in terms of its impact on economics and speed. Now that you've pointed it out, I can see it everywhere I turn.

"For example, we have one supplier in whom we have complete trust. Everything happens fast with this group, and the relationship hardly costs us anything to maintain. But with another supplier, we have very little trust. It takes forever to get anything done, and it costs us a lot of time and effort to support the relationship. And that's costing us money—too much money!"

This CFO was amazed when everything suddenly fell into place in his mind. Even though he was a "numbers" guy, he had not connected the dots with regard to trust. Once he saw it, everything suddenly made sense. He could immediately see how trust was affecting everything in the organization, and how robust and powerful the idea of the relationship between trust, speed, and cost was for analyzing what was happening in his business and for taking steps to significantly increase profitable growth.

I know of leading organizations who ask their employees directly the following simple question in formal, 360-degree feedback processes: "Do you trust your boss?" These companies have learned that the answer to this one question is more predictive of team and organizational performance than any other question they might ask.

Once you really understand the hard, measurable economics of trust, it's like putting on a new pair of glasses. Everywhere you look, you can see the impact at work, at home, in every relationship, in every effort. You can begin to see the incredible difference high-trust relationships can make in every dimension of life.

The trust tax

The serious practical impact of the economics of trust is that in many relationships, in many interactions, we are paying a hidden low-trust tax right off the top, and we don't even know it!

Probably no one really likes to pay taxes. But we do so because they serve a greater societal cause (and also because it's the law). But what if you didn't even know you were paying taxes? What if they were hidden—being taken right off the top without you even being aware? And what if they were completely wasted taxes, if they were going right down the drain and doing absolutely no good to anyone anywhere?

Unfortunately, low-trust taxes don't conveniently show up on your income statement as a "cost of low trust." But just because they're hidden doesn't mean they're not there. Once you know where and what to look for, you can see these taxes show up everywhere—in organizations and in relationships. They're quantifiable. And they're often extremely high.

You've undoubtedly seen this tax in action many times—perhaps in a conversation where you can tell that your boss, your teenager, or someone else is automatically discounting everything you say by 20 percent, 30 percent, or even more. If you think about it, you've probably been the one taxing some of those interactions yourself, discounting what you're hearing from others because you don't trust them.

The trust dividend

I also suggest that, just as the tax created by low trust is real, measurable, and extremely high, so the dividends of high trust are also real, quantifiable, and incredibly high. Consider the speed with which Warren Buffett completed the McLane acquisition and how quickly Gary Barron's massive reorganization proposal was approved. Consider the doubling of revenues for Jim, the donut and coffee vendor. Consider the speed with which you can communicate in your own relationships of high trust, both personal and professional.

When trust is high, the dividend you receive is like a performance multiplier, elevating and improving every dimension of your organization and your life. High trust is like the leaven in bread, which lifts everything around it. In a company, high trust materially improves communication, collaboration, execution, innovation, strategy, engagement, partnering, and relationships with all stakeholders. In your personal life, high trust significantly improves your excitement, energy, passion, creativity, and joy in your relationships with family, friends, and community. Obviously, the dividends are not just in increased speed and improved economics; they are also in greater enjoyment and better quality of life.

THE HIDDEN VARIABLE

One time I hired a guide to take me fly-fishing in Montana. As I looked out over the river, he said, "Tell me what you see." Basically I told him I saw a beautiful river with the sun reflecting off the surface of the water. He asked, "Do you see any fish?" I replied that I did not. Then my guide handed me a pair of polarized sunglasses. "Put these on," he said.

Suddenly everything looked dramatically different. As I looked at the river, I discovered I could see through the water. And I could see fish—a lot of fish! My excitement shot up. Suddenly I could sense an enormous possibility that I hadn't seen before. In reality, those fish were there all along, but until I put on the glasses, they were hidden from my view.

In the same way, for most people, trust is hidden from view. They have no idea how present and pervasive the impact of trust is in every relationship, in every organization, in every interaction, in every moment of life. But once they put on "trust glasses" and see what's going on under the surface, it immediately impacts their ability to increase their effectiveness in every dimension of life.

Edward Hall, much discussed already in this textbook, called Culture the "hidden dimension" too, referring to the four other dimensions of physics. The concept is here the same: you can't see it and you feel it only when you don't have it anymore.

A company can have an excellent strategy and a strong ability to execute, but the net result can be either torpedoed by a low-trust tax or multiplied by a high-trust dividend. As one eminent consultant on this topic, Robert Shaw, has said, "Above all, success in business requires two things: a winning competitive strategy and superb organizational execution. Distrust is the enemy of both." I submit that while high trust won't necessarily rescue a poor strategy, low trust will almost always derail a good one.

Perhaps more than anything else, the impact of this hidden variable makes a powerful business case for trust. According to a study by Warwick Business School in the UK, outsourcing contracts that are managed based on trust rather than on stringent agreements and penalties are more likely to lead to trust dividends for both parties—as much as 40 percent of the total value of a contract. A 2002 study by Watson Wyatt shows that total return to shareholders in high-trust organizations is almost three times higher than the return in low-trust organizations. That's a difference of nearly 300 percent! An education study by Stanford professor Tony Bryk shows that schools with high trust had more than a three times higher chance of improving test scores than schools with low trust. On a personal level, high-trust individuals are more likely to be promoted, make more money, receive the best opportunities, and have more fulfilling and joyful relationships.

One of the reasons why the hidden variable of trust is so significant and compelling in today's world is that we have entered into a global, knowledge-worker economy. As New York Times columnist Thomas Friedman observes in *The World Is Flat*, this new "flat" economy revolves around partnering and relationships. And partnering and relationships thrive or die based on trust. As Friedman says, "Without trust, there is no open society, because there are not enough police to patrol every opening in an open society. Without trust, there can also be no flat world, because it is trust that allows us to take down walls, remove barriers, and eliminate friction at borders. Trust is essential for a flat world."

This is why I again affirm: the ability to establish, grow, extend, and restore trust with all stakeholders—customers, business partners, investors, and coworkers—is the key leadership competency of the new global economy.

I suggest you ask yourself, "Is my organization paying taxes or receiving dividends? And what about me? Am I a walking tax or a walking dividend?"

Also, think about your relationships both in and out of work. Ask yourself, "Where in this summary do these relationships fit? And where can I focus my effort to make the greatest difference in my life?"

Now I suggest you take any cross-cultural project you need to work on and look at it in terms of this summary. Say you need to pull people together to have a project completed within six weeks. Ask yourself, "What's the level of trust in the culture? Am I paying a tax or getting a dividend? If so, what percent? What impact is that going to have on speed and cost and on my ability to execute this project effectively?"

Now consider what would happen if you were able to change that percentage. What if you were able to move from a 20 percent tax to a 20 percent dividend? What difference would that make in your ability to execute your project?

Think about what's happening in your personal relationships or in your family. Ask yourself, "What's the level of trust? What impact is that having on quality of life for me and for the people I care about? What if I could move from a tax to a dividend? What difference would it make?"

Trust myths

Examples such as the McLane acquisition, the Kelleher reorganization approval, and others I've shared in this chapter go a long way toward dispelling some of the debilitating myths that keep us from enjoying the dividends of high trust.

One myth, for example, is that trust is "soft"—it's something that's nice to have, but you really can't define it, quantify it, and measure it. As I hope you can tell by now, the exact opposite is true. Trust is hard. It's real. It's quantifiable. It's measurable. In every instance, it affects both speed and cost, and speed and cost can be measured and quantified. To change the level of trust in a relationship, in a team, or in an organization is to dramatically impact both time and money—and quality and value, as well. Another myth is that trust is slow. While restoring trust may take time, both establishing and extending trust can be done quite fast, and, once established, trust makes the playing field exceptionally quick. You don't have to look far beyond these examples I've given or even the speed with which you communicate and get things done in your own relationships to see the reality that truly, nothing is as fast as the speed of trust.

Conclusion

You can do something about trust! For twenty years, I've been a business practitioner. I've been responsible for building and running organizations, for developing teams, for reporting to boards, getting results, and having to "hit the numbers." During many of those years, I've also done consulting work with dozens of well-known companies, many of which had good strategies and good execution abilities but fell short of being able to accomplish what they wanted to without being able to explain why. I have been a husband, a father, a member of a large extended family with many multifaceted relationships. I have served in community situations in which I have counseled individuals and families dealing with complex trust issues. And in all of my experience, I have never seen an exception to the basic premise of this chapter, that trust is something you can do something about—and probably much faster than you think!

Trust truly is the one thing that changes everything. And there has never been a more vital time for people to establish, restore, and extend trust at all levels than in today's new global society.

Whether you approach the opportunity and challenge of increasing trust in relation to your personal life, your professional life, or both, I can promise you, it will make an enormous difference in every dimension of your life. [97]

....
RECAP

- Trust can be understood as another cultural dimension, with two extremes "Trust" and "Distrust"
- Trust influences our behavior and our relationships
- Culture and geography have an impact on trust, with clear differences reflecting on organizations
- The lack of trust is replaced by bureaucracy, and has a strong link to efficiency
- Increasing our trust towards others is a key ingredient for successful cooperation, particularly across cultures

....

---

97 If you want to know more about Trust and how it influences management, read « The Speed of Trust » of Stephen M.R Covey.

CASE STUDY 7.1: TRUST IN THE SUPERMARKET

Practically since mankind started making, trading and selling products, businesses have looked for ways to cut costs, so that profit could be increased (assuming that revenue did not go down). A smart way for businesses to cut costs is by letting their customers complete the actions that employees needed to do previously.

There are many examples of this. The recent spread of digital technology has catapulted this phenomenon. We can think of self-printing airline tickets, pre-checking in for flights, all cost-cutting measures of actions in the airline industry that used to be a service done by personnel, now by customers. Another example is pumping gasoline at a petrol station (up until forty years ago the pumping process was strictly done by employees). A later development was a gas station where there is no personnel at all. Everything is done automatically, paying in advance with a credit or debit card, then getting the gasoline oneself.

In all these processes companies have to deal with the concept of trust. Can we trust our customers, will they pay for the product and can we minimize cheating to an absolute minimum? How can we build a system that is not insulting for people who are to be trusted, and yet cannot be fooled and sabotaged by (the few) people who steal and take advantage of the situation?

Another interesting system is self-check systems in retail and supermarket stores. Since the beginning of this century, a number of stores have started using different systems of self-scanning. After testing several versions in a few pilot stores AH supermarkets decided in 2006 to use its system in a large number of its supermarkets.

AH supermarkets is a part of the AHOLD concern; in The Netherlands AH has currently 835 «regular» supermarkets in neighborhoods, 31 AH XL stores (very large), and 52 «*AH To go*" stores (small, higher prices, in train stations etc); the self- scan system is based on a shifting "trust paradigm" as checking usually means: we don't trust you.

The customer bleeps and scans each item s/he wishes to buy using a device that s/he picks up at the entrance of the supermarket. After scanning each item, the customer puts them in their shopping cart, while walking through the store. In the end the self-scanning device needs to be put in an electronic reader, which tallies up the total. After the customer pays the required amount by debit card, s/he gets a paper coupon, which enables them to open an exit gate, so s/he can leave with his groceries.

CASE STUDY 7.1: TRUST IN THE SUPERMARKET

The philosophy behind this system is based on the paradigm of "trust your customer", however, to participate as a customer, one first has to apply and go through a screening process. A form needs to be filled out, and only after the applicant has been admitted as a "self-scanning customer", they get a personalized card with a barcode. Advantages communicated to the customers of self-scan systems seemed to be mostly psychological (speed of scanning, easy, see your cumulated shopping amount instantly).

This *"bonus+"* card allows customers to use the self-scanning system, yet random verifications are conducted at the exit counter. If a customer has "made a mistake", trust is violated, and this customer can expect more frequent controls… After no new "mistakes" are registered, i.e. trust has been restored, the frequency of verifications decreases.

Other retailers are using similar techniques, mostly across Europe and in North America. Yet, this new system seems to have its own limits. A 2006 survey showed that systems like this can be used for about half the market: when asked, some 60% of customers prefer a physical check-out person.

Jacob "Rob" Laas
IMBS Business Faculty, The Hague Univ. of Applied Sciences
The Netherlands

Discussion questions:

- Link the concept of trust to checking customers, and reflect about possible improvements to this system/paradigm;

- Do you consider it a good development that self-scanning systems are becoming more and more abundant? Give at least two reasons to support your answer.

- Can you think of a method other than the one described in the article, to show how a supermarket can introduce and use a self-scanning system, one that demonstrates confidence in its customers, and at the same time detects and sanctions cheats?

CASE STUDY 7.2: INTERNATIONAL FINANCE AND TRUST

In their monthly meeting in June 2006 the board of a major US investment bank based in Manhattan, NY, is thinking about launching a new product to raise revenues and increase shareholder value. After a fruitful discussion they decided to do something special and create a fund with a variety of high risk papers. Once they finished the formal IPO process they discovered that the distribution of these papers appeared to be difficult. The customers seemed to be reserved because of the high risk.

Confronting this problem the marketing department developed the idea of increasing revenue by strengthening customers' trust in these papers.

They knew that an expensive marketing campaign, with glamorous material, would probably not be the right way to succeed in this case. They needed to create a safe environment supported by persons or institutions with a strong reputation.

So they asked a professor of finance from Varthar, one of the most prestigious Universities of the country, to write 1-2 pages about this fund in a popular finance journal. For his efforts the investment bank offered him the amount of $ 80.000,-.

Having this generous remuneration in mind, the professor doesn't wanted to be impolite and asked the bankers for suggestions. He received the "right" information and wrote the article in a scientific, and for the bank satisfying, way.

Armed with this article the investment bankers approached a well-known rating agency, Stich, to invite them to rate this fund. This rating agency is usually neutral, however they trusted the opinion of the professor as an independent specialist. As a result of this trust, Stich didn't investigate the rational of the fund thoroughly and rated the fund better than the equity of the papers.

With the benefit of the positive rating and the professor's endorsement the investment bank created a marketing package and offered their fund to banks all over the world.

The banks trusted the status of the investment bank, of the professor and of the "independent" rating agency and purchased the fund for their clients.

Dr. Rainer Wehner
Würzburg-Schweinfurt University of Applied Sciences
Germany

CASE STUDY 7.2: INTERNATIONAL FINANCE AND TRUST

Discussion questions:

- Which role plays trust in this case?
- Which role plays the status the professor?
- Nobody can blame a professor or a rating agency for doing their work, yet it lead to unethical situations. Whose behavior needs to reviewed?

Chapter 8: Organizational Culture

CHAPTER CONTENTS

Highlights
Introduction
Defining organization (or corporate) culture

WHAT IS CORPORATE CULTURE?
Why organizational culture?

MODELS OF CORPORATE CULTURE
Approaches to solve an organizational dilemma

THE ROLE OF CORPORATE CULTURE
Corporate culture in mergers, acquisitions and strategic alliances
Major tensions originating in corporate culture

THE EXTREME STEREOTYPES OF CORPORATE CULTURE
The family
The Eiffel Tower
The Guided Missile
The Incubator

Transformation away from a Guided Missile culture
Transformation away from a Family culture

Conclusion
Recap
Case study 8.1: French railways change timetable
Case study 8.2: Corporate culture changes at Steel-Roll

CHAPTER 8

ORGANIZATIONAL CULTURE
By Peter Woolliams

Highlights:

After reading this chapter, you should be able to:

– Reflect on the significance of corporate culture in explaining how organizations operate and how one organization may differ from another even in the same business segment or country
– Describe some of the frequently quoted models and means to assess corporate culture
– Understand how an assessment of the difference between current and some idealized corporate culture explains the key drivers faced by an organization and what tensions will arise
– Understand the relevance of corporate culture in mergers and acquisitions in explaining why mergers often fail to deliver the anticipated benefits, and how cultural due diligence, rather than simple financial diligence, is the key to success

Introduction

Cultural factors in business derive not only from differences across national boundaries but also within and between organizations. For many managers, the culture of their organization may dominate over national differences. Consider the young Japanese manager who typifies Japanese thinking and values in his junior role working in Japan for a US

American company. However, when he gets promoted to a significant management grade, he travels the world, visiting headquarters in the US frequently. Now he spends his time working and interacting regularly with his peers who may be of many different nationalities. It is not their country/nationality differences that dominate but what they share in terms of the "way things are done around the organization." The system of shared meaning is no longer from their country of birth and fellow countrymen but from their shared way of working together. This can include making PowerPoint slide presentations to company colleagues on this quarter's results using an in-house style with corporate logos, speaking their own corporate language, talking in terms of short-term budgets (rather than longer-term Japanese thinking), and following email protocols and resource planning systems.

So, we must now begin from the nomothetic perspective. The corporate culture of the organization is now the driver. The "management of culture" is now about creating a corporate culture in which people will work together to achieve the organization's goals as well as reconciling dilemmas that originate from issues of corporate culture. Of course, this is not (national) culture free. An organization in one part of the world, with a society that ascribes status, may choose an organization model that builds initially upon ascription rather than achievement. But what about the global company with a diverse workforce? And what is the link between corporate culture and business?

Defining organization (or corporate) culture

Organizational culture became the topic of the 1980s which was used to solve all management problems and so to increase performance. Companies seized on the notion of corporate culture as an all-encompassing panacea for corporate ills. US author and guru Warren Bennis, speaking at a conference in 1986 noted, "I think a more urgent reason for the interest in corporate cultures is the rapid changing, turbulent environment most managers find themselves in now. I have been an organization watcher for something like thirty-five years, and I can't recall a time with more volatility, complexity, uncertainty, and ambiguity than there is now. One result, I think, is that people are looking for an anchor…such as the stability a strong corporate culture provides".

WHAT IS CORPORATE CULTURE?

Geert Hofstede maintains that the attribution of a culture to an organization is a relatively recent phenomenon first appearing in English language in the 1960s. He further noted that the equivalent term 'corporate culture' was introduced through the title of the book by Deal and Kennedy[98]. Both terms are used in this chapter, and they are deemed to be equivalent.

The number of definitions of corporate culture reflect the position taken by each author in terms of how he or she views the phenomena to which they refer; the main distinction made by these authors is between those who regard culture as a metaphor and those who see culture as an objective entity. The approach that sees the idea of culture as a metaphor is one that is increasingly receiving attention. Culture is perceived as not some tangible, objective, or measurable entity[99], so much as an intellectual device that enables understanding of organizations in terms of a specific vocabulary, norms, beliefs, values, symbols, artifacts. It is a perspective that allows for every part of the organization to be regarded as a part of its culture.

Theorists seem to show a dichotomy of view, some believing that culture is something the organization *is*, an integral part of the firm that is fixed and stable and not very adaptable to change. Others believe that culture is something an organization *has*, an adaptive phenomenon that evolves and changes with the internal and external environments of the firm[100].

Goffee and Jones[101] suggest that it is culture that holds the organization together, acting as a force for cohesion in the firm. They argue that culture is embedded in the members of the organization, enabling the successful firm to continue to do what it is doing.

---

98 T. Deal & A. Kennedy, 1982, Corporate cultures: the rites and rituals of corporate life, Addison-Wesley
99 G. Morgan, 1986, Images of Organizations, Sage Publ.
100 Charles J. Fombrun et al., 1984, Strategic human resource management, Wiley
101 Goffee & Jones, 1998, The character of a corporation

Meyerson and Martin[102] also see culture as an integrating mechanism, a social or normative glue that holds together the potentially diverse members of a group.

Pedersen and Sorensen's definition, "As in traditional anthropological social entities, organizations create systems of meanings that influence the myriad behaviors, routines, and practices recognized as a distinct way of organizational life"[103], endorses the view that corporate culture is the means by which the members are able to give meaning to what they do within the firm. Camerer and Vepsalalainen support this view of corporate culture as a means of providing cohesion for employees. They are quite clear in their definition of corporate culture as "a set of broad, tacitly understood, rules which tell employees what to do under a wide variety of unimaginable circumstances"[104].

Organizational or corporate culture is defined by Conner as, "the basic patterns of shared beliefs, behaviors and assumptions organizational members acquire over time"[105].

Conner described a "culture triangle" (figure 2.3) linking the beliefs, behaviors, and assumptions held by members of a workforce into a coherent whole. The Conner triangle closely resembles the cultural onion (figure 1.5) and the Schein levels of culture (Figure 1.4) in its pictorial description of organizational culture.

The collective beliefs (see below) are a conscious set of integrated values and expectations that shape what individuals hold to be true or false, relevant or irrelevant, etc., about their environment. Belief statements, which may be oral or written, are generally messages about what it is individuals intend to do, or, think they should do; the behaviors are the observable, overt actions. They are the way that members of the workforce behave on a day-to-day basis.

---

102 Joanne Martin, 1992, Cultures in organizations: three perspectives
103 Pedersen and Sorensen, 1989, Organisational cultures in theory and practice, Avebury
104 Camerer and Vepsalainen, 1988, The Economic Efficiency of Corporate Culture, in Strategic Management Journal, Vol. 9
105 Conner, 1985, The Culture audit workbook: Corporate culture and its impact on organizational change, OD Resources

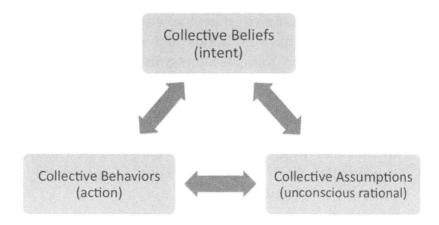

Fig. 8.1 - Culture triangle (adapted from Conner 1985)

Corporate culture is a complicated phenomenon, but it is important because it is the means by which the members of the culture, i.e. the people that work in the organization, make sense of their working lives and give meaning to their experiences of the firm. Trice and Beyer conclude that corporate culture is a collection of phenomena that in a way embody people's responses to the uncertainties and chaos that are inevitable in all areas of human existence[106]. Individuals in an organizational setting respond to the need to make sense of the world around them basically in two ways: firstly through shared belief systems and secondly through what might be called cultural forms, these being the observable entities, including actions, by which members of a culture can express, affirm, and communicate that which makes up the culture to one another. The two responses, the shared belief systems, and the cultural forms are developed by members of any group, including organizations, in order to make sense of the surrounding uncertainties and chaos.

Why organizational culture?

Implicit in research is that culture is an asset in all organizations. If culture is an asset then a large number of functions can be attributed to the corporate culture.

---

106 Trice and Beyer, 1993, The cultures of work organizations, Prentice Hall

Researchers agree that the culture of an organization defines appropriate behaviors, bonds and motivates individuals, and asserts solutions where there is ambiguity. It governs the way a company processes information, its internal relations and values.

More specifically, a corporate culture can, in a way, be said to be able to influence a number of organizational functions directly related to the members of the group. These functions could include conflict resolution, coordination and control, reduction of uncertainty, motivation, and competitive advantage.

Most cultural theorists would emphasize the important role that culture plays in fostering cohesion. Most writers on culture have tended to emphasize the positive implications of culture. However, not all corporate cultures are necessarily functional; the numbers of poorly performing and failing organizations would indicate that in these cases the corporate culture could be said to be dysfunctional. (Dysfunctional cultures have been investigated by other researchers and are outside the scope of this chapter).

Cameron and Quinn[107] title a section of their introductory chapter "The Need to Manage Organizational Culture." They note that in the United States, among the most successful firms, "those with sustained and above-normal financial returns," a number do not exhibit the conditions for success identified by Porter[108]. The question then needs to be asked as to what differentiates organizations that are successful from others that are not, given similar markets, similar business segments and similar resources. The leading research teams Cameron & Quinn and Trice & Beyer each identified the powerful effect that corporate culture has on performance and hence the long-term viability of an organization in explaining such success. Corporate culture also has visible effects on individuals in that it can affect employee morale, commitment, physical and emotional health, and hence productivity. These are all factors relevant to this study of corporate culture.

---

107 Cameron and Quinn, 2011, Diagnosing and Changing Organizational Culture, Jossey-Bass; 3 ed.
108 Porter, 1998, Competitive Advantage: Creating and Sustaining Superior Performance, Free Press

Culture is a crucial factor in the long-term effectiveness of an organization; being able to categorize it into an accepted framework provides a means of identifying the sorts of factors and variations that exist between cultures. However, the researcher recognizes that deciphering a culture is a subjective activity in that no two researchers collecting the same data will arrive at the same conclusions. Yet, in triangulating the data collected from each organization, the researcher seeks to minimize the subjectivity of the conclusions derived from the research as far as possible.

MODELS OF CORPORATE CULTURE

The number of typologies, classifications, and models of corporate culture developed provide a broad overview of the factors and variations in corporate cultures. These differ quite markedly in their degrees of complexity, the range of variables that are taken into consideration, and their applicability across organizations.

Typologies are useful ways of categorizing corporate cultures, but no organization is likely to fit any single category in a typology. What they do is to allow comparisons of an organizational culture against an ideal type.

Hofstede notes the case of a professor at INSEAD marking assignments for MBA students who recognized that the way students answered the questions was dependent upon their national culture. The different approaches taken by the students expose different organizational responses to problems in organizations and provide a starting point for the structure of a model of corporate culture.

The different approaches included a behavioral response, structural response, procedural response, together with a response that involved power, in that only the person/people at the top of an organization were deemed able to solve the particular dilemma.

Approaches to solve an organizational dilemma

Fig. 8.2 – The Organizational dilemma

The simplified diagram of culturally defined responses to corporate dilemmas is fundamental to many of the existing models and typologies of corporate culture.

Consideration of the four approaches is reflected by the various authors in terms of how their own approaches fit into the overall model. From the following diagram (Fig. 8.3), it can be seen that many of the accepted typologies fit to a certain extent and that each researcher, although they describe their various corporate cultures differently, do conform to a great extent to a general model of corporate culture. The models reviewed[109] included those of Ouchi (1982), Deal and Kennedy (1982), Mitroff and Killman (1975), Sethia and Von Gillow (1985), Kets de Vries and Miller (1984), Cameron and Quinn (1999), Handy (1985), and Trompenaars and Hampden-Turner (1997).

---

109 Collected by S. Watt, PhD thesis, University of NSW, 2005

ORGANIZATIONAL CULTURE

Author(s)	Type of Corporate Culture	Dominant Ideologies
Mitroff & Killman (1975)	Sensation – thinking Intuition – thinking Intuition – feeling Sensation - feeling	Impersonal, abstract, certainty, specific, authoritarian Flexible, adaptive, goal-driven Caring, decentralized, flexible, few rules Personal, home-like, relationship-driven, non-bureaucratic
Ouchi (1982)	Type A Type J Type Z	Hierarchical, high specialization, short-term employment, individual responsibility, and decision making Clan control, low specialization, long-term employment, collective responsibility and decision making Clan control, moderate specialization, long-term employment, individual responsibility, group decision making
Deal & Kennedy (1982)	Process Tough-guy, Macho Work-hard, Play-hard Bet-your-company	Low risk, slow feedback, rules-driven, exposure avoidance High risk, quick feedback, little structure Medium risk, active, persistent, flexible structure Very high risk, slow feedback, clear structure
Ket de Vries & Milner (1984)	Paranoid Avoidant Charismatic Bureaucratic Schizoid	Fear, distrust, suspicion Powerlessness, inaction Power, success, following leader Depersonalized, detailed, rigid Politicized, isolated
Handy (1985)	Club (Zeus) Task (Athena) Role (Apollo) Existential (Dionysus)	Entrepreneurial, few rules, empathy, trust Creative, goal orientation, group decision making Structured, rule-based, stable, predictable Individualistic, self-oriented, little structure
Sethia & Von Gillow (1985)	Apathetic Caring Exacting Integrative	Demoralizing, cynical Employee concern Performance and success orientation Concern for employees, performance orientation
Trompenaars & Hampden-Turner (1997)	Family Eiffel Tower Guided Missile Incubator	Hierarchical, personal, power oriented, high-context Bureaucratic, hierarchical, rules and regulations, rational, stable, impersonal Goal-oriented, impersonal, group decision making Individualistic, self-fulfillment, personal
Cameron & Quinn (1999)	Hierarchy Market Clan Adhocracy	Bureaucratic, efficient, formal, structured Productivity orientation, competitive, aggressive Shared values, cohesion, participative Responsive, entrepreneurial, creative

Fig. 8.3 – Corporate culture models

THE ROLE OF CORPORATE CULTURE

Fundamental to understanding culture in organizations is that we can also define culture as a series of rules and methods that an organization has evolved to deal with the regular problems it faces. Organizations face dilemmas in dealing with the tensions between the existing set of values and the desired ones—or between partners of a merger or strategic alliance. While cultures differ markedly in how they approach these dilemmas, they do not differ in needing to make some kind of response. Once the leaders have become aware of the problem-solving process, they will reconcile dilemmas more effectively and will therefore be more successful.

It is becoming more frequently recognized that organization development and business process reengineering have too often failed because they ignored aspects of corporate culture. However, simply "adding" the culture component does not suffice. This explains perhaps why culture is very often ignored. Values are not artifacts that can be added. They are continuously created by interactions amongst human actors and not "just out there" as solid rocks. As such, culture is only meaningful in the context in which the members of an organization go about their daily work.

Corporate culture in mergers, acquisitions, and strategic alliances

Globalization through mergers, acquisitions, and strategic alliances is very big business. They are sought after more than ever, not only for the implementation of globalization strategies but also as a consequence of political, monetary, and regulatory convergence. Even so, two out of three deals don't achieve anywhere near the expected benefits that prompted the venture (*Economist*, Jan. 9, 1999).

It is common to acquire an organization with less concern for full integration simply to purchase its inherent value. Increasingly, however, motives originate from a range of other expected benefits including synergistic values (cross-selling, supply chain consolidation, and economies of scale) or more direct strategic values (to become market leaders, penetrating a ready-made customer base). The emphasis in the pre-deal and post-deal management is too often focused on seeking to exploit the new opportunities quickly under a mechanistic systems or financial due-diligence mindset[110]. It is assumed that the task to deliver the benefits is to align the technical, operational, and financial systems and market approaches.

Our research reveals that the real underlying failure to deliver real benefits arises from the absence of a holistic structured methodological framework; therefore senior management does not know what to integrate or what types of decisions are important to deliver the anticipated benefits. While any integration program should be based on operational matters where the benefits are being sought, much more attention and resources need to be given to managing the cultural differences between the new partners/businesses. Indeed, relational aspects, such as cultural differences and lack of trust, turn out to be responsible for 70 percent of alliance failures. This is even more striking when we realize that building trust is a cultural challenge in itself. Lack of trust is often caused by different views of what constitutes a trustworthy partner. In addition, intercultural alliances involve differences in corporate cultures as well as national cultures. Problems can be due to more or less objective cultural differences and also to perceptions about each other, including those of corporate culture and national culture.

Human resources has a major role to play when dealing with corporate culture. Consideration must be given to leadership styles, management profiles, organization structures, working practices, and a wide range of perceptions within and outside of the marketplace. In short, culture is pervasive. Even when strategists and senior managers recognize the importance of culture, frustration continues because until now they have had no means of assessing or quantifying its causes and effects and of taking relevant effective action.

Major tensions originating in corporate culture

Much of our inductive thinking owes its origin to our portfolio of effective diagnostic and analytical tools and models and to the large and reliable database we have established based on data collected from these. This enables us either to facilitate or let organizations themselves diagnose the tensions they are facing.

Structure is a concept that is frequently used in the analysis of organizations, and many definitions and approaches are to be found.

---

110   KPMG Consulting, 1999, Mergers & Acquisition Report

Our interest here is in examining the interpretations employees give to their relationships with each other and with the organization as a whole. Organizational (nomothetic) culture is to the organization what ideographic (seven dimensions model) culture is to the individual—a hidden yet unifying theme that provides meaning, direction, and mobilization that can exert a decisive influence on the overall ability of the organization to deal with the challenges it faces.

Just as individuals in a culture can have different personalities while sharing much in common, so too can groups and organizations. It is this pattern that is recognized as corporate culture.

The corporate culture has a profound effect on organizational effectiveness because it influences how decisions are made, how human resources are used, and how the organization responds to the environment.

We can take the most useful constructs from the various and different models from the above authors and assemble a unified model that helps summarize and explain corporate culture.

In so doing we need to distinguish three aspects of organizational relationships whose meaning is dependent on the larger culture in which they emerge:

1. the general relationships between employees in the organization
2. the vertical or hierarchical relationships between employees and their superiors or subordinates in particular
3. the relationships of employees in the organization as a whole, such as their views of what makes it tick and what are its goals

The summary model identifies four competing organizational cultures that are derived from two related dimensions:

1. task or person (high versus low formalization)
2. hierarchical or egalitarian (high versus low centralization)

Combining these dimensions gives us four possible culture types.

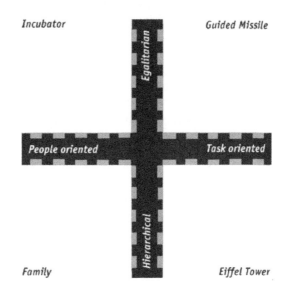

Fig. 8.4 – The corporate cultures quadrant

THE EXTREME STEREOTYPES OF CORPORATE CULTURE

The Family

The family culture is characterized by a high degree of centralization and a low degree of formalization. It generally reflects a highly personalized organization and is predominantly power-oriented.

Employees in the family seem to interact around the centralized power of father or mother. The power of the organization is based on an autocratic leader who, like a spider in a web, directs the organization.

There are not many rules and thus there is little bureaucracy. Organizational members tend to be as near as to the center as possible, as the source of power. Consequently the climate inside the organization is highly manipulative and full of intrigue. In this political system the prime logic of vertical differentiation is hierarchical differentiation of power and status.

Its main characteristics are:

- power orientation
- personal relationships

- entrepreneurial
- affinity/trust
- power of person

CRAIG'S DIALOGUE: DEDICATION	
MS. LEWIS:	As you know we've had many complaints about Mr. Barzini.
MRS. FERMI:	What kind of complaints?
MS. LEWIS:	He's very slow in his work and some of our people aren't getting paid promptly.
MRS. FERMI:	Yes. Mr. Barzini's been with us a great many years; he's not as efficient as he used to be. His age is beginning to catch up with him.
MS. LEWIS:	So you agree?
MRS. FERMI:	Definitely. After so many years of dedicated service we can't expect him to perform as he used to. We'll be hiring someone new.
MS. LEWIS:	That's good to know. But I feel badly for Mr. Barzini. How's he taking it?
MRS. FERMI:	Taking it?
MS. LEWIS:	Losing his job, I mean.
MRS. FERMI:	Oh, he's not losing his job.

The Eiffel Tower

This role-orientated culture is characterized by a high degree of formalization together with a high degree of centralization and is symbolically represented by the Eiffel Tower. It is steep, stately, and very robust. Control is exercised through systems of rules, legalistic procedures, assigned rights and responsibilities.

Bureaucracy and a high degree of formalization make this organization inflexible. Respect for authority is based on the respect for functional position and status. The bureau or desk has depersonalized authority.

In contrast to the highly personalized family, members in the Eiffel Tower are continuously subordinated to universally applicable rules and procedures. Employees are very precise and meticulous. Order and predictability are highly valued in the process of managing the organization. Duty is an important concept for an employee in this role-orientated culture. It is a duty one feels within oneself, rather than an obligation toward a particular individual.

Procedures for change tend to be cumbersome, and this role-orientated organization is slow to adapt to change.

Its main characteristics are:

- role orientation
- power of position/role
- job description/evaluation
- rules and procedures
- order and predictability

CRAIG'S DIALOGUE: BASICS

MISS. LI:	And as we have said, this was all part of the vision of our founder.
MR. HOLT:	I see. Well, Tsai International certainly has an interesting history. Perhaps now, if you don't mind, we could talk about how we might be able to do business together.
MISS. LI:	You have nothing to add?
MR. HOLT:	About us? Not really. As you know, we're a pretty young company, nothing like Tsai.
MISS. LI:	Well, then, as you say, we can talk about doing business. With your permission, we might begin by describing our organizational structure for you and how it reflects our company principles. And then perhaps you could do the same.
MR. HOLT:	I see. And then we can talk about specific terms?
MISS. LI:	Terms?
MR. HOLT:	You know, some of the basics?
MISS. LI:	But we are talking about basics.

The Guided Missile

This task-oriented culture has a low degree of centralization and a high degree of formalization. This rational culture is task- and project-oriented. "Getting the job done" with "the right man/woman in the right place" are favorite expressions. Organizational relationships are very results oriented, based on rational/instrumental considerations and limited to the specific functional aspects of the persons involved.

Achievement and effectiveness are valued above the demands of authority, procedures or people. Authority and responsibility are placed where the qualifications lie, and they may shift rapidly as the nature of the task changes. Everything in the culture is subordinated to an all-encompassing goal.

The management of the organization is seen predominantly as a continuous process of successfully solving problems. The manager is a team leader, the commander of a commando unit, in whose hands lay absolute authority. This task-oriented culture, because of its flexibility and dynamism, is highly adaptive but at the same time is difficult to manage. Decentralized control and management contribute to the shortness of channels of communication. The task-oriented culture is designed for rapid reactions to extreme changes therefore, matrix and project types of organizations are favored designs.

Its main characteristics are:

- task orientation
- power of knowledge/expertise
- commitment to tasks
- management by objectives
- pay for performance

CRAIG'S DIALOGUE: A POSSIBLE CANDIDATE	
MS. MILLER:	Have you finished writing that job advertisement yet?
MRS. DE JESUS:	Not quite.
MS. MILLER:	Don't take too long. Filling that vacancy is a priority.
MRS. DE JESUS:	I agree. Actually, I think I know of a possible candidate.
MS. MILLER:	You do? Who?
MRS. DE JESUS:	He's my youngest nephew, Eduardo. A good boy.
MS. MILLER:	Great! Tell him to apply.

The Incubator

This culture is like a leaderless team. This person-oriented culture is characterized by a low degree of both centralization and formalization. In this culture the individualization of all related individuals is one of the most important features. The organization exists only to serve the needs of its members.

The organization has no intrinsic values beyond these goals. It is an instrument to the specific needs of the individuals in the organization. Responsibilities and tasks within this type of organization are assigned primarily according to the member's own preference and needs. The structure is loose and flexible and control takes place through persuasion and mutual concern for the needs and values of other members.

Its main characteristics are:

- person-oriented
- power of the individual
- self-realization
- commitment to oneself
- professional recognition

> **CRAIG'S DIALOGUE: THE THINKER**
>
> RICHARD: Has Claude submitted his final draft yet?
> ISABELLE: No, he's still working on it. You know Claude, always thinking and pondering.
> RICHARD: But I needed that report last week.
> ISABELLE: I know. Claude never meets his deadlines; it's a real problem. But his ideas are so wonderful, aren't they?
> RICHARD: I've complained about him twice to Monsieur Cardin, but he doesn't do anything.
> ISABELLE: You've complained. Why?

The corporate culture model also has links with the ideographic dimensional model explained in previous chapters. Thus the relationship between employees in the Family or Incubator tends to be diffuse and in the Eiffel Tower and Guided Missile more specific. Status is ascribed more in Family and Eiffel Towers and achievement orientation in Guided Missile and Incubator organizations.

Studies often invite participants to describe the tensions they feel in actual business life and then relate them to the tensions between current and ideal cultures. For example, as an actual business tension: "I feel that our organization is so much focused on next quarter's results, we don't have enough time to be creative and come up with our next generation of innovations." This example would translate the current corporate culture as a Guided Missile and the dominant profile as an Incubator.

We often find that a extant organizational culture has developed because it is the context best suited the main dilemmas their leader(s) were facing in business. Thus an Incubator culture is often the result of a leader who strives for a core value of entrpreneurship and innovation while having an envisoned future of becoming the most pathbreaking organization in the field of cross-cultural management thinking and consulting. A Guided Missile culture is a much better context for leaders who want to help clients gain the highest return on their investments in the financial service sector, holding a core value of integrity and transparency.

However business environments and challenges are changing continuously. Once an organizational culture has established itself, it creates new dilemmas (or its changing environment will) on a higher level. For example, a dominant Incubator culture can create a business environment where many innovative ideas are born but where the management and commercialization of these borrows from aspects of a more market-sensitive and directed Guided Missile culture. Conversely, a dominant Guided Missile culture can lead to an environment where employees are so guided by market price that it needs a Family culture to create a necessary longer term vision and commitment.

Transformation away from a Guided Missile culture

The challenge is to find an approach that will be effective when the surrounding culture is not compatible with this type of logic. We recall an American manager of Eastman Kodak who had launched a very successful program in Rochester, New York. After launching the same formula in Europe, in great despair he said:

"These French and Germans are unbelievably inflexible. I have done a whole round of meetings in Europe and within each of the countries many seemed very much supportive of our vision. Okay, the Germans had some problems with process. They wanted to know all the details of the procedures and how they were connected to the envisioned strategy. The French, in turn, were much more worried about the unions and how to keep their people motivated. As internal consultants and management we left with the idea that we were all agreed on the approach. When I came back some three month later to check how the implementation was going, I noticed nothing had been started in France and Germany. Nothing! What a disappointment!"

Anyone with a little sensitivity for cross-cultural matters would have predicted this. Germans often believe in vision, but without the proper structures, systems, and procedures that make this vision live, nothing will happen. Germans have a "push" culture. You push them in a certain direction. They are not so easily "pulled" in a direction compared to North Americans. You give them a task and they follow as lemmings, especially when you pay them well to do so.

Transformation away from a Family culture

This is a situation we observed frequently when challenges arise for Western organizations in their effort to globalize their activities. Consider an American organization that thinks its Singaporean management takes too long to make a decision. Consensus is fine, but it doesn't serve well in times of urgency. The converse is that the Singaporeans think that the Americans make decisions too fast and with insufficient thought, which therefore (no wonder) leads to problems during implementation—partly because too few people have been consulted.

In contrast, we can all recognize the quick-on-their-feet managers, who induce a "follow me, follow me," attitude. The response is likely to be a situation where, as with lemmings, you all fall over the cliff together. At the other extreme, we can observe Asians who spend far too much of their tim involving all levels of staff to gain consensus: this is referred to as the Lost Democratic Model.

The organization culture paradigm that reconciles these extremes is best described by the notion of the "servant leader." In this person you would find the father figure that is so popular in both Latin and Asian cultures. He (stereotypically a "he") acquires his authority from the way he serves his team through formulating and specifying the tasks of his colleagues with rigor and clarity.

Are the experiences the same?

Readers may wish to consider the nature of their experiences when purchasing a product or service where there are several alternative providers.

- If you plan to travel and there is a choice of airlines offering the same route at similar prices, why might you choose one carrier over another?

- If you plan to purchase a mobile phone and there is a choice of phone operators offering the same model of phone at the same prices, why might you choose one and not another?

Even if the options are the same price and apparently identical, in reality the differences you experience are often a function of the corporate culture of the organization. Travelling by British Airways is different to travelling by Virgin Atlantic in the same model of aircraft on the same route at the same price. The staff behave differently to the passengers and small things like meals are different. On one flight to New York with British Airways the author was approached by a member of staff with a clipboard as part of a market research study

> about customer satisfaction. On the return flight with Virgin Atlantic, the CEO Richard Branson who was seated in economy (yes !) came around and spoke to the passengers about their satisfaction with travelling on **his** airline!
>
> British Airways is more of an 'Eiffel Tower' with people given the role of market researcher. Virgin Atlantic is more an Incubator/Guided Missile of course. And yes, where the author has the option, he now travels by Virgin Atlantic.
>
> Organizations do much marketing/advertising about the features of their products and services but underestimate the significance of portraying appropriately their corporate culture. This affects more than just customer satisfaction –job recruitment for example – and how much potential employees are likely to be attracted to an organization.

Conclusion

Organizations usually underestimate the importance of how they influence what is achieved, staff motivation, how they are perceived by the outside world and how difficult corporate culture is to change.

The models described in this chapter help us to structure our understanding of what goes on in different organizations even where they are offering similar products and services.

However, like any other type of culture, the organizational culture is a dynamic concept, in constant evolution. Tensions arising from globalization are likely to result in organizations adapting into hybrid cultures, combining several models presented earlier.

RECAP

- Organizational culture follows the same patterns as other cultures, it is a dynamic process
- Its key role in organizations is to shape the identity of the group
- Many models have been set-up to assist our understanding
- Understanding the difference between real and idealized corporate cultures helps increase the feasibility of a corporate strategy
- In a process of merger and acquisition, controlling the creation of a new corporate culture is one of the keys to sustainable business

CASE STUDY 8.1: FRENCH RAILWAYS CHANGE TIMETABLE

Major engineering work will disrupt train services in France until at least 2015, the SNCF (France's National Railways Company) has warned in June 2011.

Some 85% of train times were due to be revised when the new winter timetable come into effect on December 11, to meet the regularity requirements set by the state while allowing enough time for works to be carried out. SNCF's website explained: "This is unprecedented in the history of the railway in Europe. 160,000 workers are mobilizing now to meet this challenge on behalf of four million passengers daily who all want safer and more punctual trains."

The timetable changes ranged from a few minutes to a quarter of an hour for some journeys. SNCF president Guillaume Pépy said that some connections would be "destroyed" and others created. The overhaul is necessary because the SNCF is entering what it calls a "particularly delicate" phase in its improvement work.

Track operator Réseau Ferré de France (RFF) is spending €13bn on replacing ageing tracks, many of which are more than 25 years old. The work is mostly carried out overnight, late in the evening and at weekends. RFF shed light on the project by saying: " It will make the network more efficient, but also improve the flow. With so-called "in-sync timing", schedules will be more readable, there will be more frequent trains and more regular flow of goods."

"In-sync timing" has already been proven in many countries. It aims to organize and coordinate rail schedules. The principle is to have trains at fixed times and intervals on the network: trains to the same destination will have the same gap between them, e.g. 10:13, 11:13, 12:13 etc. The result is a more synchronized network and better performance.

A complete rethink of the current timetable has also been prompted by the launch of a new "Rhine-Rhône" TGV link from Mulhouse to Lyon later that year, which should have a knock-on effect on other rail services across several regions.

These changes were supported by a €10m advertising and information campaign in Fall 2011.

SNCF was aware that the proposed changes might create havoc and appointed a mediator to smooth relations between the state-owned company and its passengers: "We regularly upgrade our schedule so you can communicate as soon as possible. SNCF manages over 15,000 trains daily over 37 000 slots

> ## CASE STUDY 8.1: FRENCH RAILWAYS CHANGE TIMETABLE
>
> journeys: some have not yet got their final timetable. A mediator of the new timetable was appointed, more information can be found on the specially created website: mediateurnouveauxhoraires2012.com .
>
> Jerome Dumetz
>
> *Discussion questions:*
>
> - Which corporate culture is presented here?
> - How is change managed in such organization?
> - What do you think the results of this project were?
> - Can you think of other similar examples ?
> - How does national culture influence organizational culture in this case?

CASE STUDY 8.2: CORPORATE CULTURE CHANGES AT STEEL-ROLL

The Steel-Roll factory is situated in a small town about 500 km from Moscow, Russia. It was founded in 1965 and now 8 factories employ 9,000 employees. The products from some factories are in high demand, while others need significant improvements (especially in the field of product quality) to be competitive.

A big holding company, built by a famous entrepreneur, acquired Steel-Roll three years ago and appointed several new managers: CEO, sales director, director of supply and director of logistics (all were young, between 27 and 35 years old and had a Western business education). The rest of the management team retained their positions, some of them having worked for the factory for more than 20 years.

Some ambitious goals and a development strategy from the parent company required many changes at the factory. Top-managers have implemented a serious restructuring during last three years: they changed the organizational structure and the remuneration system, launched special programmes to attract young specialists and introduced new corporate mission and values. However, reflecting on poor results, the CEO of Steel-Roll has recently admitted that many of these changes had only reached the minds of top management. The values and the traditional behavior of the majority of employees still did not support the new goals set for Steel-Roll by the parent company.

To deal with this problem the CEO established a special organizational unit for sociological research and hired two sociologists to work there. In three months this unit delivered its first report based on a factory-wide survey of employees. The main conclusions of the report were:

- The majority of employees evaluated the current state of affairs at the factory negatively and think top-management do not have a clear plan.

- There is a significant variation in the understanding of corporate goals; that many employees were badly informed about them.

- Many employees believed nepotism influences decision-making more than skills and qualifications.

- Employees demonstrated a low level of identification with the holding company and, therefore, have a low level of loyalty.

- Employees identified themselves strongly with the departments they work for. Shop "clans" exist. There is strong confrontation between marketing and production departments in particular.

CASE STUDY 8.2: CORPORATE CULTURE CHANGES AT STEEL-ROLL

The attitude towards all innovations from the holding HQ (e.g. corporate seminars, their corporate university, exchanges of experiences, the quality management system) is either negative or very suspicious.

Considering the results from the survey the CEO decided it was time to call for professional help and invited a team of management consultants to assist with the cultural changes. When the consultants arrived the very first meeting at the factory was with CEO who wanted to brief them, in detail, about the problem. He explained the goals of the holding company, the problems he faced at "Steel-Roll", as well as the actions he had taken over last three years aimed at changing the organization's culture. At the end of his speech, he exclaimed sadly:

"We carefully formulated our new values and mission, we put the posters outlining them on walls everywhere – in the canteen, the main hall, in each of the factory shops – and ... nobody follows them! They are not applied in practice!"

So what are your values and mission? – asked one of the consultants.

After a few seconds of awkward silence, during which the face of the CEO turned pale, he angrily replied:

"The values and mission are developed for the workers, not for me! I don't have to remember them!"

Tatiana Andreeva, PhD
Graduate School of Management - St Petersburg State University
Russia

Discussion questions:

- What might be the reasons for the problems described in the case?
- What types of corporate cultures are present?
- What cultural dimensions are highlighted in the problems faced by the CEO?
- What suggestions would you make to foster the change of corporate values?

Chapter 9: Teams and culture

CHAPTER CONTENTS

Highlights
Introduction

FINDING YOUR ROLE IN A TEAM
    A long-running experiment
    Plant
    Monitor Evaluator
    Coordinator
    Implementer
    Completer Finisher
    Resource Investigator
    Shaper
    Teamworker
    Specialist
    Find out your team roles

TEAM ROLES AND CULTURE
    Combination cultures

    Conclusion
    Recap
    Workshop 9.1: Create your dream team!

CHAPTER 9

TEAMS AND CULTURE
By Meredith Belbin

Highlights:

After reading this chapter, you should be able to:

- Understand that a successful team is composed of people with different preferred behavior.
- Understand that we all have preferred team behavior, and we can talk about it in terms of Team Roles.
- Understand the strengths and weaknesses of each of the nine Team Roles.
- Understand that a team containing too many of one particular Team Role may result in a culture of its own being created.

Introduction

What makes some teams succeed, and others fail? This question resulted in years of research, culminating in the understanding that a team needs to be balanced in terms of Team Role behavior if it is to be successful. This chapter looks at; the nine Team Roles in detail, and what they contribute to a team; how to spot a team with a culture dominated by one of the Team Roles, and what to expect from it. For team work to be successful it must be remembered that a team is not a bunch of people, but a congregation of individuals, each of whom has a role that is understood by other members.

FINDING YOUR ROLE IN A TEAM

So often we need to work in teams, be it in a study group, part of a student organization/body, a field trip, or in a place of work. It is imperative that the team works efficiently, and that all members have a valued role. The main stumbling block may be that it is difficult to understand individuals' strengths; understand what they can bring to the team. The main tool you have at your disposal is language, but why doesn't this always seem to work out? Although communication is crucial, the language we use is often prone to ambiguity and misinterpretation, which can unwittingly cause offense or simply confuse. Comments about others can be subjective, simplistic, and unhelpful when it is necessary to promote an effective teamworking environment. Instead, a common, meaningful language is required to bridge the gap between ourselves and our team members.

A long-running experiment

A unique study of teams took place at Henley Management College, UK, in the 1970s. The question posed was, "What makes some teams succeed and others fail?" The upshot was a ten-year period of observational research using a simulation. The simulation was a management game designed at Henley to reproduce work life. It contained all the principal variables that typify the problems of decision making in a business environment. The experiment was designed along scientific lines with careful measurement at each stage. Those participating were invited to take psychometric tests, plus a test of high-level reasoning ability (called CTA, the Critical Thinking Appraisal). Teams of various designs were composed on the basis of these individual test scores. Every half-minute, the contribution of the person speaking was recorded and classified into one of seven categories by trained observers. At the end of the exercise, which ran off and on throughout a week, the results of each team (operating as a company) were presented financially, which allowed more effective and less effective "companies" to be compared. What was at first deemed to be likely was that high-intellect teams would succeed where lower-intellect teams would not. However, the outcome of this research was that certain teams, predicted to be excellent based on intellect, failed to fulfill their potential. In fact, it became apparent by looking at the various combinations that it was not intellect, but balance, that enabled a team to succeed. Successful "companies" were characterized by the compatibility of the roles that their members played while unsuccessful companies were subject to role conflict. Using information from psychometric tests and the CTA, predictions could be made on the roles that individuals played and ultimately on whether the company would be more likely to figure among the winners or losers. One interesting point to observe from the experiment was that individuals reacted very differently within the same broad situation. It is a common experience that individual differences can cause a group to fall apart. People just don't fit in. On the other hand, variations in personal characteristics can become a source of strength if they are recognized and taken into account. So understanding the nature of these differences can become an essential first step in the management of people, providing one can recognize what is useful for a given situation and what is not. The most successful companies tended to be those with a mix of different people, i.e., those with a range of different behaviors. In fact, eight distinct clusters of behavior turned out to be distinctive and useful. These eight were called Team Roles, and, in fact, a ninth based on specialist knowledge was to emerge later.

1. Plant
2. Monitor Evaluator
3. Co-ordinator
4. Implementer
5. Completer Finisher
6. Resource Investigator
7. Shaper
8. Teamworker
9. Specialist

These team roles have been used in organizations and teams across the world ever since. They have been immensely useful in making teams more effective. Most important is the way they can be of great use to you as a working individual. It is up to you to decide which roles to play and which to avoid. For a team to succeed, all roles must be played by at least one person, although some individuals can play several roles.

A team role was defined as a tendency to behave, contribute, and interrelate with others in a particular way The following are the nine team roles and how you will recognize each one.

Plant

Plants are imaginative and unorthodox. Plants generate initial ideas. Plants are so called for historical reasons. In the management exercise, it was discovered that there was no initial spark unless a creative individual was "planted" in each company, so giving each a chance of success. Good ideas are always valuable when problems are complex. In an office, Plants are easy to pick out. They are unconventional in their thinking, providing imaginative and original lines of thought when the team is stuck for ideas. They are there to offer the vital "eureka!" moments and, as is the nature of such thought processes, they are frequently up in the clouds as they examine things in their own particular way. Such time spent in off-the-mark thinking is needed. In order to recognize their full potential, Plants need a position where they are allowed to be creative, producing ideas like welcome fruit to be harvested by others in the team. So, for a person to be a true Plant, he or she must have a creative disposition and be able to think laterally. This kind of behavior is not always appreciated in structured organizations, however, as it tends to rock the boat. Yet it is the Plant who can offer the seed of an idea that leads to greater things, and without that seed, a team will stagnate. This said, the other extreme can cause a different kind of stalemate. With too many Plants in the mix, liaison and cooperation will be severely limited, with each off in their own little worlds.

Monitor Evaluator

Monitor Evaluators are logical, discriminating, and always make the right decision. The Monitor Evaluator is a very logical, analytical being—typically a high performer on the Watson-Glaser Critical Thinking Appraisal, which was one of the tests used at Henley to create the simulations. Monitor Evaluators will take the ideas of a Plant and subject them to the most intense scrutiny, taking into account all facets in an unemotional way. Sometimes overcritical, frequently skeptical, they nevertheless provide a reasoned mind that curbs excessive enthusiasm. Without a Monitor Evaluator to put a rein on the Plant, the most ridiculous ideas might be allowed to go further than they should, wasting time and money. Monitor Evaluators are represented by the Belbin icon as an all-seeing eye. Spatially, we often think of them as positioned slightly outside the group. This is not to say that they are isolated. They are likely to be the first to be called upon whenever a discerning view is needed. What they possess, however, is sufficient emotional detachment to prevent their judgment from becoming clouded. A good Monitor Evaluator knows when criticism is appropriate. Here is a neat test of any Monitor Evaluator. If your enthusiastic cry of, "I have an idea…" is received with thoughtful nodding, then ten tough questions on how it will work, how much it will cost, and whether it has already been done, they're doing the required job as a Monitor Evaluator. On the other hand, if your suggestion is met with: "NO! NO! IT WON'T WORK, I TELL YOU, IT WON'T WORK!" before you're through the door, you're dealing with a pessimist rather than a Monitor Evaluator. The difference? A Monitor Evaluator builds skepticism on logic; a pessimist doesn't. A mature Plant will welcome the criticism of a good Monitor Evaluator and modify a proposed strategy. But it can be a sensitive meeting of attitudes. When the Plant's originality meets the inalienable logic of the Monitor Evaluator, sparks are likely to fly. Then it's time for some mediation.

Coordinator

Coordinators clarify goals, promote decision making, and involve others in appropriate ways. The Coordinator excels in getting the best from any team of people, which is why what is needed is a mature, confident individual who will spread a feeling of calm around the group. Regardless of rank, Coordinators are naturally suited to chairing meetings because of their capacity to manage and develop other members of the team. Because they are able to identify others' talents, Coordinators possess skills at delegating work and choosing the most suitable team member to take on a particular task or responsibility. In a meeting or discussion, they make sure that everyone is given a chance to make their contribution. If a Plant is struggling to explain a new idea, and the Monitor Evaluator is proving overly dismissive, the Coordinator will hopefully step in to facilitate communication and progress between the two. The Plant, Monitor Evaluator, and Coordinator could happily work as a small unit, generating and vetting ideas in a cooperative and constructive way. But this unit would be unproductive, since none of them actually do any work! Enter the Implementer, someone who's focused on the task, and to whom the Coordinator can entrust the organization and follow-through of the project.

Implementer

Implementers are disciplined, systematic, and love structure. So nobody is getting on and doing anything. Sound familiar? This is when the diligence and the methodical approach of the Implementer proves welcome. Perhaps not the highest-profile member of the team, this is a hardworking individual, without whose efforts the team's ideas would go nowhere. It is commonly observed that people choose the bits of work they like doing and ignore the rest. Not so for the Implementer, who will do what needs to be done for the good of the company. The Belbin icon for this team role is a cog, an essential part of the infrastructure or organization—someone who gets things moving and then keeps the ball rolling. Unlike the scatty Plant, this person's desk is likely to be organized, with everything filed methodically by size and color. There is, however, a price to be paid. Once you've got a cog moving, the process of trying to make it move in another direction is difficult. Implementers should do well in the army: they like organization and effective processes that produce good, reliable results. Shaking things up and doing things differently will inevitably interrupt this efficiency at an operational level, and this can make the Implementer slow to respond to change or even resistant to it altogether.

Completer Finisher

Completer Finishers are anxious people who worry about standards and detail. They're perfect...need to find a needle in a haystack? That is the challenge to which your resident Completer Finisher is well placed to respond. Here's another team role to be found hard at work. Completer Finishers are painstakingly meticulous, investing their close attention and bringing their love of accuracy to bear on every detail of a plan, product, or report. They'll act as quality control—editing, checking, and rechecking until they are completely satisfied with the final outcome. The irony about the Completer Finisher is that they can be so obsessed with quality that they fail to finish in time. They polish rather than finish. A copy editor is highly likely to be a Completer Finisher, or you'll find it somewhere prominent in their team role profile. Whereas creative team roles might lose interest after they have penned the article and brought the initial idea to fruition, Completer Finishers see the job as just beginning. They will make sure that any spelling or grammatical errors have been removed and that all the nuts and bolts of the operation have been correctly tightened. It is important to realize, when you're dealing with Completer Finishers, that their behaviors are often driven by anxiety, even when this might be masked. The Completer Finisher will worry until a satisfactory result has been achieved and deadlines met. Anxiety is the opposite of complacency, so you can be sure your Completer Finisher won't be a cocky, laissez-faire person. The tendency to check and double-check, however, comes at a cost. That cost is to be obsessive, coupled with a reluctance to delegate work to others. This may result in an overloaded Completer Finisher who is likely to fall victim to stress unless protected by others in the team.

So you have a finished product: created by the Plant, examined by the Monitor Evaluator, produced by the Implementer, and checked by the Completer Finisher, with the Coordinator ensuring that the team is working and communicating well and that they are listening to one another. But what are your competitors up to? Could you be buying your materials more cheaply? How are you going to market the product? Can you seek advice from someone who has managed a similar project before? With only the team roles we have discussed so far, the team would be at risk of becoming very insular. What is needed is someone who is willing to branch out and look outside the team for information and ideas.

Resource Investigator

Resource Investigators are enthusiastic, inquisitive, and explore opportunities. If the Plant is the initial "eureka!" light bulb, the Resource

Investigator is more like a sack marked "Stolen!" What the Plant creates within one organization, the Resource Investigator will borrow and improve from another. The striking thing about Resource Investigators is their bold and outgoing nature, countering the Monitor Evaluator's pessimism with optimism. The downside of this optimism is that, like the Plant, they risk being euphoric and failing to follow through, losing interest, and becoming bored quickly. Yet Resource Investigators are greatly valued for their ability to attract new business with their energy and enthusiasm. They possess an inquisitive nature. Not only are they good at finding out about where to source a necessary item, they also have persuasive skills that can be ideal for selling. Studies have shown that Resource Investigators are more successful than other team roles in gaining job offers. They are also quite effective being self-employed as they source the market and spot opportunities. Resource Investigators are sometimes described as "never in the office, but when they are, they always seem to be on the phone." The other side of enthusiasm can be boredom, and this is why Resource Investigators sometimes need to be prodded in order to continue the momentum that otherwise may fade and die. Delivery can be their downside, so this is an area where they need to rely on others.

Shaper

Shapers are dynamic and make things happen. When it comes to reaching a goal, Shapers will get you there. Quickly. Shapers are often admired for the way they manage to get things done and succeed in getting people moving, but their tactics for doing this are not always welcome. They're extroverts, like Resource Investigators, but more highly strung. Being no-nonsense individuals, they are not afraid to be blunt. One of the most useful things a Shaper brings to a team is the great injection of energy and urgency. Shapers make their mark because they are achievers and are determined to find a way round any obstacle and bring others with them. Their downside is that they often come across as aggressive. Too many Shapers, like too many cooks, will spoil the party. Shapers need to be thinly spread. If they are not careful, they can win the battle and lose the war. They need an ally to work with who diffuses tension. The Teamworker would be a good choice.

Teamworker

Teamworkers are diplomatic, popular, and avert friction. Enter the Teamworker, the most diplomatic and sensitive member of the team. If you've just been offended by your resident Shaper, or had your Coordinator load work at your door, the Teamworker is the person who will make you feel better about it. A Teamworker makes sure everyone is comfortable, lightens the atmosphere, and provides an empathetic, listening ear. They use intuition to promote a good atmosphere. A gifted Teamworker is likely to be a popular member of the team. As well as caring deeply about their colleagues and the team as a whole, they offer versatility and diplomacy. When the Shaper rubs the team the wrong way, the Teamworker can act as a foil, cementing good relationships between colleagues and taking on the work that needs to be done. The downside to this is that because Teamworkers are keen to please, they can fail to impart reality when news is bad. This can also lead to indecisiveness when a course of action might upset others.

The ninth team role

In the original experimental studies at Henley, prior knowledge and experience had no part to play in the management exercise that had been designed. No team, therefore, enjoyed any starting advantage in the exercise. In practice, such a situation is entirely artificial. Every project needs to start from somewhere, which means getting someone involved who knows a lot about the subject. By nature, a specialist is someone prepared continually to expand and develop knowledge in a particular area in order to become an expert in his or her field. As Specialist is a team role, we spell it with a capital letter.

Specialist

Specialists are professionally dedicated, single-minded, and prepared to build up their knowledge. Because the word specialist is already in common usage, the Specialist tends to be the most misunderstood team role of all. The key thing to remember about the Specialist is that—in team role terms at least—it is a way of behaving just like any other team role and is not a job title. It therefore doesn't mean someone with a particular academic or technical background. A Specialist in this new sense is a self-reliant individual dedicated to an area of expertise—a real fount of knowledge determined to know absolutely everything there is to know about a particular topic. Leaving the workplace for a moment, it might be easy to think of examples of this type of behavior in everyday life. The Specialist is the kind of person who, on purchasing a new mobile phone or DVD player, reads the product manual from start to finish in order to discover how to use all of its various functions. The Specialist displays a thirst for knowledge—an attribute that makes this individual invaluable in many situations. A Specialist does not necessarily denote someone who has had a particular academic or technical education. Remember, the subject of team roles deals with natural behavior, not credentials. Technical knowledge and interest are invaluable qualities in the right place. But too much of it soon becomes off-putting to others who don't share the same fascination with the subject. Loss of interest becomes difficult to disguise, and yet you will commonly find that the Specialist will take no notice but carry on as before.

Find out your team roles

All nine team roles have now been covered. A mix of these roles is needed in every organization if it is to work well. Each of these roles can be of value in the right place. What is important is that every team member becomes a good example of a preferred type. We have also established that each role comes with its strengths and weaknesses. These weaknesses need not always present a problem. Provided they are recognized and admitted, they can be balanced by a team role strength in another. If you wish to make the most of yourself at work and be at your most effective, then you will need to identify your personal set of team role strengths. We all have our own combination of top roles. This fingerprint will underlie your own particular work style.

Measure yourself through self and observers: Why the perception of others matters

Team roles focus on behaviors. If our interests were confined to personality, it could be argued that no one else could know or understand you better than you know yourself. With behavior, however, it's a different story. While you might think you are sending out a certain message, other people might read your actions and words very differently, and in that case, it's important to know. While your self-perception can tell you what you think of yourself and what your aspirations might be, simply relying on your own perception of your behavior is unlikely to improve self-awareness (and won't prove as interesting!). What matters in the workplace is what your managers, colleagues, and subordinates think of you, since you are likely to be assigned tasks on that basis. For a broader view of how you really are and how others see you, Observer Assessments are desirable. They can indicate how others view you. They can help modify your overall team roles to give a more accurate picture of how you come across in your current team.

TEAM ROLES AND CULTURE

Once the successes of a particular individual or group are known, it is tempting to try to reproduce those characteristics that are seen to have brought the company success. The attributes of a particular employee or group are then taken further, to the organization at large. They are hailed as invaluable to the company's culture and become integral to recruitment processes, which are then set up to identify and select particular team roles. Very soon, the organization has a cloned culture, with everyone taking the same approach. Not only will the company discover that it is deficient in other roles, but also, as cracks start to appear, the weaknesses of the dominant team role are likely to become more and more pronounced. Organizations will develop in a particular way, according to the types of person they prefer to recruit. Like chooses like. Hence, some cultures are dominated by a particular team role type.

A **Teamworker** might be the model employee in an easygoing company where attention is paid to the atmosphere at work. With concern to ensure that everyone gels, conflict is avoided almost at all costs.

Contrastingly, **Shapers** are likely to be competitive. If an organization continues to recruit Shapers (and only Shapers) on the basis that they are hard-driving, high-profile, and successful individuals, they are likely to end up with a culture plagued by internal conflict. If other team roles exist within the organization, they will be neglected or overwhelmed. Shapers are used to calling the shots and nothing stirs them more than the presence of other Shapers. Because other team roles barely figure, there is no teamwork and complications multiply.

With too many **Coordinators**, a different situation will prevail. Impressed by an interviewee's broad perspective and maturity, managers may unwittingly recruit a surfeit of Coordinators, each vying to play the same role. At worst, the culture will be a manipulative one, with each person trying to persuade colleagues into doing their bidding. With Coordinators being natural delegators, productivity is likely to be low, with everyone trying to limit their own workload. The fallout is liable to cause resentment among those forced to take on more than their fair share. Any Implementers present will be reluctant to put their shoulder to the wheel when others are quick to take the credit for accomplishments. With the vast majority of Coordinators favoring a broad outlook, details may fall by the wayside, as specialized knowledge is rejected in favor of generalizations.

A culture of criticism, or even cynicism, can often be attributed to an excessive number of **Monitor Evaluators** in an organization. Like the maturity of the Coordinator, the logical, analytical brain of the **Monitor Evaluator** might prove a promising attribute at interview. However, cloning Monitor Evaluators will mean that new ideas are few and far between, since they are likely to be quashed before being given a chance to air. This dampened spirit will affect the activities of others, meaning that creative individuals, like Plants, will be afraid to speak up for fear of having their ideas ridiculed or rejected out of hand. If such "paralysis by analysis" is left to continue, the organization will soon find itself stagnating and seemingly unable to account for its unmotivated workforce.

A sales company commonly hires **Resource Investigators** for their enthusiasm, persuasiveness, and "gift of gab." With such a lively staff and all phone lines buzzing, bosses might wonder why the profits are not as high as anticipated. In spite of the enthusiasm shown for landing the initial sale, goodwill is soon lost. Few structures will be in place for ensuring customer care and follow-up. Projects will seem to have been abandoned in mid-flow. Customers may feel that they have a great contact at the company but will eventually become frustrated by their gradual loss of interest.

A culture with too many **Plants** might also prove inefficient, but for very different reasons. It might be tempting to recruit Plants for their innovative, pioneering mentality and unconventional thinking. However, where too many Monitor Evaluators cause stagnation through over-criticism, Plant culture destabilizes any structure already in place. A true Plant is a rare breed but worth holding out for—one brilliant idea far surpasses hundreds of indifferent or average ones. Process industries are usually drawn to an Implementer culture, favoring employees who are efficient at getting the job done and loyal to the company. But the upshot of this may not be what is desired.

Too many **Implementers** could mean an over-structured and inflexible culture. Routine procedures will leave little room for new ideas, and much will be sacrificed in the name of productivity. Employees will be given little scope for initiative. With Implementer managers interfering at operational levels, employees will be resentful that they are not respected or trusted to get on with the work.

In a **Completer Finisher** culture, high standards, rather than efficiency, take priority. Levels of anxiety are likely to be high, and, if there is little or no calming Coordinator influence, this anxiety could be severely detrimental to morale. At worst, the drive for perfectionism will turn into obsession. Employees are likely to work long hours, getting in early and staying late to make sure they have got every last detail right. Since so many people are competing to have the last say, a culture of penny-pinching or splitting hairs is likely to develop. Individuals will be eager to claim ownership of work and reluctant to delegate it. The price paid is that consultation will be rare, with individuals or departments operating as "lone rangers" without reference to each other.

Employing too many **Specialists** produces its own typical problems. The willingness to develop and maintain specialized knowledge might be highly desirable for a pharmaceutical company recruiting scientists and technicians, for example. But if there are no Shapers or Resource Investigators to drive the company forward or consider what is needed in the market, individuals will become bogged down in project work and overprotective of their areas of special interest.

Combination cultures

Knowing the culture of the organization will give you insight into the likely advantages and pitfalls and how you can fit in and progress. The tables below demonstrate the positive and negative features commonly produced by certain team role combinations.

Positive Features

Culture of Leaders	Culture Focus	Culture Type
Co-ordinators Team Workers	Development of Human Resources	Human Relations Model
Plants Resource Investigators	Expansion, Transformation	Open Systems Model
Completer Finishers Implementers	Consolidation, Equilibrium	Internal Process Model
Monitor Evaluators Shapers	Maximisation of Output, Competitiveness	Rational Goal Model

Fig. 9.1 – Positive features of team roles combinations

Negative Features

Culture of Leaders	Culture Focus	Culture Type
Co-ordinators Team Workers	Permissiveness Unproductive Discussion	Country Club
Plants Resource Investigators	Premature responsiveness	Tumultuous anarchy
Completer Finishers Implementers	Procedural sterility	Frozen bureaucracy
Monitor Evaluators Shapers	Exhaustive hostility	Oppressive Sweat Shop

Fig. 9.2 – Negative features of team roles combinations

The stronger the culture, the more resistant it will be to outsiders. However, sometimes it takes an outsider to provide a fresh perspective, which is why many companies use external public relations agencies.

Remember the adage: "In the kingdom of the blind, the one-eyed man is king." The one person who can see what is needed, if eventually recognized, will be much appreciated. In a "country club" scenario, practicality and organization will stand out. In a "tumultuous anarchy," you need someone who thinks about fundamentals in an organized fashion. A "frozen bureaucracy" invites an enterprising individual to bring in new life and vitality. The "oppressive sweat shop" demands a person with a humanistic outlook, who can lead others to a more acceptable way of managing people. Of course, acting as a catalyst is far more demanding than fitting in with an existing culture. A successful change agent needs moral courage, a slice of luck, and support from above.

Conclusion

Success in a team begins with self-knowledge and understanding of others. Team Roles can help gain mutual understanding, by providing a common language, and giving everyone a part to play. For a team to be successful, each team member should be able to declare their Team Role preferences, to enable the team to work out how tasks should be distributed. This process also highlights where the gaps and overlaps occur. Too many Shapers, for example, may create a team of hard driving individuals that breeds competiveness. A lack of Shapers however will mean a lack of drive and determination. Communication is key. Being prepared to play a role that may not be your preferred way of working for the good of team makes you a valuable team member.

Remember – Nobody is perfect, but a team can be.

....

RECAP

- There are a finite number of behaviors that are useful to a team.
- You should try to understand how each of these roles fit the overall need of the team
- Each of the nine Team Roles has strengths and associated weaknesses.
- Get feedback from others to understand how you contribute
- Be aware of any Team Role culture and consider where you fit in.

....

WORKSHOP 9.1: CREATE YOUR DREAM TEAM!

Working as team is frequently required, especially when working on particular projects. This short workshop will help you understand that once the elements of the project are identified, the allocation to the most effective team member, depending on their Team Role preferences, means more effective working.

First of all, think of a real or imaginary project and identify the stages that the project will follow, step by step. For example:

- A hypothesis was agreed upon
- Various approaches/solutions were put forth
- Ideas discussed - best one agreed on
- The idea was outsourced to check viability
- A plan was put in place

Then decide which Team Role(s) would be useful at each stage of the project, and which would be unhelpful (e.g. Plants and Resource Investigators for ideas, Co-ordinators and Implementers for organizing people and work, Monitor Evaluators for strategic decision making etc.).

Use the table below as a template.

TEAMS AND CULTURE

WORKSHOP 9.1: CREATE YOUR DREAM TEAM!

Stage of project	Team Roles you would like to be involved	Reasons why
Example: Brainstorming	Plant Resource Investigator	Will come up with ideas, original or 'borrowed' from others!

Fig. 9.3 Workshop template

Chapter 10: Reconciliation of Cultural Dichotomies

CHAPTER CONTENTS

Highlights
Introduction

MEASURING CULTURE IS CULTURALLY BIASED
    Dichotomizing is extremely prevalent in our studies of culture
    When cultural studies can be applied to a hard science like physics
    Reconciling dilemmas, along with most of the contributors to this book.
    The West avoids contradictions, but the East welcomes and embraces them.
    West and East are mirror images of each other.
    There are ways of measuring cultures that combine West with East

RECONCILIATION EXAMPLES
    Reconciling standard and adaptation
    Reconciling individual creativity and team spirit
    Reconciling passion and control
    Reconciling specific and diffuse
    Reconciling being and doing
    Reconciling sequential and synchronic
    Reconciling inner and outer forces

Conclusion
Recap
Workshop 10.1: Reconciling your own dilemmas

CHAPTER 10

RECONCILIATION OF CULTURAL DICHOTOMIES
By Charles Hampden-Turner, Raymond Abelin and Haihua (Helen) Zhang

Highlights:

After reading this chapter, you should be able to:

- Understand that most cross-cultural researches are biased by Western values
- Recognize dichotomies when comparing cultures
- Comprehend the fundamental dichotomies between the West and the East
- Reconcile the extremes of the dimensions already presented

Introduction

In the West we have a persistent habit of dichotomising and polarizing to create exclusive ends of linear dimensions, so "objectivity" demands detachment from others and "freedom" an oppressor to be free from. This also affects our approach to culture. We tend to slice and dice an entire continuum and to treat its ends as specifics. This owes its origins in the hard science of Newtonian physics from which we have over-generalized. Fons Trompenaars and I have done this too, along with most of the scholars in this book.

This "specificity bias" turns processes into things and makes us fearful of contradictions, lest doubt be cast on our rationality. In contrast, the East, with its yin and yang embraces opposites gladly. Ruth Benedict, a noted anthropologist, solved the puzzle of why some American Indian tribes were happy and some close to despair. It was not the relative emphasis placed on selfish vs. unselfish behavior, but the likelihood that an unselfish person would be repaid by close companions, thus transcending the distinction. This was the synergistic secret of happiness.

East and West are mirror images of each other, reversing each other's values left to right and right to left. China discovered this in 1979 when embracing the market and reconciling Western values with its own. Witness the economic surge which resulted. All this is measurable as we will see through the concrete examples of success which follow.

MEASURING CULTURE IS CULTURALLY BIASED

The West has a persistent habit of dichotomizing along linear dimensions. The problem we wish to address concerns a difficult challenge in trying to understand culture. This originates from the fact that the methodologies we use *include* our own cultural preferences and biases. The idea that there are some lofty Olympian heights from which we can "objectively" view culture, some scientific stance that is somehow "culture free," is a delusion. Our very approach to culture is steeped in culture, *our* culture, and the methods we use to assess cultures different from our own are distorted by these same preferences. We have *culturally biased ways of measuring culture*.

This is illustrated by our attitude to objectivity and freedom. Let us consider objectivity as a cultural concept. The Japanese do not have it in their language and render the idea as *kyankkanteki*, "the guest's point of view." This suggests the somewhat superficial view of a relative stranger visiting a home, while *shukanteki*, or subjectivity, is rendered as "the host's point of view," which is surely better informed and more subtle. It appears not to have occurred to the Japanese that people should be treated *as if they were physical objects*. Or take the Chinese characters for the word freedom. This translates literally into "sitting at my door looking at the moon." Clearly this means the freedom to relax briefly from a life of toil, but this is not exactly what most of those raised in the West mean when they use this word. "Give me liberty or give me death!" is a rather different approach. The Chinese see freedom as freedom *for* enjoying a bit of rare leisure. Americans tend to see freedom as freedom *from* arbitrary rule and coercion.

The first sees freedom as inclusion. The second sees freedom as independence.

Dichotomizing is extremely prevalent in our studies of culture

American and European cross-cultural studies suffer from cultural biases that are systemic, not random, and these shape all our social sciences. One of the most prevalent of these, present in the work of most of those cited in this book, is the habit of dichotomizing. Ruth Benedict, Max Weber, Claude Levi-Strauss, Edward Hall, Geert Hofstede, Fons Trompenaars, and Charles Hampden-Turner all use dimensions with polarities at their ends. Indeed, the word definition means "to put an end to." We put an end to individualism by contrasting it with collectivism, and we cannot have both tendencies. It is not allowed! Meredith Belbin puts an end to one role by contrasting it to another. Mayo and Roethlisberger contrast formal with informal systems, required interaction with emergent interaction, and so on.

Max Weber famously contrasted *Gemeinschaft*, the intimate culture of the family, with *Gesellschaft*, the rational, impersonal calculus and culture of the workplace, with its contractual-legal orientation and its objectivity. Part of industrial modernization was growing out of the first into the second. Most of us recognize this dichotomy, and the younger Marx used it to define alienation at work in factories. There is only one drawback: *it does not apply to East Asian cultures at all.*

Not only are more than 90 percent of all companies in the Chinese Diaspora family companies, but the metaphor of the family is widely used even in publicly owned companies, with "fathers," "mothers," "aunts," "elder brothers," "elder sisters," and so on. The nickname for MITI (Ministry of International Trade and Industry) in Japan is "worried auntie." The most important value in Japanese business is *amae*. It means "indulgent affection between a senior and junior person of the same gender, a kind of developmental bond." *Sempai-kohai* is used in a Japanese business setting to denote an elder and younger brother relationship between a new employee and his appointed mentor. The Confucian family is everywhere!

Not only are some of the dichotomies we take for granted not applicable to East Asia, but East Asians dichotomize far less frequently than we do in Europe and America; their whole world is less polarized. There is the old story of the professor who diced a piece of cheese with a kitchen gadget and then wrote a learned dissertation on the cubic structure of cheese! Polarizing and dichotomizing the "data" (meanings things are given) is something we **do** to reality. It is not necessarily the way reality comes to us. Even the word data, Latin for "things given", assumes the shingle on the seashore while denying the continuous waves of an unbroken ocean.

One notable exception is the work of Ludwig Von Bertalanffy[111]. Regarded as one of the most important biologists of our time, he called his general system theory "a general science of wholeness." It describes its models in a qualitative language based upon his holistic worldview. He openly challenged and moved away from the traditional reductionism and promoted a new paradigm where "the whole is more than the sum of its parts."

When cultural studies can be applied to a hard science like physics

In theoretical physics there used to be a major dispute as to whether the ultimate nature of matter consisted of particles, little things or data, or whether it consisted of waves, diffuse and unbroken wholes with amplitude and frequency. It turned out that what we observed *depended on the methodology we used.* If you used a particle detector, low and behold, you would see particles! But if you used a wave detector, waves would mysteriously appear. What was happening is that phenomena were *reacting to the methodology being used.* If this happens, even in physics where phenomena are dead, it must be even more prevalent when what we are looking at is something alive. After all, the people we are studying have their own nervous systems and, if we approach them with professional detachment, they will surely respond in similar ways. If we approach them with engaging smiles, they will attach themselves to us. There is no way of *not* disturbing what we are studying.

---

111 L. von Bertalanffy, 1968, General System theory: Foundations, Development, Applications, New York

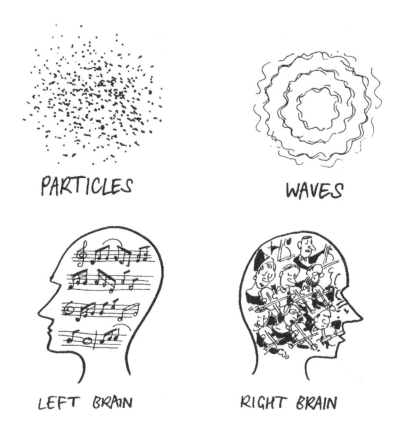

Fig. 10.1 - **Dual hemispheres and dual phenomena**

It was Niels Bohr who suggested the Principle of Complementarity[112]. Both views were equally valid, but each depended on the methods being used. Science was an *interaction* between the investigator and what was being investigated, and what was found would depend on the tools and the paradigm being used. He incorporated the Tao in his coat-of-arms. Werner Heisenberg also contributed his Uncertainty Principle[113]. We could exactly locate the *position* of a particle, but when we did so we would lose sight of its *momentum*. Or we could measure its momentum precisely but then we would lose sight of its position. It seems there are several precedents for the problems we face in measuring culture.

---

112 N. Bohr, 1985, A Centenary Volume, edited by A. P French and P.J. Kennedy, Harvard University Press

113 W. Heisenberg, 1927, Über den anschulichen Inhalt der quantentheoretischen Kinematik und Mechanik, Z. Phys.

We know that our brains are laterally specialized and that the left brain reduces and analyzes phenomena to bits and pieces, like the music notes seen above, while the right brain immerses itself in the whole experience. It is at least likely that what we see depends on which hemisphere we use most of the time. Helen Zhang (2008) reports that Chinese research subjects make greater use of their right-brain hemispheres compared to Western counterparts.

Reconciling dilemmas, along with most of the contributors to this book.

Trompenaars, Woolliams, and I have, for more than twenty-five years, presented our respondents with *dilemmas* (two propositions in conflict). So everything we have discovered is a *response to being presented with these dilemmas.* We sought to drive a wedge between values and then look at the pieces. I believe this analytic technique can be justified, but it certainly does *not* give us an unbiased view of culture. We have discovered dichotomies because we first produced them by pushing our respondents and forcing them to choose!

For example, in game theory, the Prisoner's Dilemma game presented by Juliette Tournand in the Prologue confronts the respondent with the stark choice of exploiting a fellow prisoner, being exploited by him, or compromising and receiving a lesser sentence. This dilemma is *imposed* on the prisoner by a researcher who seems to think we are all in jail at the mercy of a prosecutor and that those who successfully betray fellow captives will win. Is this an accurate portrait of American culture? One hopes not, but it clearly is what the investigator is assuming; otherwise its findings would be irrelevant.

The specificity bias identified by Trompenaars is a case in point. One of the more fruitful distinctions Trompenaars (1992) makes is between cultures that are specific (as in specific taxonomy of things) and cultures that are diffuse (as in a continuous wave-like process). I argue that this is a *very* crucial distinction, but notice the bias that has already crept into the distinction he has made. *He is assuming that specificity is something apart from diffusion.* In short, he is treating specificity—diffusion *in a specific manner,* chopping it in two. He is entitled to do this, of course, but he cannot at the same time claim to be free of cultural bias. He is steeped in it. Why should not specificity—diffusion be considered to be a continuum, a process, and everlasting movement, a circle of eternal return, as in the Tao or the yin yang symbol? Is this not every bit as real?

Note that specificity—diffusion helps to describe some of the dichotomies we have already touched on. Objectivity is specific while subjectivity is more diffuse. Freedom *from* is specific; freedom *for* is diffuse. Formal systems are specific, but informal systems are diffuse. Max Weber's *Gesellschaft* is specific while *Gemeinschaft* is diffuse. Particles are specific and waves diffuse. The left hemisphere reduces phenomena to specifics; the right hemisphere makes them into diffuse wholes.

The West avoids contradictions, but the East welcomes and embraces them.

Another major difference that we fail to notice is that we in the West tend to resist and dismiss contradictions of any kind. For example, most economists believe that at bottom we are all selfish and that sovereign self-interest is at the roots of our rational behavior. They embrace the dictum of Adam Smith, that the butcher and baker care for their customers not at all and are really bent on maximizing their own profits, so that serving customers is but a means to an end.

The whole point of Adam Smith's "invisible hand," pictured below, is to explain away one side of a contradiction. We all pursue self-interest but then a phantom hand transforms this into public benefit by accident! We benefit others as a side effect of competition. It is better not to think about cooperation at all but just about trying to get the better of our rivals. If we had to admit that our motives were mixed, sometimes concerned for others, sometimes for ourselves, how could "rational" conduct ensue?

Note just how far economists will go to maintain the concept of rationality! They will excise one half of human nature, ignoring that even self-interested American millionaires seem to renounce their riches and spend much of their lives giving these away.

The popularity of such books as *The Selfish Gene*[114] is that they explain away our willingness to die for those we love as a plot to perpetuate our own genes in preference to those of others! Our genes are selfishly perpetuating themselves when we save our child from drowning. In contrast, the Confucian ethic has no trouble with contradictions at all. We are partly self-seeking and partly unselfish, and the aim of life is to combine the two. There is no invisible hand. There are two *visible hands*, working together.

---

114   R. Dawkins 1976, The Selfish Gene, Oxford University Press

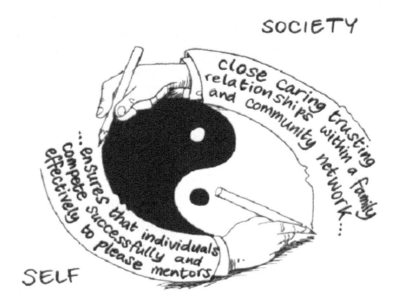

Fig. 10.2 – Two visible hands: the Confucian ethic

Ruth Benedict found her answer at the heart of contradiction and dilemma. An anthropologist who faced up to the lethal dichotomy at the heart of Western culture was Ruth Benedict, also featured in this book. She examined several American Indian tribes and recognized two as relatively happy and three as sunk in despair to the point of self-destruction. Unfortunately, a lifetime of methodology taught to her by her studies at American universities proved incapable of distinguishing the reasons for these very different outcomes. She especially concentrated on whether a tribe advocated or censured conduct that was selfish and whether they counseled unselfishness. She found that all the tribes varied in this respect, but the variance failed utterly to predict their differing levels of morale.

Perhaps it was because she was also a poet or perhaps it was her female consciousness. It could have been her exposure to Japanese culture about which she wrote *The Chrysanthemum and the Sword*, but she began to think diffusely, and when she did, the solution came to her. It was not the sheer amount of emphasis on selfishness, nor the strength of the norms promoting unselfishness. The answer lay in the space *between* these values. In the happy tribes, those *exhibiting unselfish behavior were promptly rewarded by reciprocity, gratitude, and increased social esteem, so that they were in effect benefiting themselves, and the difference between egoism and altruism*

RECONCILIATION OF CULTURAL DICHOTOMIES

was transcended. Benedict called this synergy, from the Greek *syn-ergo*, "to work together."

So Adam Smith got it half wrong. It is not simply that selfishness turns into selflessness when you enjoy helping another or when he or she increases your profits, but selflessness turns into self-regard when that person in turn expresses love and admiration for you. The two values *are one diffuse process* in addition to being polarities.

West and East are mirror images of each other.

By now, the mirror image hypothesis should be presented. This is illustrated below. I have taken Trompenaars' first three dimensions: universalism—particularism, individualism—community orientation and specific—diffuse, and held these up to a mirror. What this does is switch these values from left to right and from right to left, and it alters their relative priorities. This is what happens to your face when you look in the mirror. A slight mark on your left cheek is now on the right. An earring in your right ear is now on the left. One might think this would lead to rejoicing. They are very like us after all. In fact, the word sinister means left-handed. It is all very sinister, indeed! What are those astute Orientals up to?

Fig. 10.3 – The Asian mirror

For most Western cultures, the universal law or standard comes first, and the unique or exceptional occurrence comes second. Individuality precedes community, to the extent that Mrs. Thatcher doubted the very existence of society! Analyzing phenomena into supposed specifics precedes their reassembly into diffuse wholes. Yet in all or most of East Asia, this preference is reversed. Particular differences come first as do communities and diffuse wholes. In short, East Asia has the same values as we do but in a different sequence and order of priority. But the contrasts do not end here.

What is the opposite of a dichotomy? Surely it is a continuum. What is the opposite of a polarity? Is it not a relationship or connection? What is the opposite of linearity? Is it not circularity? So the cultural differences between West and East are as follows:

DICHOTOMY--------------------------CONTINUUM

POLARITY--------------------------RELATIONSHIP

LINEARITY--------------------------CIRCULARITY

We see this in the Tao or yin yang symbol where the dichotomy has become a continuum, the polarity has been joined into one relationship, and the lines have bent into arcs and from there into a circle. All this represents a challenge as to how we measure culture and assess it in a way that is fair to both. We must **not** abandon Western methodologies. We are what we are, and it is too late to change. On the other hand, we need to give full respect and credence to another way of thinking.

There is a most important distinction, a matter of life and death, between a diffuse culture that *excludes* specificity and a diffuse culture that *includes* specificity. China has always been diffuse in its thinking, but up to 1979, the death of Chairman Mao and the rise to power of the Gang of Four, this diffuse style adamantly rejected all Western-style specificity, especially markets with their tens of thousands of specific prices, far more than even the most intelligent government officials could handle.

China had suffered two extreme catastrophes, the Great Leap Forward and the Cultural Revolution, which between them left many millions dead. The ideology of pure Marxist-Leninism rejected any values derived from the West, along with business practices that had long been successful in the Chinese Diaspora, which when combined constituted even then the fourth largest economy in the world. The advantages of diffuse thinking are largely lost where this concept is polarized with specificity. What has happened is that diffuse thinking has been extolled but in a specific polarized manner.

How could this happen? We must remind ourselves that Marxism is a Western, enlightenment doctrine, penned by Marx in the British Museum. It was hostile to traditional Chinese culture and sought to overcome it. When Mao died, the country was exhausted and near bankrupt. Its ideology had failed. The Gang of Four was despised. It fell back on its ancient roots, on the ingenuity of its citizens living abroad but anxious to help.

In the countryside, peasants returned to the safety of their extended families, and Deng Xiaoping began to speak of the dual values of the Tao. It did not matter whether the cat was black or white so long as it caught mice. One country could have two systems. You must cross the river by feeling for the stones, i.e., every idea needed to be tested for its practicality. Intellectuals were proletarians after all! He wanted party members to get to the top through practical deeds not just pure thoughts. Socialism did not mean being poor. Socialism must and should prosper. He encouraged a flood of investment into free-trade zones. He invited the Diaspora with its traditional Chinese roots to come back home and reinvigorate the country. A diffuse system that *included Western values alongside Chinese ones* had been born. The socialist market-driven economy was part socialist, part capitalist, a potent new combination never seen in the world before.

In short, China's extraordinary feat of economic development owes its dynamism not to particularism replacing universalism, not to community orientation overcoming individualism, not to diffuse ways of thinking swamping specifics, but to these sets of twin values working with each other in synergy.

There are ways of measuring cultures that combine West with East

How then can we take the measure of East Asian cultures that will reveal their true power and significance? To illustrate our meaning, we have designed a methodology that is part Western and part East Asian. We will start with the very familiar Western method and then discuss how we might adapt this to our purposes. It begins with two Likert scales. We are measuring a desire for realism at work compared with the value of idealism. We ask, "Please indicate the extent to which you agree with the following statements."

➤ "Our work is realistic, practical, and very necessary"

Not true at all   Very true indeed

    1   2   3   4   5   6   7   8   9   10

➤ "Our work is idealistic, aspiring and inspiring."

Not true at all   Very true indeed

    1   2   3   4   5   6   7   8   9   10

We then invite the responent to locate him or herself on the grid below. Since we have changed the question somewhat, he or she may change the answer. To assist with placement on the grid, see the pop-up balloons.

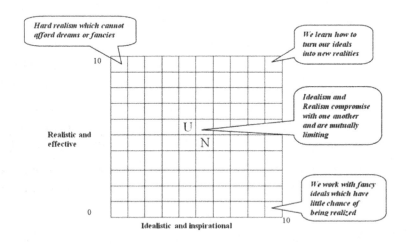

Fig. 10.4 – Realism and idealism on a two-dimensional grid

At top left, realism has got the best of idealism. At bottom right, idealism has got the best of realism. In the center, the two have had to compromise, and the result is moderate degrees of both values, which have frustrated one another. Only at top right have aspiring ideals become realities. The point is **not** that East Asians are more idealistic than we are in the West. The point is that it takes a diffuse, non-dichotomizing concept of culture to achieve our ideals. It is here that we find the saving wisdom of East Asia.

Note that we have given new meaning to the Chinese concept of *guanxi*, to the Japanese search for *wa* or harmony, to Ruth Benedict's search for the synergy at the heart of human happiness, to Maslow's "peak experience" where duty and pleasure, egoism and altruism, were transcended, to the "flow experience" of Mihaly Csikszentmihalyi[115].

The quantum revolution in physics has given us "packaged waves" or quanta, a fusion between particles and waves. There comes a point where contrasting values fuse and for a few short years cultures sparkle. Note we have captured the capacity of contrasting values to constitute a positive-sum game, to break out of dichotomy and create value not present before. Here is the secret of the world's Golden Ages, from the Greece of Pericles to the Tang dynasty of China, to the European Renaissance, to Shakespeare's England, to the Dutch Masters, to Paris at the turn of the nineteenth century, to the Apollo moon landing and the Camelot years of Kennedy. I suspect this may turn out to be the Chinese century, with six hundred million rescued from poverty and endless, ever-cheaper energy from the sun shining on us all.

But we must learn to look in the right place for such things and that place is in the "between" of contrasting phenomena. My one-time colleague Phil Slater put it well, "We keep searching for the star-gate, but it is not hidden. Hovering delicately in the spaces between things, it has been there all the time."

We will next turn to practical examples but let me us give the reader one succinct case of a bitter disagreement and a clever, creative reconciliation:

> Australian-Japanese reconciliation process
>
> Back in the Seventies the Japanese confectionary industry undertook to buy Australian cane sugar at five dollars a ton below the then market price. Hardly was the ink dry on the contract when Brazil threw quantities of sugar on the world market and the price slumped by ten dollars. The Japanese now faced the prospect of paying five dollars more than all their competitors. Being particularistic and diffuse in their values they asked the Australians to renegotiate. Were they not all friends? This was an exceptional occurrence. If the Japanese suffered then in time so would the Australians. If they could not sell their confectionary they would be ruined and the sugar growers would suffer too. Were we not really a community needing each other, two parties in one diffuse relationship?

---

115   M. Csikszentmihalyi, 1975, Beyond Boredom and Anxiety, Jossey-Bass

> Being universalistic and specific in their cultural values the Australians refused. « Is this your signature? Is it worth the paper it's written on? "What is the point of a contract if you dishonor it within days? We will look after our individual self-interest if you look out for yours. That is all that is needed. We cannot be responsible for your decisions. A contract is a contract. You gave us your word. Suppose the world price had risen? We would not have come crying to you! You must learn to accept individual responsibility for your actions."
>
> The reader can imagine the fit of moralizing which took another six years of litigation. Then a solution occurred to someone. Let the Japanese agree to pay five dollars below the market price for twenty years whatever that price might be at the moment payment was due. A universal, specific promise had been tied to particular, diffuse, relational contingencies.

RECONCILIATION EXAMPLES

by Fons Trompenaars and Peter Woolliams

It is not enough to just show the differences across cultures. The contribution that our field needs to make is how to help you to deal with the differences across cultures. In other words, what could a specific, low-context person do to criticize the work of a diffuse, high-context person? Obviously, try to do what the Japanese would do over a glass of sake after work. And the English would go for the pub, where privacy is combined with a little alcohol to overcome great inhibitions.

Reconciling standard and adaptation

While we have often used dilemmas such as the car accident (which everyone can relate to), there are many equivalent real-world dilemmas that have an impact on international managers. The most dominant and frequently occurring is the global-local dichotomy. Shall we have one standardized approach or shall we try the local, more particular approach? If we have a single universal model that appears to work in our own country, can we just replicate it across the globe? There are differing views on whether we are becoming more globally universal and alike or whether we are becoming more influenced by particular and unfamiliar national cultures.

In hindsight, this global-local dilemma was one that very much jeopardized the success of the KLM–Alitalia alliance. The Protestant Dutch were sticklers for following the contract. The prepayment of some $100 million for the development of Malpensa airport was one of the central conditions. The Italians saw it as a sign of the seriousness of the alliance rather than of the financial evaluation of the investment. When the investment failed to go to schedule, the Dutch began discussing prepayments; a contract is a contract. The Italians had all kinds of reasons why it was not going as planned. Life is hectic and might offer unexpected particular exceptions: "What's the problem? We'll do it in another way." But what a difference when Air France bought KLM. From the outset, the new French CEO Jean-Cyril Spinetta focused clearly on the things the new integrated company needed to share in order to allow as many differences as possible. The conclusion has been very simple: we focus on IT, marketing/sales, purchasing, and top management so that the brands, operations, and crew can be unaffected. It can be called a successful integration, so much so that a few years later Alitalia was invited to become a member of the family. What can we learn from these types of successes and failures in the process of internationalization?

The bounding outcome behaviors in intercultural encounters can be identified as the following:

Ignoring other cultures: The global corporation

One type of approach is to ignore the other orientation. You are sticking to your own (cultural) standpoint. Your style of decision making is to either impose your own way of doing things because it is your belief that your way of doing things and your values are best, or because you have rejected other ways of thinking, or, you are doing things because you have either not recognized them or have no respect for them. Our aim is to help you to both recognize and respect cultural differences as the first step to reconciling the differences. The Ford Mondeo (meaning "world car"), for example, was envisaged as a model to be both made and sold in an identical way across the world. Another great example in consulting is McKinsey, where local influences are minimized for the sake of their dominant approach. Even clients are frequently excluded from co-designing strategic interventions. It is "my way or the highway" at McKinsey. This is the global organization where headquarters reigns and cultural diversity is ignored.

Abandon your own orientation: The multi-local organization

The second type of response is to abandon headquarters' orientation and go native wherever you can. Here you adopt a "when in Rome, do as the Romans do" approach. Acting or keeping up such pretenses won't go unnoticed—you will be very much an amateur. People from the other culture will mistrust you, and you won't be able offer your own strengths to any alliance.

This has been the approach of the big four accountancy firms, and for good reasons. The laws on financial transactions and tax were and are often local. These firms have great difficulty in globalizing, as we can see with KPMG and Deloitte. The only thing people share is that nobody seems to carry a passport.

Compromise: The international organization

Sometimes do it your way. Sometimes give in to the others. But this is a win/lose solution or even a lose/lose solution. Compromise cannot lead to a solution in which both parties are satisfied; something has to give. It leads to the international organization where most things are shared but there are some local adaptations.

Some organizations were forced to do this because of the nature of their product or service. A good example is the theme parks of Disney, where in Paris they serve wine, in Japan you can get sushi at lunch, and in the US it is the burger and Coke that dominate. It is the international organization with the Statue of Liberty holding a local flag.

Reconciliation: The transnational organization

In an increasingly more subtle and complex process of internationalization, the above approaches show growing inefficiencies. What is needed is an approach where the two opposing views can come to fuse or blend—where the strength of one extreme is extended by considering and accommodating the other. This is reconciliation and is the approach that leads to becoming more effective, especially in situations of diversity or working across cultures. One approach is to start from your own natural orientation but to accommodate the alternate viewpoint to achieve reconciliation. An alternative approach is to start from the opposite orientation to your normal values, but then to embrace your own orientation and thus achieve the reconciliation you need.

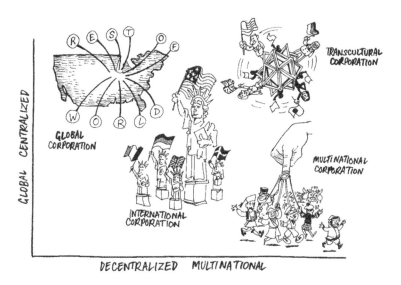

Fig. 10.5 – Reconciling management dilemmas

Hence, a company can adopt a global strategy in the extreme by ignoring other cultures and replicating its original and successful universal approach across the world. It may run into problems, for example when trying to sell beef hamburgers in countries whose primary religion may forbid beef. Or it can adopt a multi-local approach, where it adapts to each particular location in which it is trading. But as a consequence of this latter course, costs may rise because of loss of economies of scale to support different particular systems. In addition, the organization may well lose any single corporate identity or brand image.

At the corporate level, an organization needs to reconcile the single universalistic global approach with the multi-local particularistic approach. As we have demonstrated above, compromise, as in a multinational company, is not enough. What is needed is the reconciliation between the universal and the particular. In general, international success depends upon discovering special veins of excellence within different cultures. Just because people speak English does not mean they think alike. That no two cultures are the same is what brings richness and complexity to multi-nationalism. To achieve this reconciliation, an organization has to make a conceptual leap. The answer lies in transnational specialization, allowing each nation to specialize in what it does best and become a source of authority and leadership within the global corporation for that particular vein of excellence. The reach is truly global, but the sources of major influence are national. Leadership in particular functions shifts to whatever nations excel at those tasks. This cycle is, in fact, helical.

Transnational organizations need to look for a similar logic: it is the result of connecting particular learning efforts into a universal framework, and vice versa. It is the connection between practical learning in a context of intelligent theories. In this dialectic, the best integration processes are developed, disadvantages made into advantages. However, it is not easily achieved and needs the involvement of senior managers. This is known as the anti-clockwise helix, meaning that you start at the horizontal (particular) axis and work your way to reconciliation by accommodating the vertical axis.

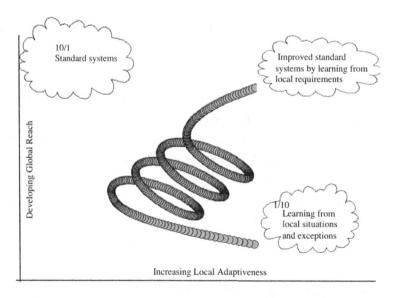

Fig. 10.6 - Learning from Best Practices

When training managers across the globe, Heineken was faced with delivering their training program in the various countries in which they had a presence. But should they deliver one standard program in each destination (universal) or a different (particular) program to meet local needs? They successfully reconciled this dilemma by continuously approaching from both extremes. They used local knowledge as input to the design of a standard training program, but then also adapted the improved generic program to meet their local needs.

Even the icon of globalization and consistency throughout McDonald's has started to develop transcultural traits. One of the most successful markets in the Western world has been France. Analyses showed that part of the success of McDonald's in France is the design of its restaurants. And what can you say about McDonald's now that they invited the French interior designer to Manhattan to help refurnish all New York restaurants? A sign of sharing best local practices and applying it globally!

In some situations, marketing strength derives from universal world branding. Thus, Coca-Cola is Coca-Cola everywhere and represents the American dream, although the list of ingredients on the can or bottle may be in a local language. Similarly, British Airways are selling safe, reliable, quintessential Englishness supported by local agents in the different destinations it serves.

There is an alternative to taking the best practices and globalizing them. When Fons Trompenaars was asked to give a presentation for Applied Materials in Santa Clara, California, he was struck by the fifty-seven nationalities in the top one hundred of the company. An American CEO shared power with his cofounder, who is Israeli. We met an Argentinean HR manager of Russian descent, a German head of technology, and a French marketing VP. If what you deliver globally is developed by a multicultural team, the helix has become clockwise again. You start with a global approach that is sensitive to local circumstances because of the variety in your top team.

Reconciling individual creativity and team spirit

The effective manager knows how to mold an effective team out of creative individuals. In turn, the team is made accountable to support the creative genius of individuals as they strive to contribute the best for the team. This has been described as "co-opetition."

In many companies, there is no problem finding enough individuals to generate enough ideas. The challenge lies with the business system or community, which has to translate those ideas into the reality of viable products and services. While ideas originate with individuals, it is not enough to simply pass these down for implementation to subordinates, who may be inhibited in their criticism. It is far more effective for the originator to work with critics, implementers, and builders of working prototypes to help debug the idea, where necessary. It is a question of reconciling idealization with realization, which is at least as important. In this dilemma concerning individual versus community, the membership of teams must be diverse, consisting of people whose values and endowments are opposite, yet these teams must achieve a unity of purpose and shared solutions. The problem with highly diverse competing individuals is that they may behave like so many prima donnas.

The problem with unity and team spirit above all is that diverse and novel inputs get squeezed out. A way of reconciling these polarized opposites is to make the ultimate goal so exciting, and the process of creating new shared realities so enjoyable, that diverse members overcome their differences to realize a unity of diversities, which makes the solution far more valuable.

Reconciling passion and control

Some leaders happen to be very passionate and others very controlled. When we observe the expressive behavior of Richard Branson, we have noticed that his colleagues praise him for his very controlled attitude when necessary. On the contrary, colleagues of Michael Dell warn you about his passion, while normally he comes across as very controlled. This is a matter of reconciling through foreground or background. To be effective as an international leader, it does not really matter what is fore- or background, as long as they are connected to each other.

Reconciling specific and diffuse

Let's look at some other differences where the diffuse and specific cultures clash. The difference shows itself clearly in the various alliances that can be observed between many of the major airlines. In our work with British Airways and American Airlines, the model helped the parties recognize and respect different ways in which they define the relationship with their passengers. It is typically American to emphasize core competencies and shareholder value. In contrast, British Airways and Cathay Pacific emphasize service with hot breakfasts, champagne, and the like.

Thus in this alliance of "One World," the options are:

1. Go for "serving the cattle with Coke and pretzels"

2. Serve not only hot breakfasts but add some massage and shoe polishing and "go bankrupt on the flight"

3. Compromise and "serve the hot pretzels" so it becomes certain that they lose all clients

4. Reconciliation: try to specifically define those areas to provide a more personal service and deepen the relationship. Jan Carlzon from SAS (Scandinavian Airlines) called this "moments of truth."

The future of the alliance will depend on this very reconciliation: the competency of the employees of the airlines to consistently choose those specific moments to deepen the relationship in the service being provided. A compromise will lead to disaster—and how often have we seen them in alliances of any kind.

Some years ago, Merrill Lynch was facing fierce competition from Charles Schwab on the Internet. While the financial consultants of Merrill Lynch were used to developing expensive relationships with their clients, Charles Schwab decided to put its efforts in helping clients online. After a couple of years, dramatic market share was lost by Merrill Lynch to the online traders. The specifics of the Internet were winning from the diffuse relationships that were quite a bit more costly. After long deliberations, Merrill Lynch decided to introduce Internet services but with much more sophistication than Charles Schwab. The sophistication was in how they combined Internet and financial consultant cultures. First of all, consultants trained their clients, making a great effort to get to know their wishes through the Internet training. And conversely, regular clients were helped with installing a web cam, allowing them to contact their consultants more quickly while on the Internet. They created clicks that stuck. The market share has been gained back against even better prices.

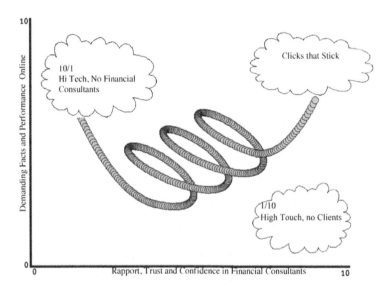

Fig. 10.7 – Moments of truth

People from specific cultures start with the elements, the specifics. First they analyze them separately, and then they put them back together again. In specific cultures, the whole is the sum of its parts. Each person's life is divided into many components: as a newcomer, you can enter only one component at a time. Interactions between people are highly purposeful and well defined.

The public part of specific individuals' make-up is much larger than their private space. People are easily accepted into the public area, but it is very difficult to get into the private space, since each area in which two people encounter each other is considered separate from the other, a specific case.

Individuals within a culture that is specifically oriented tend to concentrate on hard facts, standards, measures, contracts. In specific cultures (such as the United States or Australia), business can be done without individuals having to form a relationship first.

People from cultures that are diffusely oriented start with the whole, and see each element in perspective to the total. All elements are related to each other. These relationships are more important than each separate element, so the whole is more than just the sum of its elements. Diffuse individuals have a large private space and a small public one.

Newcomers are not easily accepted into either. But once they have been accepted, they are admitted into all layers of the individual's life. A friend is a friend in all respects: at work, in sports, in domestic life, and so on. The various roles that someone might play in your life are not separated. Diffuse cultures cherish such qualities as style, demeanor, empathy, trust, and understanding.

In diffuse cultures such as in the Gulf countries, you have to develop a relationship first before you can do business. A high level of involvement is required as a precursor.

Reconciling being and doing

Research shows that what leaders *are* is not different from what they *do*. They seem to be one with what they do. It is recognized that an important source of stress is when being and doing are not integrated. Successful leaders do things in harmony with whom they feel they are, and vice versa. They have been able to reconcile private and professional life.

One of the best illustrations of a reconciliation between **achievement and ascription** is the concept developed by Greenleaf[116] called the Servant Leader. In business, the concept of the servant leader is appropriate wherever it is an inherent mission of the company to develop a leadership culture that works globally and in multi-cultural groups. When any leader serves his or her subordinates, he or she is modeling how they should do likewise for customers. If the leader is not too proud or too high to serve others, why shouldn't employees imitate this by mirroring his or her behavior? Servant leaders are forever trying to give away their status only to get it back again through gratitude and admiration. The more you serve, the more you lead fellow servers.

Servant leadership is a powerful vehicle for the transition from the family and ascriptive culture to an achievement-oriented culture. The

---

116 Greenleaf, Robert (2002). *Servant Leadership*, Paulist

leader "gives" followers more than they could conceivably repay; thus they become obligated and even more compliant to the leader's wishes. Is the servant leader at the bottom of a deep shaft, or at the apex of a truncated pyramid? The answer is both. The leader has reversed the organizational hierarchy and is serving subordinates as if they were superiors.

The apparent modesty of this style of leadership is especially important in reconciling the need for intention and the need for invasion. Those who have weight do not throw it around. Indeed, they behave as if they were eager to learn from you, as if they had nothing to boast about. High-status people exude modesty, which enhances their status. They have nothing to prove. We shouldn't underestimate the concept of servant leaders in making globalization sustainable to the next evolutionary phase.

Reconciling sequential and synchronic

Effective leaders can plan sequentially, but they also have a strongly developed skill in stimulating parallel processes. "Just in Time" management is widely recognized as the process in which processes are synchronized to speed up the sequence. Furthermore, an effective international leader is able to integrate short- and long-term; past, present, and future; tradition and potential. And it is obvious that if the long-term vision gives you a context for the short-term actions, you will be successful.

And, finally, we all live in a present, but we reconcile them in our mind by having a present of things past, a present of things now, and a present of things in the future.

Reconciling inner and outer forces

The final core quality of an effective manager is the ability to integrate the feedback from the market with the technology developed in the company. Again, it is not a competition between technology push and market pull. A push of technology will eventually lead to the ultimate niche market: one without customers. A monolithic focus on the market will leave the business at the mercy of its clients. Values are not "added" by leaders or managers, since only simple values "add up." Leaders combine values: a fast and a safe car; good food yet easy to prepare; a computer that makes complex calculations but is also customer friendly. Combining values is not easy, but it is possible. The more extended system of values is the context where international leadership will prove its excellence.

Conclusion

If our Western way of conceptualizing culture is biased, then it behooves us to do more than simply note the differences that set us apart from Asia and the Far East. (This latter expression is rather Eurocentric !) It is necessary to *see through the eyes of those we are studying*. When we do this much of our methodology comes into question. Our polarities turn into continua, our divisions become connected, our values relativized and our straight-line thinking is bent into circles. Our objective universe dissolves into a web of relationships.

The truth is that we are *largely responsible for what we discover*, because the universe responds to our methodologies, especially when what we study is alive. Dilemma theory for example enforces the divisions it then explores, while the Tao models a universe of complements. We fear the very contradictions that many in the East welcome. We resort to invisible hands to conjure public benefit out of selfishness, while East Asia sees connectivity as competitive. Is the secret of happiness to be found *between* these cultural orientations? Ruth Benedict pointed out that where unselfish conduct is swiftly reciprocated the difference between egoism and altruism disappears and the self is restored to her or him who gave it.

Although East and West are mirror images of each other, one culture can learn the strengths of another. The rise of China testifies that this culture has learnt apace from us, while we have failed to learn the virtues of connectivity from them. Is this why they look like overtaking us? All this is measurable. We can measure the salience of values, Western style, AND their degree of fusion and inter-penetration Eastern style. Fierce ideological struggles between Japan and Australia can be creatively reconciled.

RECAP

- There isn't a unique way to manage that would be valid across the world, and the Western countries would be wise to understand it.
- Most cultures have differences that separate them at first sight, but they offers opportunities for reconciliation
- Reconciliation is a creative process which brings many positive outcomes when done sincerely

RECONCILIATION OF CULTURAL DICHOTOMIES

WORKSHOP 10.1: RECONCILING YOUR OWN DILEMMAS

Many examples of dilemmas reconciliation have been presented in this chapter. It is time to think creatively and to isolate your own dilemmas and your own reconciliation process!

A dilemma often appears as two semingly opposite concepts. It can be represented as a simple axis.

Fig. 10.8 Linear dilemma

Then, you need to fold the rope in order to turn it into a two-axis grid. You are ready to come out with your reconciliation!

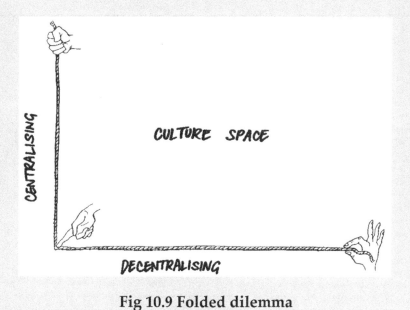

Fig 10.9 Folded dilemma

WORKSHOP 10.1: RECONCILING YOUR OWN DILEMMAS

Set-up:

In small groups, discuss ways to reconcile the following dimensions:

- Polychronic Vs. Monochronic time when planning group work
- Flat Vs. High hierarchy when dealing with the University faculty
- Ascribed Vs. Achieved status when deciding who should represent your class to the outside world.
- Can you think of your own dilemma? What reconciliation can you come up with?

Assignment:

- Discuss in small groups the possible reconciliation solutions
- Present the outcome of your group work and how you proceeded to the class
- Discuss with the audience for feedback

Chapter 11: Culture and Marketing

CHAPTER CONTENTS

Highlights
Introduction

CULTURAL ASPECTS OF PRODUCT AND SERVICES DECISIONS

CULTURAL ASPECTS OF PRICING DECISIONS

CULTURAL ASPECTS OF PLACE (DISTRIBUTION) DECISIONS

CULTURAL ASPECT OF THE PROMOTION DECISIONS

CULTURAL NORMS AND IMPOSED STANDARDS

TRUST AND MARKETING

Conclusion
Recap
Case study 11.1: Of, Audi, how could you?
Case study 11.2: Puma's intercultural gaffe

CHAPTER 11

CULTURE AND MARKETING
By Olga Saginova

Highlights:

After reading this chapter, you should be able to:

– Understand how cultural dimensions affect marketing decisions
– Compare culturally biased (local) and culturally neutral (international) marketing messages
– Explain the reasons for using (or avoiding) foreign names for products and companies
– Choose appropriate communications models to appeal to specific cultural groups of consumers

Introduction

Everything you have read so far in this book about culture can, of course, meet your personal curiosity and need for novelty and new information. People do explore new countries, learn languages, and read books just for the fun of learning and exploring. However, the majority of these undertakings are triggered and fueled by more prosaic and down-to-earth reasons—business needs. "International" is probably the most widely used word both in research papers and glossy magazines. Companies are producing internationally, placing their factories in China or Mexico and using software developed by Indian and Russian programmers; are relocating their staff to fill vacancies in their overseas branches; are selling internationally, with their domestic markets often representing only a small part of their sales; are promoting their brands internationally to become known and loved across the world—in short, companies are doing business across national borders and hence across cultures.

This chapter is aimed at demonstrating how cross-cultural differences affect business strategies and marketing decisions and which cultural dimensions should be taken into account when making important marketing decisions. We shall be using the classic Marketing Mix 4 Ps approach[117] with some additional elements, such as language, trust, cultural norms, and imposed standards.

CULTURAL ASPECTS OF PRODUCT AND SERVICES DECISIONS

Any international marketing textbook should include a standardization and adaptation section emphasizing the importance of following specific consumption patterns and environment variables of a specific country or region. It started with David Ricardo's comparative advantage concept explaining the benefits for England to specialize in the production of linen and for Portugal to concentrate on the production of wine[118]. However, these benefits ignored the cultural implications of the consumers' choices. As soon as we include culture into the decision-making process, the economic benefits would not be so simple and obvious: the Portuguese would probably easily distinguish between the English and domestic linen because of its colors, ornaments, and other culturally based details. The English, on the other hand, would probably reject Portuguese wine not for its quality or price but because they would prefer locally brewed ale or beer.

Some local products, part and parcel of their national cultures, have successfully spread all over the world. Italian pizza, French onion soup, Argentinean steak, Chinese duck, and Austrian strudel are a few to name.

---

117 E. J. McCarthy, 1972, Basic Marketing. A Managerial Approach, Irwin
118 R. Cameron, 2003, A concise Economic History of the World, 4th ed.

These national specialties became internationally recognized and loved by the customers thanks to their cultural connections and meanings. Pizzas cooked and served in North America or Middle East would still be surrounded by some Italian-looking clichés like checked tablecloths, and "trattoria" or "pizzeria" instead of "brasserie" or a simple "café" in the name of the eatery.

However, even for what may look like a perfect international product, local culture can unexpectedly get in the way. A lower literacy level or different level of technical expertise of the population can affect the way product instructions are interpreted and understood, like what happened to Nestle baby food in Africa. The fact that local culture did not include the habit of boiling water before drinking it led to babies' getting sick after they were fed with Nestlé's instant baby food diluted in unboiled and hence contaminated water[119]. European producers did not include using boiled water into the product instruction, thinking from its own European cultural perspective.

A clear difference in culturally biased motivation to use the same product was demonstrated by the famous Sony Walkman, which was understood by the European and American consumers (mostly individualistic cultures) as listening to music undisturbed by the others, while the initial motive of its Japanese inventor was to listen to music without disturbing the others (very logical to a representative of a collectivistic culture).

Culture may affect the way a product is used and hence lead to a difference in product attributes. Japanese housewives prefer lighter irons because they iron their linen, not standing over the ironing board as their European counterparts, but rather sitting by it.

Very often customers' satisfaction depends not only on the physical product bought and its characteristics but also on the service level accompanying the product (after-sales service and repair, installment and delivery service, possibility to return the product, etc.). Dependence of car owners on the repair services of small private repair shops was seen as a barrier for European car producers' expansion into the African market. IKEA's policy of easy return without explanation of any product purchased impressed Eastern European customers who were accustomed to a lengthy and very tiresome process of making any claims about a

---

119   P. Cateora, 1993, International Marketing, Irwin

defective product, let alone just taking the purchased product back because one changed his or her mind.

Adaptation of services deals with opening hours of retail chains to fit the local traditions and norms. For example, a usual schedule for the US and some European countries of being open twenty-four hours a day, seven days a week is unacceptable for Germans or Austrians who are keen on keeping a balanced split between work and private life, including for sales people.

Customers from individualistic cultures expect more individualized service, while collectivistic culture representatives expect more formalized service procedures clearly explained to the customers.

An important service satisfaction factor is waiting time to be served. Customers with polychronic time perception and present time orientation tend to perceive waiting as time wasted and expect immediate service or, if this is not possible, a clear indication of service sequence. To get an example of this, it is worth remembering how passport control lines are organized in US airports. Officials there are regulating not only who goes next, but which desk the passenger should go to. Customers from low-power-distance cultures would expect to get a ticket with their number in a bank and will wait until this number is on a special screen. High-power-distance culture representatives will attempt to jump the line or get some preferences.

> Misako Kamamoto, head of a Japanese tourism committee, shared a number of observations concerning Japanese tourists' behavior and attitudes. At European restaurants, they are often dissatisfied with the time it takes to get the food, and even if the food is excellent they are not happy. When shopping in Paris, the Japanese tourists expect the same personal attention from the shop assistants and are disappointed to find what they perceive as a condescending and arrogant attitude. They are surprised that the shop assistants are not interested in serving every individual customer.
>
> Losing face for the Japanese is unacceptable so they never show mistrust to the others, always trusting the bills they are served in a restaurant or a hotel, while for many Europeans it is absolutely normal to check what was included in their bill before paying it. And this is not because they do not trust the waiter or a hotel receptionist.

> A Japanese railway station is more noisy than a station in Europe; there is far more information for the passengers, both written and verbal, over the station radio. This is because the European railway's mission is to provide maximum comfort and convenience for the passengers, while their Japanese counterparts aim at providing travelers all possible information they might need during the journey[120].

An interesting differentiating factor between cultures is attitude to domestic and imported products, or the importance of country of origin effect. Country of origin is important for product differentiation and quality assurance in South East Asia, Latin America, and East European countries. Customers from Russia, Poland, and Hungary value the quality of their domestic products less than imported ones. Hence, local producers often use foreign-looking names as a disguise. A Russian producer of fashion footwear used an Italian name, Karlo Pazolini, for its retail outlets; a Russian producer of home appliances called itself Bork and registered its brand in Germany to be able to claim "German quality," which was highly appealing to the Russian consumers.

Some countries are linked to stereotypes for some of their products. For example, Scandinavian furniture is usually perceived by consumers as made of natural materials. German products enjoy the reputation of advanced technologies, and "made in Italy" is associated with fashion and style. Retail outlets selling perfumes and toiletries in Russia often bear French names, and it is true not only for "Isle de Beauté" or "Rive Gauche" coming from France, but initially Russian retailers "L'Etoile" and "Rivoli." These stereotypes should be considered by companies when planning their communications in foreign markets.

Global companies often study the ways customers in different countries use their products to adapt them to national cultures. Unilever and Procter & Gamble collect information about the ways people take baths and showers in different countries, how they wash dishes and cook food, where and how they store foodstuffs. These patterns may differ from country to country and should never be taken for granted. Using domestic patterns to market products abroad can lead to expensive mistakes.

---

120   Dr Mooij M. Global Marketing and Advertising. Understanding Cultural Paradoxes. 2005. SAGE Publications

CULTURAL ASPECTS OF PRICING DECISIONS

Price is an important means to communicate cultural values. Relationships between a seller and a buyer can be seen through different bargaining rituals. Price sensitivity is different in different cultures. Price—value balance is also culturally biased. In some cultures, prices for products and services are not openly shown, buyers are expected to haggle with the seller, a buyer's readiness to pay the first price announced by the seller may not only be unwise but may be interpreted as lack of serious intent or lack of interest in the product sold. If bargaining on price is expected, it is important who will announce the first price—the seller or the buyer; it will show the bargaining power and will set the range within which bargaining is possible.

Price is used as a sign of product quality in a number of occasions:

- when product quality cannot be estimated objectively
- when perceived quality is not directly connected to the product, but rather is emotionally colored
- when perceived quality is linked to other value characteristics and influences the decision-making process.

Spending money is perceived differently in different cultures. Following Max Weber's[122] approach (see chapter 2), one can deduct that Northern Europeans, who are mostly Protestant, view money wasting as a sin, so customers are price sensitive even when their disposable income allows them to afford more expensive things, and they prefer durable products, good value for money. For southern Europeans—mostly Catholic cultures—spending money is not shameful. People there spend more time outdoors and are keen to demonstrate their wealth and possessions to neighbors and friends.

In emerging markets, demonstrative spending is often misinterpreted. With high inflation rates, people in these countries prefer to spend money now as any savings will lead to loss of value. As soon as the economy stabilizes, spending becomes more reasonable.

---

122 M. Weber, 2003, *The Protestant Ethic and the Spirit of Capitalism*, Dover Publ.

Some of the factors that raise the cost of serving poor consumers in emerging economies are actually acute forms of challenges that businesses confront across all consumer segments. When low disposable incomes limit the amount consumers can buy at any one time, it becomes extremely important to deliver products and services in affordable parcels, such as single-use packets of products like shampoo or detergent. Consider the problem faced by Globe Telecom and Smart Communications, operating in a country where a mobile handset costing roughly sixty dollars might represent 20 percent of an average low-income consumer's monthly wages. Acquiring new customers was virtually impossible without radical changes in the parceling and pricing of services.

Besides monetary perception of price, which is demonstrated by spending or saving, customers have non-monetary perception, which includes time spent to find and purchase a product, possibility to bargain on price, and getting a discount. All these factors add to the perceived quality and hence to the evaluation of price as reasonable, affordable, or too high.

CULTURAL ASPECTS OF PLACE (DISTRIBUTION) DECISIONS

Channels of distribution can act as cultural filters as culture impacts consumers' behavior in a number of ways. When evaluating the perception of time spent on making purchases, in some cultures it is perceived as time wasted and should be minimized. In these cultures, retailers do their best to facilitate the process through efficient merchandising, placing additional cashiers' desks, providing guiding signage, etc. In other cultures, this process is perceived as entertainment so the environment should be arranged correspondingly, providing not only convenience and efficiency but also an opportunity for customers to enjoy the process, and get all the attention of the shop assistants and consultants. Customers take their time, have a drink or a snack, enjoy some music or performance. The purchasing process can be viewed as education; French mothers would take their daughters shopping to teach them taste and style.

Retail outlets' working hours and customers' expectations are influenced by culture. "Siesta time" in Spanish or Greek supermarkets and department stores is not only a matter of climate when it is too hot to shop in the middle of the day but also the perception of retailers' right to take a break during these hot hours, just as other citizens have.

Loyalty to a producer or a retailer can be perceived as a benefit earned by special measures because customers are entitled to choice and variety (this generally is characteristic for individualistic cultures), or can be taken for granted unless something goes wrong (mostly in collectivistic countries).

The assortment of products sold in retail outlets is regulated by religion (alcohol is restricted in most Muslim countries) or government-imposed norms based on the understanding of certain values (strong alcohol in Finland can only be bought in specialized shops outside high streets or central shopping malls).

The perception of retail trade as a service also depends on culture. In some cultures, shop assistants are friendlier and smile easily because serving customers is perceived as an honorable occupation. In other cultures such as former communist countries, but not only, retail trade was looked down on for a long time, and shop assistants are not known for their friendliness or service quality.

Waiting time to be served is linked to the perception of shopping time in general, but queuing is an organized process in some countries (UK) or a mess in others (India or Senegal). Customers may expect the full attention of the shop assistant when their turn comes, so would not distract him or her by questions when another customer is being served.

Shoplifting, of course, happens in different countries, but the cultural impact of the attitude to shoplifting varies from being perceived as a shameful act or some kind of acceptable entertainment.

Culture through language

Of course, most vividly the impact of culture can be seen in verbal communications. Languages reflect cultural characteristics and influence the way consumers understand and express themselves.

A comparison of different writing styles can be a vivid example. Writing patterns, or the socially accepted ways of writing, differ significantly between cultures. In English and northern European languages, there is an emphasis on organization and conciseness. Here, a point is made by building up to it through background. An introduction will often foreshadow what is to be said. In Roman languages, such as Spanish, French, and Portuguese, this style is often considered boring and inelegant. Detours are expected and are considered a sign of class, not of poor organization. In Asian languages, there is often a great deal of circularity. Because of concerns about potential loss of face, opinions may not be expressed directly. Instead, speakers may hint at ideas or indicate what others have said, waiting for feedback from the other speaker before committing to a point of view.

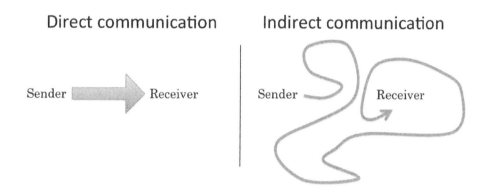

Fig. 11.1 – Language directness

Because of differences in values, assumptions, and language structure, it is not possible to meaningfully translate word-for-word from one language to another. A translator must keep unspoken understandings and assumptions in mind. The intended meaning of a word may also differ from its literal translation. For example, the Japanese word はい (hai) is literally translated as "yes." To Americans, that would imply, "Yes, I agree." To the Japanese speaker, however, the word may mean, "Yes, I hear what you are saying" (without any agreement expressed) or even, "Yes, I hear you are saying something even though I am not sure exactly what you are saying."

Differences in cultural values result in different preferred methods of speech. In American English, where the individual is assumed to be more in control of his or her destiny than is the case in many other cultures, there is a preference for the active tense (e.g., "I wrote the marketing plan") as opposed to the passive (e.g., "The marketing plan was written by me").

A number of cultural dimensions are expressed through communications and should therefore be taken into account when planning communications with consumers. The first dimension to be aware of is context Vs. content as already presented in Chapter 4 (check still chp 4). In low-context cultures, the message is understood at face value and should be formulated verbally, while in high-context cultures, the verbal message communicates only part of the meaning. The remaining meaning is taken from the context: situation, social roles of the sender and receiver, their physical positions in the visuals accompanying the message, etc. High-context cultures may have a variety of words that seem to have the same meaning. For example, in Japanese there are twenty words of politeness to be used with people of different age, gender, and social standing. A habit of checking the context first before making an important decision, or just contacting a person, makes consumers look for additional signs in marketing communications, so all messages should be double-checked to not contain any inadequate or unwanted signals and meanings.

Languages are all meant to communicate meanings from one person to another, but they do it with their own means. Language structure and characters are used to influence not only the way people speak but also the way they think, memorize information, and perceive signs and signals. Chinese, for example, stimulates visual memory, while English is more focused on phonetics. This explains a lot of wordplay and puns in English-language advertising: "Candy. Can do." When adapting these messages to another culture, advertisers tend to do it through vocal, that is, phonetic correspondence, which is not the best way for Chinese consumers, who perceive and remember advertising slogans as an integrated visual image.

The French agency Sofres, together with Nielsen research agency, compared 210 words in four European languages (German, Italian, Spanish, and English) used to communicate common human values. Research showed that twenty of these words could not be used in international advertising, as they had different associations in different languages: duty—*obeying the rules* or *satisfying your wishes*; individuality—*connecting with people* or *attracting attention to your personality*; culture—*earthly pleasures* or *spiritual values*. Apart from common values, researchers found a number of specific values more important for a certain culture. For the Spaniards it was love, family, and idealism; for the Germans, pragmatism and satisfaction; for the English, personal freedom, individuality, and even eccentricity.

Language reflects the power distance of the culture. In English there is no pronoun of the second person singular, as "tu" in French or "ty" in Czech, which is used for relatives or people who are younger. The same applies to using titles like mister, mademoiselle, or Herr.

In Vietnamese, respect towards seniority status is such, that in the Vietnamese language there exist distinctive ways to address people depending on their gender but also their status, often age (It's not unusual for strangers to ask each other about age when they first meet, in order to establish the proper terms of address to use). There are more than fifteen kinship terms (pronouns) reflecting the relationship between the persons talking to each other!

CULTURAL ASPECTS OF THE PROMOTION DECISIONS

Many difficulties in cross-cultural communications are the result of entocentricity, unconscious use of your own norms and cultural criteria when perceiving and evaluating communication messages. Stereotypes are commonly used to simplify cross-cultural interactions, but they often communicate wrong images of the culture and its representatives. Stereotypes should be checked and used carefully; otherwise, they may turn into prejudices.

In marketing, the language of the message should be communicating the values and benefits the advertiser wants to promote. Cultural impact can be seen in a very simple standard example: "A tiger in your engine," a slogan used to communicate the power of the car. In German, the tiger was in the tank, while for the Thai and Vietnamese, the slogan was improper, as a tiger is perceived in these cultures as a symbol of danger, not power.

Channels of communication can vary across cultures. Their availability may be similar, but their perception and credibility is different. Eurostat researched the use of different communication media by the population of European countries. It turned out that masculine cultures with high power distance watch more TV. It is integrated into consumers' everyday lives, and TV often serves as a background to all family activities. But watching TV can be different in different cultures. Children in France, for example, watch TV less often in their own rooms than their counterparts in Sweden.

Printed media preferences are related to such dimensions of culture as power distance and uncertainty avoidance. People in high power distance cultures and with a high uncertainty avoidance index less frequently read newspapers. TV as a source of news is preferred in collectivistic cultures, while in individualistic cultures, newspapers are in the first place, according to the Eurobarometer research.

Advertising models can also be related to cultural dimensions. Giep Franzen[123] described 7 models of how advertising affects customers: the sales-response model, the persuasion model, the involvement model, the awareness model, the emotions model, the likeability model, and the symbolism model. To explain how advertising works in different cultures M. de Mooij[124] added some cultural implications to each model.

- The sales response model is based on the simple stimulus-response and gives a direct message to buy now. This model is suitable for individualistic cultures with small power distance and weak uncertainty avoidance

- The persuasion model is aimed at short-term attitude change, using arguments and explanations to change consumers' attitudes, demonstrating the product, or giving an expert's opinion. This model is suitable for individualistic cultures with low power distance and short-term thinking.

- The involvement mode: is aimed at establishing relations between the customer and brands and developing favorable brand associations. This model is effective in feminine individualistic cultures like the Netherlands or Scandinavia.

- The awareness model is based on creating an awareness of differentiating brands using associations, metaphors, and humor. This model is effective for collectivistic cultures where awareness is part of building trust (Spain or Latin America) and may also

---

123 Percy L., Rossiter J. And Elliott R. (2001) Strategic Advertising Management, Oxford University Press
124 De Mooij M. Global Marketing and Advertising. 2005, SAGE Publications

work in individualistic cultures which do not favor persuasiveness (England or US)

- The emotional model is aimed at building positive attitudes and loyalty by establishing emotional connections and trust. This model is effective for feminine collectivistic cultures, and the intensity of emotions will vary according to the level of uncertainty avoidance.

- The likability model is based on the assumption that when customers like advertising, they will like the product. This model is not suitable for cultures with preferences for rational appeals and explanations of the reasons to buy. The model is characteristic of Japan, where advertising should create a positive mood, and information about the product will be provided in the shop.

- The symbolic model is developing a symbol for the brand, differentiating the consumers, not products. This model is effective for cultures where status and success are important. Symbols are used to communicate in cultures with large power distance and strong uncertainty avoidance.

Cultural dimensions are linked to the images advertising uses. High power distance cultures use images of older people (mothers, grandparents) to advise on the product usage, while low power distance cultures rely on images of young people or children. This can be seen in the Ace brand advertising by Procter & Gamble in different countries. In Russia, a mother-in-law is instructing her daughter-in-law, which fully agrees with the high power distance in the Russian culture, but neglects another cultural implication: mothers-in-law are traditionally depicted in Russian folklore as too-demanding faultfinders, nagging their in-law daughters and sons with petty nitpicking.

The image of a small boy struggling with his bicycle in the Dutch (low power distance culture) advertising of margarine was meant to be a symbol of independence and maturity. In high power distance cultures, this image can be pitied: isn't there anyone to help the poor child? This happened to one of Danone's ads in Russia promoting yogurt for children with extra calcium for growth. A small boy returning home couldn't push the elevator's buttons because he was too small, but gradually (after eating Danone's yogurt) he was able to do it. This ad was criticized by the Russian public; parents thought that small children should not be allowed to operate elevators on their own.

Advertising, showing that one person managed to do something the others did not think about, would be accepted as positive in individualistic cultures and as negative in collectivistic. Collectivistic cultures react positively to images of people doing something together. A person enjoying some product alone is perceived as lonely, neglected by his friends and family. For individualistic cultures, the image of a person enjoying a cup of coffee alone is a symbol of satisfaction and relaxation. A Portuguese sweetener, Hermesetas, used the slogan meaning, "It is so good you want to share it," while Danish biscuits' manufacturer Evers claim, "They are so good you want to keep them." The former Philips slogan, "Make things better," in Spain was, "Together we make things better." For collectivistic cultures, popular advertising words are modern, contemporary, and international, as they mean people are following trends and tendencies together with the others.

Bearing in mind that about 70 percent of the world population belongs to collectivistic cultures, advertising ideas developed in London or New York should be carefully checked on their adaptation to cultural norms. An interesting result was produced by the analysis of advertising coming from cultures with different attitudes to risk and uncertainty. High uncertainty avoidance cultures tend to show perfect people in advertising: with even teeth, perfect skin, well-toned muscular bodies. For high risk and low uncertainty avoidance cultures, ordinary people are acceptable, as are sometimes even people with evident imperfections; Stella Artois beer advertising in Australia depicted two laughing elderly peasants who were almost toothless.

European consumers do not understand why Asian computer producers use butterflies and flowers to promote their products. These natural beauty images are important for long time orientation cultures as they mean harmony and high quality.

The dependence of advertising style on some cultural dimensions is summarized in Fig. 11.2.

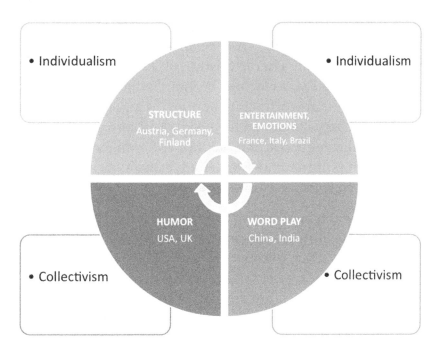

Fig. 11.2 - **Advertising style and cultural dimensions**

Culture affected the schools of national advertising, so one can see a difference between advertising developed by German, French, and British agencies. British advertising is known for the use of humor, puns, and creative verbal messages. German advertisers prefer explanations and appeal to natural and environmental issues. French advertising is often associated with the promotion of luxury goods, and there is a special style called "pornochic." This advertising is not politically correct and often balances on the edge of socially accepted images. The term was coined in the early 1970s when erotic films were shown in French cinemas. Now it is used for creative ads excessively using sexual attractiveness appeal. These ads in early 2000 shocked French consumers, and the French government even published a special report accusing companies of the exploitation of female images in advertising.

During this controversial debate, Eram, a French shoemaker, presented a naked man wearing only sport shoes with the headline stating "no female body was exploited in this advertisement" promoting the new shoes. Not sure such a billboard would be as easily accepted in many other countries...

"Where US advertising is persuading consumers, the French ads are seducing them." A special advertising research in 1993 found that the four main characteristics of French advertising were seduction, demonstration, love, and humor. Seduction does not only mean sexual appeal but also attracting and involving. French advertising attracts and involves consumers in the product advertised. Advertising is similar to a good theater performance. Love and romance are important values of the French culture, and French advertising stresses romantic relationships between consumers and products.

German advertising fully exploits the tendency for healthy lifestyles and a healthy environment. To promote Becks beer in Germany, for example, advertisers used a "green ship" image and a sea world reference. In Russia, however, where young consumers are keen on entertainment and communication rather than environmental issues, a different commercial was used: "The city is waiting," featuring nightclubs and parties. In Russia, no beer brand is promoted as natural or close to nature, while in Germany these account for more than half of the beer brands. In Russia, Bavarian beer advertising was used without adaptation, as it referred to friendship, communication, and sharing values.

Even cultures speaking the same language can differ in communication perception, and hence need an adaptation of marketing communication messages. In August 2007, Richard Branson, founder of the brand Virgin, opened the American office of his Virgin Atlantic airline. Virgin Atlantic has operated flights from Europe to the US since 1984. Virgin America was set to operate domestic flights between big cities in the eastern and western coasts (New York, Washington, Seattle, and several cities in California). The British Virgin Atlantic focuses on low prices and entertainments on board with its slogan, "The class of the sky." Its American version—Virgin America—emphasizes modern planes and new equipment, though it offers the same entertainment opportunities on board.

The British retail chain Tesco entered the American market under a different name, Fresh & Easy Neighborhood Market. Research done by the company before entering the US market showed that 73 percent of American customers are not satisfied with the quality of products offered by local markets and greengrocers. Tesco used the new name to compete, not with the retail chains, but with these local greengrocers offering a friendly "neighborhood" service.

Media Markt, a retail chain selling home appliances and electronics, used its traditional logo—a cute piglet, to advertise its newly opened Russian stores. In Germany, this image is very popular and is used to promote different products and services, including fitness centers and real estate services. In the German culture, a pig is associated with good luck, well-being, and income. In German, there are numerous idioms using pigs: "Er hat Schwein," he is lucky; "saubillig," very cheap; "das Schweinegeld," big money; "das Schweineglueck," happiness; etc. This is why Media Markt used the image of a piglet in communications designed by the German Red Blue agency. However, in Russia, the associations with pigs are very different—dirt, laziness, boorishness—nothing positive. The Russian phrase "подложить свинью" means "to let down, a bad turn." Russians prefer cats instead of traditional pigs as money boxes (piggy banks). No wonder the Media Markt logo surprised the Russian consumers and did not communicate the company values as planned.

CULTURAL NORMS AND IMPOSED STANDARDS

We often use terms norm and standard when discussing culture. However, in the business context, it would be useful to differentiate between the two. Social norm in its initial natural meaning is a stable social standard that is formed over a long time before it is perceived as such by the majority of the population. Cultural norms are formed and change very slowly and are often not written or registered anywhere, which is why it is difficult for people outside a culture to understand them. There are different norms, or standards, that are established by governments or other organizations coercively, and these are not always positively perceived by people[125]. To help a person in need is a cultural norm of human civilization, to give food and shelter to a traveler, even if you do not know him, is a cultural norm of some middle-Asian nations. Receiving two hundred grams of bread per person per day was a norm (standard, normative) imposed on people in Leningrad during the Nazi

---

125 V. L. Makarov, 2010, « Social klasterism », Business Atlas

blockade. Dress code is also a norm (standard, normative) imposed by some businesses as well as entertainment organizations (face control). These dual norms and standards reflect the dual character of human society and economy always divided into soft (unregulated, market) and hard (regulated, planned) parts or segments. There are many terms used to define this: double-track economy, two- floors economy, dual economy.

It is important to understand and clearly define, each time, which type of norms and standards we are dealing with—natural or imposed. Within many modern cultures there are several ethnicities living together. A dominant culture gains supremacy at the expense of the rights of ethnically rich local cultures. A dominant culture often tends to dictate to ethnic groups by determining or restricting the vernacular, other spiritual culture, and material culture. Ethnic identity, and the rights and obligations of a local ethnic inhabitant or a migrant, may be viewed from the perspective of Ajzen's theory of intended behavior[126]: a culture bearer's decision to influence the profile of his own identity and local position depends on his/her confidence and ability to improve their status, that is, on his/her cultural competence and intention to develop his/her own culture and tradition. These are affected by cultural norms and the culture bearer's attitudes toward their own ethnic culture and tradition. The culture bearer's ability to control their own behavior thus influences at least their intention and may also have a direct effect on their behavior and tradition.

Aspects of cultural competence[127] are:

- cultural instinct of self-preservation,

- cultural self-confidence (unconscious reliance on the strength of one's cultural background and tradition),

- cultural self-consciousness (to be aware of and able to analyze the basic elements such as values, tradition, beliefs of one's own culture),

---

[126] P. Suojanen, 1992, *Aspects of Identity: Rights and Obligations of Ethnic Groups*. Nordic Journal of African Studies.
[127] ibid

- cultural self-esteem (high appreciation of one's culture), and finally,
- cultural right of self-determination (national independence, political action).

Culture is part of the *external* influences that impact the consumer. That is, culture represents influences that are imposed on the consumer by other individuals. Culture has several important characteristics[128]:

- Culture is *comprehensive*. This means that all parts must fit together in some logical fashion. For example, bowing and a strong desire to avoid the loss of face are unified in their manifestation of the importance of respect.
- Culture is *learned* rather than something we are born with.
- Culture is manifested within *boundaries* of acceptable behavior. For example, in American society, one cannot show up to class naked, but wearing shorts and a T-shirt would usually be acceptable.
- Conscious awareness of cultural standards is limited. One American spy was intercepted by the Germans during World War II simply because of the way he held his knife and fork while eating.
- Cultures fall somewhere on a continuum between static and dynamic depending on how quickly they accept change.

Culture is a problematic issue for many marketers since it is inherently nebulous and often difficult to understand. One may violate the cultural norms of another country without being aware of this.

TRUST AND MARKETING

Trust-based marketing is a marketing theory based on building consumer relationships through trustworthy dialogue and unbiased information.

---

[128] Lars Perner, Ph.D., Marshall School of Business University of Southern California, http://www.consumerpsychologist.com/international_marketing.html

The concept was originated by Dr. Glen L. Urban[129], professor and former dean of the MIT Sloan School of Management. Trust-based marketing focuses on customer advocacy techniques that assist consumers in making informed purchase decisions based on comprehensive marketplace options and equitable advice.

Customers have increased consumer power through Internet access to product information and competitive pricing. Companies therefore can no longer rely on traditional models of "push marketing," in which a product's positive attributes may mask unsuitable characteristics. Companies that provide consumers with comprehensive product options, including their competitor's, will earn the trust of the consumer even if it does not result in an immediate sale.

Dr. Urban argued that his theory is not simply a marketing concept but also an interdisciplinary strategy, a philosophical approach, and a behavioral method; a vital business competency he calls the "trust imperative." Dr. Urban originally tested his hypothesis with a prototype site for General Motors called TruckTown which provided unbiased comparisons of competing truck products. He found that more than 75 percent of TruckTown visitors said they trusted TruckTown more than the dealer who had sold them their last vehicle.

Cultural differences play a key role in the creation of trust, since trust is built in different ways and means different things in different cultures. For instance, in the US, trust is "demonstrated performance over time.". In many other parts of the world, including many Arab, Asian, and Latin American countries, building relationships is a prerequisite for professional interactions. Building trust in these countries often involves lengthy discussions on non-professional topics and shared meals in restaurants. Work-related discussions start only once your counterpart has become comfortable with you as a person.

Conclusion

Globalization is based on technological advances, which explains the supply side: economies of scale, experience curve, transportation and communication advances. Globalization of consumers and demand is

---

129 http://mit150.mit.edu/infinite-history/glen-l-urban

more long-term and slower. Cultural coherence must not be forgotten and neglected by marketers.

Consumers buy meanings, not products. Meanings are shared by the cultural community. At present there are many things that are shared among cultures of the world, but just as many remain culturally specific. True globalization means not denying differences but being aware of them and responsive to them. The law of comparative advantage we referred to in this chapter imposes a paradigm of international trade that assumes preeminence of utility over identity. In reality, people live not only with what is useful but with what helps the self-actualization of their identity.

This is why it is so important to integrate the dimension of culture into all marketing strategies' planning and implementation. It is important not only for companies focusing on international markets but also when targeting ethnic segments in the domestic market.

RECAP

- The chapter described how cultural dimensions such as power distance, collectivism/individualism, emotional/neutral attitudes influence consumer behavior
- These cultural dimensions should be considered when making marketing decisions about product characteristics, pricing, distribution and communications.
- Marketing communication, especially advertising is most affected by culture and communication models
- Appeals, targeting clients, should be carefully chosen by marketers to achieve the desired results and limit misunderstanding and ambiguity.

CASE STUDY 11.1: OH, AUDI, HOW COULD YOU?[129]

Marketing missteps in naming cars quickly become legendary. There's the urban myth that the Chevrolet Nova failed in South America because in Spanish, "no va" means "won't go." (It's not true.)

But now it turns out that Audi may have committed a blunder in naming its line of electric cars **e-Tron**. Especially since they're about to be shown at the Paris Motor Show.

As one Francophone just pointed out to us, the French word *étron* is a particularly unfortunate choice in that language. Online translation tools give French synonyms for étron that include *caca* and *excrément*. Or to put it a tad less delicately, in English, it means "crap, dirt, droppings ... muck, poop ... shite, turd".

Yes, it appears Audi may have named its entire line of electric cars after ... errrr ... dung. Sigh.

French seems to pose frequent problems for automakers in naming cars. When Buick famously rebranded its midsize sedan from Regal to LaCrosse for 2004, its marketers were mortified to learn that in French Canadian slang, *lacrosse* was used by Québec teenagers to refer to the practice of masturbation.

Thus, in Canada, the midsize car otherwise known as the Buick LaCrosse was sold as the Buick Allure from 2005 until the 2010 model year. In an effort to unify global Buick model names, Francophone Canadian buyers will now have to be willing to say they drive a LaCrosse. *Quelle horreur.*

Other such gaffes globally include the Mitsubishi Pajero (in Spanish-speaking countries, pajero is a slang word for masturbator) and the Ford Pinto, which in Brazilian Portugese slang turns out to mean "small penis." And there are more.

Over to you, Audi.

John Voelcker
Sept. 2010
www.greencarreports.com
© 2011 High Gear Media

---

129   Link to article: http://www.greencarreports.com/news/1049196_oh-audi-how-could-you-the-french-like-electric-cars-but

> ### CASE STUDY 11.1: OH, AUDI, HOW COULD YOU?
>
> *Discussion questions:*
>
> - How do you think companies could prevent such mishaps?
> - Are there colors, numbers or sounds in your culture that could be misinterpreted with others'?
> - How would such a marketing blunder influence your purchasing decision?

CASE STUDY 11.2: PUMA'S INTERCULTURAL GAFFE[130]

In December 2011, the federation of United Arab Emirates (UAE) celebrated the fortieth anniversary of its birth. On this occasion, the equipment manufacturer Puma had the idea to create a special model of sports shoes taking up the colors of the flag of the UAE.

The launching of this model in Emirates' stores immediately provoked a wave of indignation, which forced Puma to withdraw it from the market and publish a statement to apologize. Here is an extract from this statement: "The shoe was never intended to upset or offend our customers here in the Middle East, but to give the people of the UAE a piece of locally created design as a symbol of recognition of this great occasion."

The reaction of an Emirates media specialist, Aida Al Busaidy, is particularly interesting: "A national flag represents a country and what it stands for and it is strictly not right for depicting it on shoes or anything that is worn on the feet. It is highly disrespectful."

This indignant reaction seems strange to many in the West. Indeed, many brands of shoes incorporate the colors and patterns of national flags, especially for special occasions. For instance, during the football World Cup of 2010, the brand Superga released six models with the flags of the United Kingdom, South Africa, France, the United States, Jamaica and Italy.

So, if in some countries it is acceptable to reproduce the national flag on shoes, it is not the case elsewhere. According to Aida Al Busaidy, Puma officials have not understood anything of the local culture: "They really need to understand a nation's cultural values. On what basis did they decide to use these colors? Did they conduct any research and speak to any of the Emirati population to find out if it was okay to place the flag on the shoes?" she said adding that the practice might be acceptable to other nationals in Europe or elsewhere but it is definitely not here. "May be the Italians are okay with it. But we are not," she added.

---

130   Link to the article: http://gestion-desrisques-interculturels.com/risques/puma-s-intercultural-gaffe/

CASE STUDY 11.2: PUMA'S INTERCULTURAL GAFFE

If the Emiratis felt offended by the model designed by Puma, it is because the shoe does not have the same status in Arab countries as in Western countries. The shoe is actually in contact with two impurities: the ground with dirt and filth, and the foot that every Muslim must wash before prayer. It is unthinkable to enter a mosque with your shoes on your feet, alternatively the shoes must be held in your hand sole against sole.

It is extremely rude to show the soles of your shoes to your interlocutor. Hence, the throwing of a shoe as the ultimate insult and expression of revolt. Everyone remembers the press conference in December 2008 when George W. Bush had to avoid the shoe of an angry Iraqi. Since then, this gesture has been imitated many times.

In other words, Puma made the mistake of concentrating on the symbolic value carried by the shoe, and of overlooking the fact that the "shoe" as an object could also be the support of symbolic meanings, including negative ones.

Puma's premise is that the shoe, and in this case the sports shoe, is necessarily a positive symbol (performance, efficiency, originality, distinction). This positive side has a story – which I have already mentioned in the article *Entreprises et influence culturelle: les origines* (Business and cultural influence: the origins). I would just repeat that the explosion in the sale of sports shoes in the 80's is inseparable from the emergence of the rap industry.[131]

The year of that explosion is very clearly identified. It is the year 1986 with the hit My Adidas by the rap band Run DMC. That year, the band had invited the top management of Adidas to one of their concerts: when they were about to sing My Adidas, they asked those wearing them to show one of their Adidas shoes ... and twenty thousand shoes were waived in the air. Run DMC went on to be the first rap band to sign a sponsorship deal worth one million dollar with Adidas, who previously only signed contracts with athletes. From then on each rap band claimed a brand or a particular type of sports shoes.

---

131 http://gestion-des-risques-interculturels.com/points-de-vue/enterprises-et-influence-culturelle-les-origines/

CASE STUDY 11.2: PUMA'S INTERCULTURAL GAFFE

This wave finds cultural obstacles in its path. It is the case with the Arab countries where the shoe is inseparable from the notion of impurity. As a result ignorance of a cultural gap that has led to a gaffe by Puma.

Benjamin PELLETIER

Trainer

© Gestion des Risques Interculturels

Discussion questions:

- Can you think of any object that has a different meaning in your culture from another one?

- Do you think it is a good idea to use the national flag as a marketing symbol?

- Can you think of other objects displayed by opinion makers, such as music bands, that are not employed for their original use?

Chapter 12: The challenge of culture in expatriation

CHAPTER CONTENTS

Highlights
Introduction

CULTURE SHOCK
Tips to better adjust to the cultural shock
How to hold a conversation anywhere in the world?

THE PERPETUAL EXPAT
Expatriating… Again?
When in Rome…
Who to involve?

POST-GLOBAL WORLD

REPATRIATION
Personnal repatriation challenges
Professional repatriation challenges

Conclusion
Recap
Workshop 12.1: Expats checklist
Workshop 12.2: Ask around

CHAPTER 12

THE CHALLENGE OF CULTURE IN EXPATRIATION
By Dean Foster

Highlights:

After reading this chapter, you should be able to:

- Relate your own experience when in a new culture
- Gain knowledge to better communicate across cultures
- Get an insight on a new phenomenon called perpetual expatriate
- Understand how preparing one's repatriation is becoming as essential as expatriation's

Introduction

In the 21st century, the first century of the global millennium, the ability to communicate, work, and live across, among and with cultural differences is the critical "tipping point" for successful individuals, organizations and nations. This will be the fundamental differentiator between success and failure, as every individual, organization and nation in today's world is interconnected in ways that exceed any previous experience in human history. However, increased cultural contact, as a result of interconnected technology, increased travel and migration, the fall of national boundaries to powerful global economic and social forces, etc., does not automatically lead to increased understanding, collaboration and positive all-round enrichment.

In fact, unfortunately, history shows us that whenever there has been increased cultural contact, the first typical response is misunderstanding, suspicion, conflict and hostility. Only through often many painful interactions and over much time do individuals, organizations and nations develop the mechanisms for understanding, tolerance and collaboration, and then only if there is the will, individual, organizational or political, to do so.

We do not have a choice but to face this intercultural challenge, and fundamental to grappling with the intercultural realities of work and life in the 21st century, is the need for all individuals, organizations and nations, to deeply understand cultural differences and how to manage them for positive results. This is a powerful requirement for the expat and their family, the international student, businessperson, the international diplomat, and even the casual traveler.

In today's world, there is no "wiggle room" for cultural ignorance, and every individual must also be an ambassador of understanding by virtue of the very fact that they will and must work and live with colleagues of different cultures every day.

CULTURE SHOCK

Adjusting and adapting to the cultural differences in daily life and work can be one of the hardest challenges facing expatriates and their families. Cultural differences may not be recognized, yet their impact is often viscerally felt. Cultural differences often challenge our most basic assumptions of how the world is supposed to work, how people are to behave with one another, and yet may do so in subtle and almost unconscious ways.

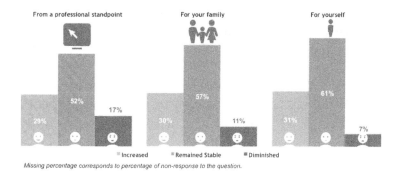

Fig. 12.1 – Evolution of optimism when on assignment abroad[133]

Over time, while we might find such differences enchanting and exotic at first, the dissonance caused by continuously needing to interact with fundamentally different ways of being, can become overwhelming. Coping with this cultural dissonance has often been illustrated as a wave, beginning with naïve enchantment, plummeting through the depths of misunderstanding (and all the behavioral "fall-out" from such misunderstanding), and pulling-out again to a level of acceptance, sometimes even extending to valuing and integrating differences into one's own persona.

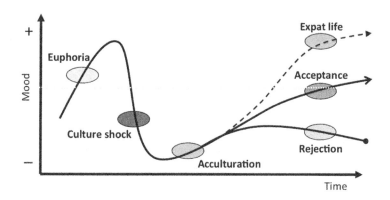

Fig. 12.2 The cultural adaptation curve

---

133   *All the graphics of this chapter (except Fig. 12.2) are coming from the study « Expatriation Study White Book » published by Berlitz Consulting, BVA, EuRA, Magellan & INSEAD. Reproduced with the permission of Patricia Glasel.*

The process of acculturation means to weigh-up the pros and cons of the situation, and to increase your knowledge about the new culture in order to better adapt to it.

As may or may not have been done the first time, reviewing essentials such as values, history, background, people, language, politics, economics, demographics, school systems, daily life, work habits, negotiation, managing, the worlds of men and women, children and adults, socializing, making friends, dealing with conflict and differences, etc., all need to be explored, this time specific to the culture to which you will be moving.

Tips to better adjust to the cultural shock

1. Self-awareness is crucial. Be aware of where you are on the curve. Remember that your reactions and emotions are normal.

2. Meet people who have already gone through the adjustment curve—and survived! They can give you suggestions and remind you that the end is in sight.

3. Don't hang around with expatriates who exhibit a consistently negative attitude toward your host country. Misery loves company, and they will soon drag you down to the depths of their despair.

4. Make an effort to meet people and make friends with people in your host culture.

5. Look for the positive aspects of every experience.

6. Set small goals for yourself initially; adjustment is gradual.

7. Take care of yourself physically. Make sure you get enough sleep, keep a proper diet, etc.

8. Adjust your schedule to the rhythm of the host culture (meal times, work, time off, etc.)

9. Try out the new language. Don't be afraid to make mistakes.

10. Make plans to stay in touch with friends and family at home. Some ideas for maintaining contact:

THE CHALLENGE OF CULTURE IN EXPATRIATION

- Set a time for a monthly telephone call (10:00 a.m. on the last Sunday of each month).
- Start a round-robin letter with your family (one person begins the letter and each family member adds to the letter).
- Set aside time on a regular basis (monthly, weekly, or biweekly) to record a few minutes of digital film (a camera or even telephone allows that). You can send movies to your family and friends. If you have children, they can send movies to their friends (a teacher might also like to show the film in class).
- Establish a letter or e-mail writing routine.

11. Even with a positive attitude, moving abroad is a very stressful experience. Maintain your usual stress outlets, such as exercise.

12. Keep your sense of humor!

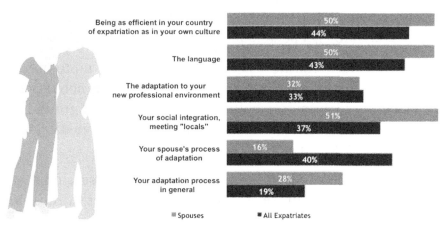

Fig. 12.3 Challenges of living in a foreign country

How to hold a conversation anywhere in the world

Demonstrate genuine interest in the culture of your host country: food, art, sports, music, current events, architecture, etc. If you don't know, ask humbly; and if you do know something about their culture, show it, but admit it is just a start and that you welcome their help. People love to show off their country's culture. All you have to do is ask.

In some cultures, personal questions may be asked of you that you may find intrusive and embarrassing to answer (e.g., "How much do you make?" "Are you married?"). Handle this by speaking in the general ("Just enough to pay my mortgage!" "In [your country], many people do not marry," etc.). Treat personal questions for what they usually really are—requests for information about life in your country.

Do not talk business during business social situations unless they bring business up first. Talking about family is usually okay, as long as it's about the family and family background in general.

Do not admire personal things unless you want them delivered to your doorstep the next day. Admire things in general ("Vases that beautiful can be found in museums in [my country]") not specifically ("I really love that vase you have over there"). Guest/host relationships often obligate your host to give you something you gush over.

If personal comments about you and your possessions are made, try not to take it personally. It is usually a sign that they are comfortable enough to "get personal" with you; take it as a compliment.

In most cultures, people want to know more about who you are. Avoid jumping into statements and questions about one's work; instead seek to learn more about the personality, background, and interests of your foreign counterparts! (Except in the United States, where people tend to talk more about what they do.)

Count on the three traditional taboos (sex, religion, and politics) to be brought up probably sooner than later at most social occasions. Depending upon the culture, it may be referred to more or less, but sooner or later, cross-cultural curiosity will overwhelm one or both of you, and a sensitive topic will be brought up. When this occurs… Do not opine. Most people do not appreciate foreigners (i.e., you) opining about their country.

Seek information, be a student, and inquire about what you do not understand or need further information about.

When people in your new country volunteer their ideas, opinions, or questions about your country, be a teacher: speak in the general, not about yourself but about your country.

THE PERPETUAL EXPAT

> Peter and Jacqueline Carter and their three children made their first international relocation from upstate New York to Paris in 2005. Jacqueline was then a senior manager at a large multinational, and when her company offered her an international assignment in Paris for three years, she knew it would be a great professional move but had serious concerns about the implications such a move would have for her husband and their children. Wisely, her company's HR department arranged for the Carters to attend a cross-cultural orientation prior to their departure, which, in addition to providing important information about the social and business requirements for succeeding in France, also provided the Carters with the opportunity to explore their own private concerns and questions in regard to the impact that living and working in France would have on each member of the family. By the end of the training, the Carters felt they were fully prepared for a new and exciting adventure in France, and, in fact, after three years in Paris, had developed a love affair for their new home, new neighbors, and new country. Most importantly for Jacqueline's employer, she had succeeded masterfully on her assignment in France, so much so, in fact, that the company has just asked Jacqueline if she would repeat her success in Singapore. Yes, move the family again, this time to Asia.

For a number of reasons, many first-time expatriates choose to expatriate again at the end of their first assignments abroad rather than return home (returning home being, for most of them, their initial intention when they first began their assignment). Many repeat this pattern again after the second assignment as well, and perhaps again, and yet again. In fact, the number of perpetual expatriates seems to be on the rise, as the end of the first and second wave of corporate expatriates on traditional two- to four-year assignments approaches.

Often the reasons are complex: an ambivalent mix of concerns and feelings about returning "home," going back to a job and a place that may no longer be familiar or satisfying, an unexpected comfort—even affection—for new friends and country, as memories and relationships back home have faded, and an appreciation for the challenge of living and working internationally.

Sometimes the reasons are more prosaic: the company simply does not have a position back home that values the new skills that the assignee has developed, skills that can be better applied in yet another foreign location. In this case, the wise employer offers another opportunity abroad. Sometimes, (and this happens far more frequently, unfortunately), the employee simply takes another assignment abroad...with another company, rather than return home. With the investment being well over a million dollars per family per average international assignment, the employer has a vested interest in retaining the global talent of the company and of making sure that the international assignee stays with the company at the end of the first assignment. Reassigning them to another foreign location often mitigates the problems of repatriation and avoids the risk of losing repatriates to a risky return process. However, does merely assigning the so-inclined and soon-to-return expatriate to another location abroad ensure a second or third successful international assignment? Just as adequate preparation for the first assignment is usually necessary to ensure success, what kind of preparation and training should the "onward" employee and family receive to ensure that they succeed on their second and third and, sometimes, fourth assignment abroad?

Expatriating... Again?

All too often, the assumption is that since the expatriate and family already succeeded in their first international assignment (with or without formal preparation training), their success obviates the need for any formal training prior to their "onward" move. Certainly this is the thinking in the case where the family received no training prior to their first move yet managed somehow to succeed in their first transition abroad. Unfortunately, it also remains the prevailing thinking (at least in many organizations) for those families who did receive training prior to their first move, as well—the thinking being something like this: the cross-cultural training the family received prior to their first move gave them everything they needed to know about how to transition to international life and work, and the success of their first move proves they mastered these skills. Therefore, with such experienced expatriates, there really is no need for any further preparation training with their subsequent onward moves. The assumption couldn't be more wrong.

Most experienced expatriates and their families will tell you that if there was one thing they learned both in their formal pre-departure cross-cultural training and in their on-the-ground life and work experiences as expatriates abroad, it is that the cultural (and sometimes language) issues were typically significantly more challenging than what they had first expected.

> When providers of cross-cultural training offer pre-departure cross-cultural training to expatriates who have been authorized for the service by their sponsoring organizations, it is almost 100 percent of the time guaranteed that expatriates who have already completed at least one assignment abroad (regardless of the location), will actively seek to arrange their cross-cultural training for themselves and their family prior to their onward move to yet a second or third location. When there are difficulties getting authorized assignees and families to actually commit to a cross-cultural training, it is almost always with families on their first move. This indicates that ignorance of the critical adjustment issues associated with crossing cultures is fairly high among first-time assignees, but that once an assignment has occurred, awareness of the need for and importance of formal cross-cultural training is high among onward assignees and families.

Curiously, the high awareness for cross-cultural training among onward assignees is often not met with a similar level of awareness on the part of the sponsoring HR department. Many organizations incorrectly assume the onward assignee doesn't need any further cross-cultural training and support in advance of their onward assignment. While the first assignment heightens the awareness of the need for the assignee for further cross-cultural training in preparation for their onward move, it often serves as a justification for the company for not providing future cross-cultural training in advance of the onward move. It is never a good situation for the employer and employee to be working at cross purposes, especially when the need for support is as critical the second, third, or for each subsequent, regardless of how many there are, international assignments as it was valuable for the first.

> **Leveraging the first international experience to the advantage of the second**
>
> Most importantly, however, is the need the assignee and family may have to reflect on how they may have changed now that they have gone through their first international experience, and how these changes may help them in preparing for their next, onward, expatriation. This is important for both expatriates who received formal training prior to their first move as well as for those who received no formal training at any point. However, if the assignee and family did not receive formal cross-cultural training prior to their previous assignment, affording them the opportunity to systematically reflect in a structured and guided format on their adjustment, warts and all, can help considerably toward ensuring the success of the next assignment. We know that formal cross-cultural training helps reduce failure rates on international assignments substantially. Having a successful first assignment without any formal, structured understanding of why or how it was successful provides no insurance that the next assignment will succeed. Systematically reflecting on the causes of the success (and the bumps and difficulties, as well) of the first assignment, through a guided, structured, and formal cross-cultural training program in preparation for the onward assignment, can leverage the first assignment experience to the benefit of the second, ensuring a smoother and more successful transition onward. As might have been the case with the first, not providing this opportunity risks the million-dollar assignment the second time around.

When in Rome...

The information one needs to have about life and work with Romans is simply different from the information one needs to succeed day-to-day in Shanghai. Knowing (whether attained through formal pre-departure training or through the more difficult and risky on-the-ground school of hard knocks) the questions one needs answered when on international assignment still do not provide the country-specific (and most importantly, city-specific) answers that will ensure success for the assignee and family. This information is best presented in an efficient and structured manner through a cross-cultural program that both presents the essential questions and provides the critical answers for successful life and work in the new country, prior to the move there, so eliminating the costly and dangerous on-the-ground learning curve and maximizing return-on-investment almost immediately. Knowing how to do business with Romans in Rome, all the issues, all the intricate topics, as well as where to get the children' clothes and how to find the kind of food they like in the neighborhood in Rome where one happens to live, can only be provided objectively and accurately (no colored war stories from jaded expats already on assignment, please!) in a cross-cultural program specific to, of course, Italy and Rome. And if that's where the onward assignment happens to be, no previous cross-cultural program on, say, Sao Paulo, will do.

Who to involve?

As is the case with first-time cross-cultural training programs, every stakeholder in the international relocation process needs to be involved in some way in the program. This means that all family members who are relocating need to attend a component of the program that is specific to their issues, including the "trailing" partner and the children, as well as the assignee. But it also means that the organization itself, with its need for rapid and measurable return-on-investment, and a dependable insurance against a failed international assignment, needs to have a cross-cultural training program that it can rely on.

POST-GLOBAL WORLD

Organizations and individuals working across cultures have long known the value of cultural training. Most companies with a presence in global markets have, either through bitter experience or wise awareness, come to appreciate the bottom-line advantages that cultural preparation provides for the expatriate and family being assigned to a foreign location or to the global team attempting to work more effectively across time and culture zones.

Cross-cultural training is no longer considered a nice to-do, but for most companies with any international experience, it is recognized as an essential tool for business success.

Accordingly, the art and science of cross-cultural training has developed over the last twenty or so years from an infant discipline to a mature management training intervention, with a body of knowledge and a training methodology all of its own.

There's just one problem: most of the research, methodology, and orientation that is the bread and butter of most cultural training programs was designed in what would be called the "pre-global" world, while most organizations needing global skills training today are operating in a "post-global" world.

Most organizations working across borders today need not only the information about cultures that was researched and developed over the last twenty or so years, but more significantly require information and skills that allow them to also deal with the post-global realities of cross-border work today.

This does not mean that what traditional cultural training has been providing up to this point is incorrect or invalid but rather that a larger context has now developed, a bigger box in which cultural information must now be placed.

The newer issues of working in a global matrix, with certain global forces that may be more powerful than the individual cultural ones about which traditional cultural training was solely concerned, must now be addressed.

In fact, cross-cultural training, while new and important in the pre-global world, in today's post-global is suddenly not enough. Today, organizations do not require merely cross-cultural training: the post-global world requires global skills development training.

What are the differences? What are the additional benefits that global skills development training provides that pick up where traditional cultural training leaves off? Let's explore: TCT (traditional cultural training) for relocating expatriates and families has typically, and correctly, focused on making all members of the relocating family aware of fundamental cultural dynamics that they will experience, each in their own way, as they adjust to their new host culture.

The problem is that in today's post-global world, many individuals have lived in powerfully multicultural environments all their lives, define themselves and their families as multicultural, and may have had extraordinary international experiences themselves prior to even their first relocation abroad.

Most major world cities today, where many assignees have grown up and worked, are more international cities than they are representative of the majority of the population of the country that hosts those cities, and many potential assignees come to their first assignment abroad with an existing awareness of cultural differences and dynamics.

Correspondingly, there is an increasingly greater likelihood that the world into which the expatriate and his or her family will be moving will be more familiar than different to the world that they are leaving, both often being major multicultural, international cities.

Additionally, TCT traditionally focused on this adjustment (again, in the pre-global world, correctly) as it mainly affected the non-working partner, the goal being to assist that individual most at risk for not being able to adjust to cultural differences. And, in fact, the non-working partner, in the pre-global world, often was the most at risk individual making the move abroad (the assignee, after all, had a raison d'etre, but the partner often was ripped from his or her moorings, with no connection to the new host culture, bereft of family, friends, and in the new location solely to support the assignee).

However, in today's post-global world, over 70 percent of all expatriate families are dual-income families, and the non-assignee partner is more inclined to maintain a career (or develop a new one) than not.

Technology spawns the proliferation of networks of support that assist with adjustment and career development issues for the non-working partner, and it allows for career maintenance and management anywhere in the world by circumventing any existing restrictive local employment regulations that prohibit non-assignee partners from being employed in the new country (these regulations additionally will increasingly disappear between major trade partners, as reciprocal treaties with large, supra-national regulatory bodies such as the EU permit partners to find work as well).

But, if TCT is primarily focused on the needs of the traditional "trailing spouse" and family, it often does so at the expense of the professional training needs of the assignée. Today, over 80 percent of all international assignees have work responsibilities for multiple cultures (e.g., Ms. Smith is being relocated to Prague, but she is vice president of her company's Eastern European operations), yet TCT typically addressed the cultural phenomena one needed to be familiar with only for one's host country (in this example, only Czech Republic and the issue of working with Czech colleagues in a Czech office).

If Ms. Smith is not provided with important cultural information about how to work effectively with the ten other Eastern European countries she is responsible for, then cultural training is not doing its job.

More profoundly, in today's post-global world, most international work locations are themselves multicultural environments. In combination with the ubiquity of global teams, spread out as they are across continents, they create a total work environment for the majority of expatriates assigned abroad that are in and of themselves far more multicultural than the original culture in which they are located.

Ms. Smith would be hard-pressed to succeed in work from her office in Prague if she were only trained to work with the Czech, as most managers in Prague offices today are responsible for staff from cultures around the world and for global teams flung far and wide across all cultural horizons.

Finally, there is the issue that in the pre-global world, cultural training focused on, well, the culture, while in today's post-global world, global skills development must also provide awareness of how to work with cultural change and global dynamics (not merely cultural dynamics).

Not only are cultures today different from the traditional stereotypical outlines that TCT all-too-often drew, but perhaps what is more important for global managers today to master—more important than understanding the cultural attributes of any one particular culture (or even several)— is global behavior, or understanding a way "to be" globally, of working with a global mindset.

Global skills development represents a paradigm shift in thinking about providing the organization and its global managers with the skills they need for truly successful global work.

But why not a paradigm shift? The world has shifted in front of us: from an "international" to a "global," and now perhaps, a "post-global" place. It only stands to reason that the training needed to succeed in this new world also needs to shift: forward from traditional cultural training to cutting-edge global skills development.

REPATRIATION

The current economic emergency has suddenly forced a spotlight on the previously often unacknowledged, yet formidable, challenge of managing the repatriation process for international assignees. Until recently, companies recognizing the need for cross-cultural training for outbound assignees might not have been taking seriously the importance of cross-cultural training for assignees returning home from abroad. Today, however, in response to the economic challenges facing most organizations, significant numbers of assignees abroad are being recalled back home, some sooner than expected. Just as organizations learned the importance of cross-cultural training in order to ensure the success of the assignment abroad, organizations are now beginning to recognize that cross-cultural training is absolutely essential to ensure the success of the surprisingly challenging return home.

It's understandable that organizations place greater emphasis on the successful preparation of the assignee and family for outbound assignment, and less, historically, on the return. It seems counterintuitive that returning home should present any challenges that require training and preparation; after all, the family is coming back to a culture and environment they are intimately familiar with, right? Well, they might remember a place like that, but the truth is quite the opposite: in study after study, return shock is typically more difficult an adjustment for both the assignee and the family than outbound shock, and the degree to which assignees and their families are able to adjust to returning to their original home country dramatically affects the bottom line, or return on investment, of the organization. There are a number of reasons for this phenomenon, and they are, for the most part, hidden and unexpected. Nevertheless, unless these repatriation challenges are managed, a failed repatriation can undermine the significant investment that has been made in the success of the international relocation. There are a number of reasons for the repatriation challenge, and they fall into two areas, the personal and the professional.

Personal repatriation challenges

Personally, assignees and family members alike tend to idealize home while they are abroad, and now that they are going back, they tend to remember home as it was, not as it is, even though they have made home trips periodically while on assignment abroad. When it comes time to return home for good, idealization tends to kick in strong, and with it, severe disappointment with the inevitable reality that home is not the "white picket fence" (it never was) or the perfect nurturing environment the repatriating family may imagine it to be. And assignees may not understand the changes that have occurred back home while abroad; nevertheless, now they have to make sense out of them. In effect, they have to learn what home is now all about, all over again. There is also an expectation that friends and family will be there (they often are not, having moved away or died), breathlessly waiting to hear all about the adventures the assignee and the family experienced while on assignment abroad.

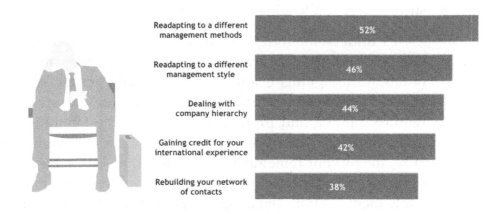

12.4 – The repatriation Blues: Upon your return from expatriation, did you encounter difficulties in... ?

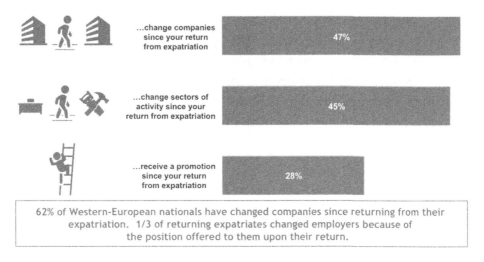

Fig. 12.5 – Life after expatriation: In the end, did you …?

The disappointment can be profound when assignees learn that there is, in fact, very little interest in learning about what happened to them while away, but rather, friends and family are far more interested in telling the assignee about all the things that happened to them while the assignee was gone. Children come back with accents; some may have been born abroad, and they speak their parents' home country language as a second language, if at all. Children may feel disoriented, not being able to find groups with whom they feel comfortable: the school system may be very different, the local home country child culture may be mystifying and uninteresting (going to the mall is usually very boring for repat children), and often they express a real desire to return to the country of their expatriation. Most importantly, there is a general failure on the part of the assignee and the family to recognize the fact that they have individually changed, substantially, but often in ways that they only recognize once they return to their home country. The shock can often be overwhelming.

Professional repatriation challenges

These professional challenges, perhaps, have the greatest impact on the success of the repatriation. The partner, who initially may have had to forsake his or her own career in order to accompany the assignee partner on assignment abroad, now is more eager than ever to return to a career and reenter the workforce. However, having been out of it for several years, the partner often struggles to find a way to pick up the thread of his or her career, and the frustration, after expecting to be able to do so, can be difficult. Most importantly, the assignee returns with the expectation to find a position in the company that values the new skills he or she has gained while on assignment abroad.

> Working abroad, most expatriates must wear lots of different hats, and they are often big fish in small ponds, wielding much authority. Back home, often at headquarters, they find themselves as small fish in a big pond, often with their authority far more circumscribed and dependent on the decisions of others.

While abroad, the assignee may lose touch with what is really happening at the home office, and the home office may not be able to assess the degree to which, and the areas in which, the assignee has developed new and important skills that can be applied when brought back to work at the home office. In short, there is often a severe disconnect between the kind of position and work that the repatriate expects to do and the position and responsibilities that the company actually has for them to do. This is probably even more the case in an economically challenging time, where organizations are rapidly downsizing and where repatriation may itself be occurring because there is now significantly less work to do, or certain projects are put on hold or eliminated, or the organization that the repatriate is returning to is simply smaller, leaner, and meaner than the one he or she left. Nevertheless, the repatriate has the global knowledge, skills, and savvy to advance the globalization of the organization in ways that simply do not exist elsewhere in the organization, and to not provide the repatriate with a position that makes the most of these new global skills wastes the dollars that the company has already spent on the expatriation and the repatriation. Inevitably, unless this disconnect between the professional expectations of the repatriate and the resource needs of the organization are resolved, the company risks losing the repatriate. Statistics show that on average almost 48 percent of all repatriates leave their companies within two years of returning home.

And they often take a new position with an organization that does value their skills and global knowledge - an organization that is often the competition. If an organization does not retain its global talent, it will have a very hard time succeeding in the global market, especially when its competition is benefiting from the investment that was made in their global managers.

In short, successful repatriation is the insurance policy that the "million-dollar investment" that is being made with each and every assignee and family is maximized. "Bring 'em back alive" is no longer a viable measure of the success of an international assignment, and the failure to retain global talent after they return home significantly impacts the overall success of the assignment. Statistics also show that when **repatriation training** programs are administered, repatriation attrition, one measure of a failed repatriation, dramatically drops from 48 percent to less than 10 percent. This translates into retained global talent, maximizing the return on the investment in the global assignment. The cost of repatriation training, therefore, is not an expense. It represents, rather, savings: saving the organization (and its people) the dire and very real expense of a failed assignment back home, and the risks associated with an organization losing its most valuable global talent.

Conclusion

As we indicated when we began this chapter, there is no more important knowledge needed, and set of skills to develop, than the critical understanding of how to manage cultural differences in the 21st century.

Not only do these skills accelerate success when working and living abroad, for individuals and organizations, but those who possess this understanding and these skills help to advance this knowledge for others. With this knowledge comes responsibility, and while such knowledge advances individual and organizational success, it also requires those who possess it to share it, pass it on, and become the "ambassadors" of understanding, so that this information becomes as global as our lives.

If we have globalized work and life, we need to now also globalize intercultural information and effectiveness, so that all individuals, organizations and nations, can better manage the intercultural challenges they face. Those who hold the torch must also pass it on.

RECAP

- While discovering a new culture is exciting at first, it is always stressful and it exposes us to a cultural shock
- There are ways to blend into a new culture, all it takes is to pay attention to cultural details
- A new trend is emerging among international managers, the perpetual expatriate, moving from one assignment to another
- As disturbing as expatriation itself, repatriation needs to be carefully prepared for so not to face a cultural shock when back in the home culture

WORKSHOP 12.1: EXPATS CHECKLIST

Whether this is your first or fifteenth international move, whether it's just across the border or halfway around the world, packing up and moving yourself, sometimes with your family, and your life across time zones and culture zones is **always** stressful. Acknowledging and exploring those aspects of your expatriation that are most stressful are the best ways to deal with them before they grow too big to handle.

So, for each of the ten major international relocation stressors listed below, circle the comment (a, b, c, or d) that most closely reflects how you currently feel. Then, in small groups, ideally made of participants from various backgrounds, compare and discuss your choices.[134]

1. Language
a. Should not be a problem…I already speak it, more or less!
b. Don't expect it to be a problem, although I don't really know it.
c. My inability with the language may keep me from making friends and necessary contacts.
d. I am terrified of not being able to do even the simplest of things because I cannot speak or read the language.

2. Building personal relationships
a. This is definitely **not** a problem. I make friends everywhere I go.
b. It may not happen so quickly, but that's okay…I can get along on my own until I meet some nice people.
c. Making friends is very important to me, and I am concerned that I do not know how they do it over there.
d. I'll never make any friends, and this worries me a great deal…I don't want to be alone.

---

[134] This workshop is copyrighted by Dean Foster Associates. It is permitted to use it only in association with this textbook, for a non-commercial assignment. More information about DFA at www.deanfosterassociates.com

WORKSHOP 12.1: EXPATS CHECKLIST

3. What about the food?

a. I eat absolutely anything. This will not be problem, even if I cannot find what I want.

b. I am concerned about where to go to find the kind of food that my family and I like.

c. I don't think I will like the food they have there. It will be too _____.

d. I am sure I will lose weight, because I will not be able to buy or eat anything I like.

4. Where am I going to live?

a. I am delighted with my housing arrangements. Everything is perfect, just like home or maybe even a little better!

b. Even though the arrangements have not yet been completed, I feel sure things will turn out okay.

c. I am concerned that I don't know much about the neighborhood, the size of my apartment, how to buy a kitchen, the electricity, air conditioning and heat, lease terms, how to get a phone, all those little but important things...

d. The housing issue is a major problem for me. I am very worried about it.

5. Adjusting to differences

a. I expect to fit right in. I've got a great sense of humor, and I am not a very judgmental person; I expect an easy adjustment.

b. Even though I am excited about the differences, I am afraid I might have a hard time adjusting to them all.

c. I am afraid adjusting to things I don't understand will be hard and that I will be homesick for familiar things back home.

d. I am going to be very depressed. I don't plan to go out much and will somehow try to carry on as best I can.

6. Will I be safe and secure?

a. Absolutely. In fact, probably safer than at home!

WORKSHOP 12.1: EXPATS CHECKLIST

b. I guess it's as safe as home, but I do have some concerns about how to behave on the street, when alone, being in a car, etc.

c. I am seriously concerned about safety and security, for myself and for my family.

d. This is a major problem. Do I go outside ever at all? How do I deal with all these risks?

7. Will I be healthy?
a. Of course, as healthy as I have been.

b. I need more information on doctors, hospitals, the health system, dentists, dealing with emergencies, and such.

c. I am worried about the health risks I have heard about. Can I even drink the water?

d. Health is my greatest concern because _____.

8. How will I stay busy?
a. Everything will be intriguing and interesting. This is definitely not going to be a problem.

b. I have thought about this quite a lot. Maybe language lessons, travel, volunteer, school courses, maybe additional work?

c. I worry about this a lot, and I am not sure how to go about getting the information I need on what is available for me.

d. I am going to be terribly bored and frustrated. This is a real problem.

9. What about returning home?

a. Don't even want to think about this right now; after all, when it's time to come home, I'll be enlivened and enriched. This won't be a problem at all.

b. I wonder how I will fit in again back home.

c. I worry about reconnecting at work and with friends.

d. It's going to be another adjustment ordeal that I do not look forward to.

WORKSHOP 12.2: ASK AROUND

This workshop requires some preparation as participants need to collect information from others.

- Find a foreigner living nearby and ask this person about their experience.
- Review positive issues and negative ones alike.
- Ask whether they received any specific preparation.
- Present the findings to the class and give recommendations as to how to best prepare and live one's expatriation.

A final word

Throughout this book, each author has brought to you a piece of the bigger jigsaw puzzle that is cross-cultural management.

It is up to you to react with empathy to the cultural characteristics of others, as each context is unique. However, we would like to share a few tips in conclusion that could help you better navigate cultural waters.

Do not assume. Anything.

When we are confronted with a cultural misunderstanding, its genesis is often our assumption that the other is thinking like us, with the same norms and values. They don't.

Question. Everything.

When confronted with a different culture, ask questions. Any. There is no stupid question. Not only will you learn a lot from the answers, but you will also limit future blunders. Also, you will please your host who, most certainly, will be overjoyed to share with you some details about their culture.

Document yourself.

The more you develop your knowledge about a culture, its history, geography, traditions, language, religion habits, political system or even fairy tales; the more you will understand the way people communicate. You are also likely to be more accepted by the hosts if you know their fundamental cultural cues.

Respect others.

Others think differently from you, they live differently from you, accept it. You will not change them, only *you* can adapt. Others a have different values? So what! Respecting others' view is a prerequisite for successful cross-cultural communication and management. You don't need to accept everything, nor to adhere to the others' opinions, only to respect their ideas as equally valid as yours. Try, that feels good!

Be creative.

Cultural misunderstandings stem mostly from the different perception of a problem, and therefore lead to different solution proposals. Learn to reconcile those views into a creative outcome; it is the best way to satisfy both cultures. Remember, good communicators are creative people, this is ever more true across cultures.

Have fun.

Accept the other's mistakes with humor: you could be next! By deflating a nascent offence, you guarantee yourself a tolerant attitude from others when you'll act "strangely". We all make mistakes, most often involuntarily. Those blunders can become an invaluable source of friendship. A good laugh, followed by a brief and delicate explanation, is the best way to respond to someone else's unusual actions!

PART 3
APPENDICES

ABOUT THE CONTRIBUTORS

Edgar H Schein

Country of origin: Switzerland

Countries you have lived in: Switzerland, Soviet Union, Czechoslovakia, USA

Family status, children: three children, seven grand children

Studies: Social Psychology

What is your definition of culture: What a group has learned to solve its problems of external survival and internal integration.

What is your definition of cross-cultural management: I have none, it is our biggest problem.

A personal cultural anecdote: Making an intervention in another culture which led to the ruin of my client because I did not understand the cultural dynamics

Favourite quote (s): "Everything happens through conversation" (A Company CEO said this)

Favourite movie: *Lawrence of Arabia*, 1962, with Peter O'Toole, Alec Guinness and Omar Sharif, directed by David Lean

Published books:

- Helping: How to offer, give and receive help, 2011, Berrett-Koehler Publishers
- Organizational Culture and Leadership, 2010, 4th edition, Jossey-Bass
- The Corporate Culture Survival Guide, 2009, Jossey-Bass
- Career Anchors: Participant Workbook, 3rd Edition, 2006, Pfeiffer
- Process Consultation Revisited: Building the Helping Relationship, 1998, Prentice Hall
- Organizational Psychology, 3rd Edition, 1979, Prentice Hall
- Career Dynamics: Matching Individual and Organizational Needs, 1978, Addison-Wesley

Website: www.facebook.com/edgarschein

ABOUT THE CONTRIBUTORS

Juliette Tournand de Rouyn

Country of origin: France

Countries you have lived in: France

(Juliette is a seasoned sailor, she has sailed across the Atlantic Ocean with offshore sail racers)

Family status: Married

Studies: EDHEC business school, INSEAD « diploma in Clinical Psychology of Organisations » with *magna cum laude*.

What is your definition of culture: The vision of what is good and bad inspired by a specific environment that we don't question until we meet another one.

What is your definition of cross-cultural management: The talent to manage the creation of the culture of "us" where each person and culture feels respected and improved.

A personal cultural anecdote:

First trip to the London agency of the group I worked for, at a meeting with the client's and agency's international coordinators whom I had never met. The traffic outside the airport is solid. I hope that the client will be delayed too. I am relieved as soon as I am introduced in the meeting room. People speak in such a cool and relaxed way it's as if there is no client here.

But after a short while the agency's coordinator finished the conversation and introduced me to everyone. Half of the people were from the client's company.

My national sense of client-supplier relationship had to be completely reconsidered for the better.

Favourite quote (s): "The acme of skill is to win without fight - the winner wins before the fight, the looser searches victory in the fight" Sun Tzu.

Favourite movie:

- *A beautiful mind*, 2001, with Russell Crowe, directed by Ron Howard
- *Das Leben der Anderen (The Lives of Others)*, 2006, with Ulrich Mühe, directed by Florian Henckel von Donnersmarck

Published books:

- *La Stratégie de la bienveillance ou l'intelligence de la coopération (The Bienveillance Strategy or the Intelligence of Cooperation)*, 2nd edition, 2010, InterÉditions
- *Sun Tsu sens dessus dessous – Un Art de la paix (Sun Tzu upside down – An Art of Peace)*, 2010, InterÉditions/Dunod
- *Secrets du mental (Secrets of offshore racers' mental)*, 2011, InterÉditions/Dunod

Chapters in collective books

- "De la prophétie à la prospective" (From Prophecy to prospective) in *Réenchanter le futur par la prospective RH (Renchanting the future with the HR prospective)*, 2010, Village Mondial
- "L'éthique du métier du changement, en movement" (The ethics of the job of changes, in movement) in *Le Coaching en Mouvement*, 2011, Dunod

Contact: Website: http://fr.linkedin.com/pub/juliette-tournand/0/28b/635

Craig Storti

Country of origin: USA

Countries you have lived in: Morocco, Tunisia, Sri Lanka, Nepal, the UK

Family status, children: Married, no children

Studies: English literature

A personal cultural anecdote: I was invited to the home of one of my Moroccan students for dinner. At one point an older woman passed by the door of the guest room where I was being entertained. "Is that your mother?" I asked my student. "No," he said. "It's one of my father's wives."

Favourite quote (s): It's a funny thing; the French call it a *couteau*, the Germans call it a *messer*, but we call it a knife, which is after all what it really is. Mark Twain

Favourite movie: *Lawrence of Arabia*, 1962, with Peter O'Toole, Alec Guinness and Omar Sharif, directed by David Lean

Published books:

- *Cross-Cultural Dialogues*, 1994, Nicholas Brealey Publishing
- *Culture Matters: The Peace Corps Cross-Cultural Workbook*, 2nd edition 2011, Peace Corps Publishing
- *The Art of Crossing Cultures*, 2nd edition, 2007, Nicholas Brealey Publishing;
- *Figuring Foreigners Out: A Practical Guide*, 1998, Nicholas Brealey Publishing

- *The Art of Coming Home*, 2001, Nicholas Brealey Publishing
- *Old World/New World: Bridging Cultural Differences: Britain, France, Germany and the U.S*, 2001, Nicholas Brealey Publishing
- *Americans at Work: A Cultural Guide to the Can-Do People*, 2004, Nicholas Brealey Publishing
- *Speaking of India: Bridging the Communication Gap When Working With Indians*, 2007, Nicholas Brealey Publishing

Website: craigstorti.com

Jérôme Dumetz

Country of origin: France

Countries you have lived in: France, Netherlands, USA, Canada, Russia, Czech Republic

Family status, children: Married, two very multicultural daughters

Studies: BTS International Trade (France), BA International Business (Holland), Specialist (Master) of Economics (Russia)

What is your definition of culture The other can *also* be right.

What is your definition of cross-cultural management: Empathy applied to international business

A personal cultural anecdote: When I was a student in the north of the Netherlands, I lived in a students' dorm with mostly Dutch students. One day, a roommate invited me and others to have dinner. She would cook.

Having already overcome the early time for dinner (around 6pm), I enjoyed the simple meal composed of classic students' food such as ham, cheese and bread, and maybe spaghetti.

The shock came at the end of the dinner, when the "hostess" asked for everyone to tip-in to cover the cost of the food! I remember the share per "guest" was very small, even by students standard; maybe 1,5 Guilder (around 1 USD at that time).

It was my first cultural shock and the first lesson to the Dutch egalitarian culture!

Favourite quote (s): « We have a strategic plan, it's called doing things. » Herb Kelleher (CEO of SouthWest Airlines) quoted by Tom Peters

Favourite movie: *Wag the Dog*, 1998, with Dustin Hoffman and Robert De Niro, directed by Barry Levinson

Published books:

- *Cross-cultural Marketing* (co-author), 2011, Infra-M. (In Russian)

Website: www.cultureandcompany.eu

Fons Trompenaars

Country of origin: the Netherlands

Countries you have lived in: Netherlands, France, USA

Family status, children: Married, 3 daughters

Studies: Business Economics in Amsterdam and PhD Social Systems Sciences at Wharton

What is your definition of culture: The way we solve problems

What is your definition of cross-cultural management: How to reconcile dilemmas

A personal cultural anecdote: "Introducing myself as a father of three daughters and saying it doesn't explain why I am looking old....to two American participants walking out of the room....It still makes me laugh"

Favourite quote: "What is defined as real is real in its consequences", W. I. Thomas

Favourite movie: *Neil Young & Crazy Horse - Rust Never Sleeps - The Concert Film* Starring Ralph Molina, Frank 'Pancho' Sampedro and Billy Talbot (2002)

Published books:

- *Riding The Waves of Culture: Understanding Diversity in Global Business* (3rd Edition), 2011, McGraw-Hill
- *Riding the Waves of Innovation: Harness the Power of Global Culture to Drive Creativity and Growth*, 2010, McGraw-Hill

- *The Global M&A Tango: How to Reconcile Cultural Differences in Mergers, Acquisitions, and Strategic Partnerships*, 2010, McGraw-Hill
- *Innovating in a Global Crisis Servant Leadership Across Cultures*, 2009, Infinite Ideas
- *The Enlightened Leader: An Introduction to the Chakras of Leadership*, 2009, Jossey-Bass
- *Servant-Leadership across cultures*, 2009, Infinite Ideas publ.
- *Riding the Whirlwind*, 2007, Infinite Ideas publ.
- *Managing Change Across Corporate Cultures* (Culture for Business Series), 2005, Capstone
- *Business Across Cultures* (Culture for Business Series), 2004, Capstone
- *Managing People Across Cultures* (Culture for Business Series), 2004, Capstone
- *Marketing Across Cultures* (Culture for Business Series), 2004, Capstone
- *Did the Pedestrian Die: Insights from the World's Greatest Culture Guru*, 2003, Capstone
- *C??21 Leaders for The 21st Century*, 2001, McGraw-Hill
- *Mastering the Infinite Game: How East Asian Values are Transforming Business Practices*, 2001, Capstone
- *Seven Cultures of Capitalism*, 1995, Piatkus

Website: www.thtconsulting.com

ABOUT THE CONTRIBUTORS

Joerg Thomas Schmitz

Country of origin: Germany

Countries you have lived in: Argentina, Mexico, India, United States

Family status, children: married, one daughter

Studies: cultural anthropology with ethnographic fieldwork in South Carolina (USA) focused on documenting social change in a mill village, and the efficacy of drug prevention efforts in a group home, and Yucatán, Mexico focused on health, health care utilization in the context of economic transformation in a Yucatec Maya community.

What is your definition of culture: *"What is expected, reinforced, and rewarded by and within a group"* (short version); *"The complex patterns of ideas, emotions and symbolic expressions that are expected, reinforced and rewarded by and within a particular group"* (long version)

What is your definition of cross-cultural management: pursuing objectives and goals with people of differing cultural backgrounds and social identities, including national, ethnic/religious, organizational and functional/professional.

A personal cultural anecdote:

"The Nazis of the Jungle" or *"Discovering Context"*

When I was travelling through the lowland jungle of Bolivia in the late 80s, right after my "Zivildienst" (social service instead of military service provided by 'conscientious objectors'), I learned an important lesson in the context-dependency of meaning and the depth of the emotional roots of cultural conditioning:

I found myself repeatedly in a curious and bizarre situation: when meeting indigenous villagers I was always asked where I was from. Upon mentioning I was from Germany, they would click there heals together, extend their right hand and say "*Hi Hitler*" in a curiously accent and with a big smile full of expectation of my enthusiastic response. I was deeply shocked and offended. After all, I was deeply aware of the burden my national history imposed and committed to being a different kind of German.

Why was I stereotyped in this way? I explained myself, my discomfort with this greeting and made myself accountable for the committed atrocities. However, the greeting ritual continued and my explanations seemed to make little impact. Could it be that this indigenous population had subscribed to a Nazi ideology? …. Perhaps infected by some Nazis who fled to South America and hid in the Bolivian jungle? Was there a secret enclave of Nazis hidden in the jungle?

My attempts to find out yielded no such discovery; nor did I find any other evidence of Nazi ideology. So, what could possibly explain this recurring – and increasingly aggravating greeting ritual?

The answer came to me by accident. Once a week, a travelling merchant put on a "jungle cinema" to which one of my local contacts invited me. The movies he projected were old black and white Hollywood World War II movies. Everyone enthusiastically booed the US victors and cheered the Nazi losers. They identified with the losing party as it reflected something about themselves and their own situation in the Bolivian reality.

Favourite quote(s):

- A small group of thoughtful people could change the world. Indeed, it's the only thing that ever has. *Margret Mead*

- As human beings, our greatness lies not so much in being able to remake the world - that is the myth of the atomic age - as in being able to remake ourselves. *Mahatma Gandhi*

- Behavior is the mirror in which everyone shows their image. *Johann Wofgang von Goethe*

Favourite movie: *Insignificance*, 1985, by Director Nicolas Roeg, with Gary Busey, Tony Curtis and Theresa Russell

Published books:

- Doing Business Internationally, 2002, McGraw-Hill
- The Cultural Orientations Guide, The Roadmap to Cultural Competence, 2006, 5th ed, Princeton Training Press;
- Transcendent Teams (author)
- The Guide for Inclusive Leaders, 2006, Princeton Training Press;

Website: www.schmitzandassociates.org

Peter Woolliams

Country of origin: United Kingdom

Countries you have lived in: United Kingdom

Studies: B.Sc (Hons) Maths/Science, B.A. Systems Management, PhD Data mining

What is your definition of culture: if you both agree on something, you share the same culture

What is your definition of cross-cultural management: the same as any management, there's nothing 'special' about cross-culture, that's just another factor to be included

A personal cultural anecdote: At the end of a meal in a UK restaurant, I pay the bill with a check. First time in the US, I found you pay the check with a bill. Even at the basic level and if you think you are speaking the same language, it can be difficult to communicate accurately with other cultures.

Thus, in preparation for an overseas assignment, Americans may ask about the cross-cultural competencies of a potential expat, whereas Europeans would ask about their cross-cultural competences. In fact this is not simply differences in spelling but are two totally different concepts pronounced the same.

Cross-cultural competencies are about the skills and knowledge a person must acquire to achieve levels of performance. In other words, what you know.

In contrast, cross-cultural competences are a collection of standards of effective behaviours demonstrated by high performance. In other words, what you do.

Imagine how many HR managers of international companies have talked about the suitability of candidates for a global assignment without realising their overseas colleagues were talking about something different!

Favourite quote: "The problem with conforming is that everyone loves you except yourself". Rita Mae Brown

Favourite movie: *Rififi*, 1955, with Jean Servais, directed by Jules Dassin

Published books: Extensive research publications (including 18 refereed journals), four books, some 40 practitioner publications.

- The Global Tango: Reconciling cultural differences in mergers and acquisitions (with F Trompenaars), InfIdeas, May 2010
- Riding the Worldwind of Innovation (with F Trompenaars), InfIdeas, May 2008
- Marketing across Cultures (with F Trompenaars), Wiley Capstone, 2004
- Business across Cultures (with F Trompenaars), Wiley Capstone, 2004

Website: www.pwoolliams.com

Meredith Belbin

Country of origin: United Kingdom

Countries you have lived in: Temporarily many countries round the world

Family status, children: A son and a daughter and five grandchildren.

Studies: Greek, Latin and Ancient History: Psychology, Gerontology, Engineering Production

What is your definition of culture:

The way we do things round here and how what we believe in affects what we do

What is your definition of cross-cultural management:

Developing an in-house culture while taking care not to offend prevailing cultural sentiments

A personal cultural anecdote:

Being discouraged from personally changing money in Kano (Northern Nigeria) on the grounds that without local, tribal knowledge I would not know which counter to approach.

Favourite quote (s):

- The only enemy of man is man himself (Sophocles)
- It is a race between education and catastrophe (H.G. Wells)

Favourite movie: *Les enfants du paradis* written by Jacques Prévert, with Arletty, Jean-Louis Barrault and Pierre Brasseur; directed by Marcel Carné

Published books

- Management Teams: Why They Succeed or Fail;
- Team Roles at Work;
- The Job Promoters;
- Beyond the Team;
- The Coming Shape of Organisation;
- Changing the Way We Work;
- Managing Without Power;
- The Evolution of Human Behaviour;
- Managing Genetic Diversity

Website: www.belbin.com

Charles Hampden-Turner

Country of origin: United Kingdom

Countries you have lived in: USA, Austria, Italy

Family status, children: Married, two sons

Studies: BA history Cambridge, MBA Harvard, DBA Harvard

What is your definition of culture:

Mental programming shared within a group of people.

What is your definition of cross-cultural management:

The capacity to recognise, respect, reconcile and root the cultural preferences of others.

A personal cultural anecdote:

In a Singaporean bookshop the cashier took my credit card and then started to serve the person behind me! I protested. She pointed out that it took twelve seconds for my credit card number to be OK'd. Why not save time?

Favourite movie: *Casablanca*, 1942, with Humphrey Bogart and Ingrid Bergman, directed by Michael Curtiz.

Published books:

21 in all, most significant are:

- *Riding the Waves of Culture* with Fons Trompenaars
- *Maps of the Mind*

Website: www.thtconsulting.com

Olga Saginova

Country of origin: Russia

Countries you have lived in: Many countries visited on temporary basis

Family status, children: married with two sons and a grandson

Studies: Doctor in Economics (*Доктор экономических наук*), PhD

What is your definition of culture:

The system of shared beliefs, values, customs, behaviors, and artifacts that the members of society or group use to communicate with their world and with one another, and that are transmitted from generation to generation

What is your definition of cross-cultural management:

A system of approaches, principles and methods that helps to manage people and groups across cultures

A personal cultural anecdote:

On a sunny Sunday in a quiet Dutch town I walked into a square full of weird people (to my taste), mainly men aged 7 to 70 all long-haired and clothed in black leather tending to ugly looking (to my taste) and too loud motor bikes. This happened to be a EU Harley Davidson club meeting and my first encounter of a brand and group culture.

Favourite quote: Don't fear anything, something will always work out (my grandmother's advice)

Favourite movie: Покровские ворота (Pokrovsly Gates), 1982, with Oleg Menshikov, Leonid Bronevoy, directed by Mikhail Kozakov

Published books:

- Cross-cultural Marketing, Infra-M, 2011 (in Russian, with co-authors I.Skorobogatykh, J.Dumetz)
- Marketing Management. International Perspectives. Editors: Raju M.S., Xardel Dominique. Vijay Nicole imprints Hagar. 2006 and 2010 (chapters in the book)
- University International Strategy, Rus. Econ.Acad., 2005 (in Russian)
- Managing Transformations in Higher Education, Paleotip, 2005(in Russian)
- Organisation of Advertising Activity, Akademiya, 2005 and 2006(in Russian with co-authors V.Khapenkov, D.Fedyunin, J.Pirogova)
- EU Economy, Ekonomika, 2003 (in Russian with co-authors V.Gromyko, G.Gagarina, Z.Okrut)

Website: http://business.rea.ru/sep/teachers/saginova/saginova.htm

Dean Foster

Country of origin: USA

Countries you have lived in: USA, United Kingdom, France, US Virgin Islands.

Family status, children: Married, one daughter, one son.

Studies: MA, Sociology; PhD ABD, Sociology/Anthropology, Graduate Faculty of the New School for Social Research, NY, NY.

What is your definition of culture: The sum total of all environmental influences on the behavior of identifiable human groups.

What is your definition of cross-cultural management: The ability to manage cultural differences to the positive benefit of all involved.

Published books:

- Bargaining Across Borders (McGraw-Hill);
- The Global Etiquette Guide to Europe;
- The Global Etiquette Guide to Asia;
- The Global Etiquette Guide to Latin America;
- The Global Etiquette Guide to Africa and the Middle East (John Wiley & Sons)

Website: www.deanfosterassociates.com

Bibliography

Adler, Nancy (2007). *International Dimensions of Organizational Behavior*, South-Western College Pub.
Axelrod, Robert (1984). *The Evolution of Cooperation*, Basic Books
Bateson, Gregory (1978). *Steps to an Ecology of Mind*, Jason Aronson
Belbin, Meredith (2010). *Management Teams: Why they Succeed or Fail*, Taylor & Francis, 3rd ed.
Belbin, Meredith (2010). *Team Roles at Work*, Taylor & Francis, 2nd Ed.
Benedict, Ruth (1934). *Patterns of Culture* Boston: Houghton Mifflin
Benedict, Ruth, (2006). *The Chrysanthemum and the Sword: Patterns of Japanese Culture*, Mariner Books
Bertalanffy, Ludvig von (1960). *Problems of Life* New York: Harper Torchbook
Cameron and Quinn, (2011). *Diagnosing and Changing Organizational Culture*, Jossey-Bass; 3 ed.
Cateora, Philip (1993). *International Marketing*, Irwin
Conner, Daryl (1985). *The Culture audit workbook: Corporate culture and its impact on organizational change*, OD Resources
Covey, Stephen M. R. (2008). *The Speed of Trust*, The Free Press
Custine, Marquis de, (2002), *Letters from Russia*, NYRB Classics
Csikszentmihalyi, Mihaly (1990). *Flow the Psychology of Optimal Experience* New York: Harper
Damen, Louise (1987). *Culture Learning: The Fifth Dimension in the Language Classroom*, Addison-Wesley
Deal & Kennedy, (1982). *Corporate cultures: the rites and rituals of corporate life*, Addison-Wesley
Dichter, Ernest (2002). *The Strategy of Desire*, Transaction Publishers
Early & Soon, (2003). *Cultural Intelligence: Individual Interactions Across Cultures*, Stanford business books
Fombrun et al., (1984). *Strategic human resource management*, Wiley
Fukuyama, Francis (1995). *Trust: The Social Virtues and the Creation of Prosperity*, The Free Press.
Goffee & Jones, (1998). *The character of a corporation*, HarperBusiness

Greenleaf, Robert (2002). *Servant Leadership*, Paulist

Hall, Edward Twitchell (1931). *Beyond Culture*, Anchor Books Double Day, New York

Hall, Edward Twitchell (1992). *The Hidden Dimension*, Anchor Books Double Day, New York

Hampden-Turner & Trompenaars (2000). *Building Cross-cultural Competence*, John Wiley

Hampden-Turner, Charles (1994). *Charting the Corporate Mind*, Basil Blackwell

Hampden-Turner, Charles (2009). *Teaching Innovation and Entrepreneurship* Cambridge University Press

Handy, Charles (1994). *The Age of Paradox*, Harvard Business School Press

Hofstede, Geert H. (2001). *Culture's consequences: comparing values, behaviors, institutions and organizations across nations*, Sage Publications, 2nd Ed.

Hofstede, Geert H. (2010). *Cultures and Organizations: Software of the Mind*, McGraw-Hill, 3rd Ed.

House, Robert J. (2004). *Culture, Leadership and Organizations: the GLOBE Study*, Sage Publications

Kluckholn, F and F.L. Strodbeck (1961). *Variations in Value Orientations*, Petersen

Lewis, Richard, (2005). *When Cultures Collide: Managing successfully across cultures*, Nicholas Brealey Publishing; 3 ed

Martin, Joanne (1992). *Cultures in Organizations: three perspectives*, Oxford

Maslow, Abraham (1954). *Motivation and Personality*, Harper and Row

Mead, Margaret (2001). *Sex and Temperament of Three Primitive Societies*, Harper Perennial

Mehrabian, Albert (1972). *Silent Messages*, Walsworth Publ.

Mooij, Marieke de (2005). *Global Marketing and Advertising. Understanding Cultural Paradoxes*. Sage Publications

Morgan, (1986). *Images of Organizations*, Sage Publ.

Morrison, Terry et al (1994). *Kiss, Bow or Shake Hands. How to Do Business in Sixty Countries*. Adams Media Corp.

Parsons, Talcott (1970). *The Social System*, Routledge & Kegan Paul PLC

Pedersen and Sorensen, (1989). *Organisational cultures in theory and practice*, Avebury

Porter, Michael (1998). *Competitive Advantage: Creating and Sustaining Superior Performance*, Free Press

Rapaille, Clotaire, (2006). *The Culture Code*, Broadway Books

Sapir, Edward, (2010). *Language*, HardPress Publishing

Schein, Edgar H. (2010). *Organizational Culture and Leadership*, Jossey-Bass

Slater, Philip (1974). *Earthwalk*, Doubleday

Sun Tsu, (1971). *The Art of War*, Oxford University Press

Ting-Toomey, Stella (1999). *Communicating across Cultures*, Guilford Press.

Trice and Beyer (1993). *The cultures of work organizations*, Prentice Hall

Trompenaars & Hampden-Turner, (2011). *Riding the waves of culture: understanding cultural diversity in global business*, McGraw-Hill, 3rd Ed.

Trompenaars & Hampden-Turner (2009). *Innovation in a Global Crisis*, Infinite Ideas Press

Usunier, Jean-Claude, (2009). *Marketing across Cultures*, Prentice Hall, 5th ed.

Veblen, Thorstein (2008). *The Theory of the Leisure Class*, Oxford University Press

Waal, Frans de, (2006). *Our Inner Ape*, Riverhead Trade

Walker & Walker, Schmitz, (2003). *Doing Business Internationally*, McGraw-Hill

Weber, Max (2001). *The Protestant Ethic and the Spirit of Capitalism* Routledge Classics

Zhang, Haihua and Geoff Baker (2008). *Think Like Chinese*, The Federation Press

Index

A

Adidas 327
Adler, Nancy 26, 62
Advertising 29, 247, 312, 323
Air France 287
Al Busaidy, Aida 326
Alitalia 287
American Airlines 293
Ang, Soon 28
Anthropology 39, 53, 56, 81, 151
Applied Materials 291
Art of War 6, 14
Arteau, Jean-Claude 20
Artifacts 20, 30, 49, 66, 78, 102, 229, 236
Audi 324
Axelrod, Robert 7, 9, 10, 14

B

Backchanneling 96, 98
Baron Cohen, Sacha 54
Barron, Gary 213, 216
Bavarian (Bier) 318
Becks (Bier) 318
Benedict, Ruth 57, 274, 280, 284, 297
Bennis, Warren 228
Berkshire Hathaway 213
Berlitz 75, 333
Bertalanffy, Ludwig von 276
Boas, Franz 57, 58
Bohr, Niels 277
Bork 307
Branson, Richard 247, 292, 318
British Airways 246, 291, 293
Buffet, Warren 213, 216
Buick 324
Bush, George W. 327

C

Caesar, Julius 54
Camerer, Colin 230
Cameron, Kim 232, 234, 304
Candy 312
Carlzon, Jan 293
Cathay Pacific 293
Chevrolet 324
Coca-Cola 123, 291
Conner, Daryl 230
Context, High/Low (Cultural Dimension) 56, 64, 76, 97, 134, 192, 196, 286, 312
Cottle, Tom 157
Csikszentmihalyi, Mihaly 285
Cultural Archetypes 33, 106
Cultural Gap 12, 37, 38, 43, 105, 328
Cultural Intelligence 26
Cultural Matrix Model 65
Cultural Orientations Indicator (COI) 75
Culturally Endorsed Implicit Leadership Theory (CLT) 72
Custine, Astolphe de 55

D

Danone 315
Darwin, Charles 56
Deal, Terrence 229, 234

Dell, Michael 292
Deloitte 288
Dichter, Ernest 29
Disney 288
Durkheim, Emile 59, 60

E

Earley, Christopher 27
Edelman 204, 208
Emotions (Cultural Dimension) 69, 91, 129, 140, 314, 323
Englund, Terje 31
Enron 212
Eram 317
Ethnocentrism 25, 45
Ethology 41, 58, 78
Etic/Emic 62, 72
Evers 316
Expatriation 331

F

Fayol, Henri 60
Ford 287, 324
Franzen, Giep 314
Friedman, Thomas 218
Fukuyama, Francis 184

G

General Electric 201
General Motors 322
GLOBE Project 70, 128
Globe Telecom 309
Goffee, Robert 229
Greenleaf, Robert 295

H

Hall, Edward 20, 56, 64, 69, 75, 78, 103, 112, 119, 149, 176, 182, 217, 275
Hampden-Turner, Charles 69, 75, 78, 119, 171, 175, 182, 234, 275

Haptics (Touching) 103
Heineken 291
Heisenberg, Werner 186, 277
Helman, Cecil 151
Hermesetas 316
Herzberg, Frederick 61
Hofstede, Geert 20, 22, 29, 30, 39, 43, 67, 72, 75, 78, 119, 139, 186, 188, 229, 233, 275

I

IBM 67
IKEA 305
Individualism (Cultural Dimension) 36, 67, 69, 76, 78, 95, 126, 190, 275, 281, 283, 323
Intraturn pauses (silences) 94
Involvement in Relationships (Cultural Dimension) 131
Isle de Beauté 307
Iterative Prisoners' Dilemma 7, 278

J

Jelly Belly Candy Company 105

K

Kamamoto, Misako 306
Karlo Pazolini 307
Kelleher, Herb 213, 219, 326
KLM 287
Kluckhohn, Florence 22, 24, 63, 69, 75, 78, 119
Kohls, Robert 20
Koori Mail 85, 97
KPMG 237, 288

L

Levi-Strauss, Claude 56, 59, 275
Locus of control 69, 170, 193, 194
Lorenz, Konrad 41, 58

M

Maeda Corporation 144
Malin, Shimon 169, 192
Marketing Mix 304
Martin, Joanne 230
Marx, Karl 60, 275, 282
Maslow, Abraham 61, 285
Mayo, Elton 61, 275
McDonald's 291
McGregor, Douglas 61
McKinsey 287
McLane Distribution 213, 216, 219
Mead, Margaret 57, 58, 370
MediaMarkt 319
Mehrabian, Albert 85
Merrill Lynch 293
Michels, Robert 55
MITI (Japan's Ministry of International Trade and Industry) 275
Mitsubishi 324
Monochronism (Cultural Dimension) 64, 153, 300
Montesquieu 54
Mooij, Marieke 314

N

Nestlé 305
Nielsen 312
Nin, Anaïs 44
Non-Verbal Communication 56, 82, 88, 98, 107, 111

O

Organizational culture 28, 64, 66, 72, 78, 227, 252

P

Paralanguage 88
Parsons, Talcott 69, 119, 123

Pedersen, Jesper 230
Philips 316
Porter, Michael 130, 232
Potter, Harry (Character) 34, 105
Power Distance (Hierarchy) 67, 78, 139, 182, 190, 196, 306, 313, 323
Primatology 39
Procter & Gamble 307, 315
Proxemics 56, 64, 103, 176, 178
Puma 326

R

Rapaille, Clotaire 34, 106
Rapoport, Anatol 8, 13
Reconciliation of dichotomies 273
Religion and culture 4, 35, 38, 60, 73, 139, 152, 173, 289, 310, 336, 355
Repatriation 331, 338, 345, 350
Ricardo, David 304
Roethlisberger, Fritz 61, 275
Rotter, Julian 170
Royal Dutch Shell 136
Run DMC 327

S

Sanders Peirce, Charles 59
Sapir, Edward 58
SAS (Scandinavian Airlines) 293
Saussure, Ferdinand de 59
Schein, Edgar 23, 28, 30, 66, 78, 230
Schutz, Alfred
Securities and Exchange Commission (SEC) 212
Semiotics 59, 78
Servant leader 246, 295
Shaw, Robert 217
Short/Long term time (Cultural Dimension) 67, 118, 159, 228, 296, 314
Siljerud, Peter 99
Smith, Adam 279, 281
SNCF (French Railways) 249
Sociology 7, 39, 55, 59, 60, 78, 81

Sofres 312
Sony 305
Southwest Airlines 213, 266
Spinetta, Jean-Cyril 287
Standard method 62
Status (Cultural Dimension) 4, 55, 56, 69, 73, 118, 137, 179, 228, 295, 313
Stella Artois 316
Stereotypes 19, 25, 36, 49, 57, 63, 73, 92, 102, 178, 239, 307, 313
Steyr Intercultural Management Model (SIMM) 73
Strodtbeck, Fred 22, 24, 63, 69, 75, 119
Sun Tzu 6, 8, 10, 14
Schwab, Charles 293
Schwarz, Ernst 40

T

Taboos 34, 101, 112, 336
Taylor, Frederick 60
Team Roles 255
Tesco 318
Thatcher, Margaret 282
Thomas, Alexander 62
Thomas, William Isaac 367
Timbuk2 165
Time (types of) 151
Time Orientation (Past, Present, Future) 75, 147, 153, 296
Tinbergen, Nikolaas 58
Tocqueville, Alexis de 55
Triandis, Harry 62
Trice, Harrison 231
Trompenaars, Fons 27, 29, 69, 75, 78, 132, 171, 175, 182, 234, 273, 275, 278, 281, 291
Trust (Cultural Dimension) 64, 175, 199, 237, 321
Turntaking 92, 94, 96, 98

U

Uncertainty avoidance (Cultural Dimension) 67, 76, 78, 169, 186, 193, 232, 314
Unilever 307
United Nations 3
Universalism (Cultural Dimension) 69, 121, 281, 283
Urban, Glen 322

V

Values Orientation Theory 22, 63, 78
Veblen, Thorstein 55
Verbal Communication 56, 81, 85, 87, 98, 107, 310
Virgin 246, 318

W

Waal, Frans de 39, 41
Walmart 213
Weber, Max 55, 60, 174, 275, 279, 308
Welch, Jack 201
Wolf, Erich 184
Work Goals 47
WorldCom 212
Wyatt, Watson 217

X

Xiaoping, Deng 283

Y

Yosemite National Park 160

Z

Zedong, Mao 282

Made in United States
North Haven, CT
25 January 2024

47870714R00228